Pioneer Days
in the Early Southwest

FORT SMITH

From an original drawing by H. S. Mollhausen, made soon after the Mexican War

PIONEER DAYS IN THE EARLY SOUTHWEST

by

GRANT FOREMAN

Introduction by Donald E. Worcester

University of Nebraska Press
Lincoln and London

Introduction copyright © 1994 by the University of Nebraska Press
Manufactured in the United States of America

First Bison Book printing: 1994
Most recent printing indicated by the last digit below:
10   9   8   7   6   5   4   3   2   1

Library of Congress Cataloging-in-Publication Data
Foreman, Grant, 1869–1953.
Pioneer days in the early Southwest / by Grant Foreman; introduction
by Donald E. Worcester.
p.   cm.
Originally published: Cleveland: A. H. Clark, 1926. With new introd.
Includes bibliographical references and index.
ISBN 0-8032-6883-2 (pbk.)
1. Southwest, Old—History.   2. Frontier and pioneer life—Southwest,
Old.   3. Indians of North America—Southwest, Old.   4. Houston,
Sam, 1793–1863.   I. Title.
F396.F72   1994
976'.03—dc20
93-45372   CIP

Reprinted from the original edition published in 1926 by the Arthur H.
Clark Company, Cleveland

∞

To my wife CAROLYN, whose sympathetic interest and
assistance have made this book possible,
it is affectionately dedicated

Contents

Illustrations

Introduction

By Donald E. Worcester

As a young attorney from Chicago, Grant Foreman arrived in Indian Territory shortly before 1900 to work for the Dawes Commission, which was liquidating the Five Civilized Tribes. He left it in 1903 to practice law, and by the early 1920s he was able to leave his legal work and devote his life to researching and writing about Oklahoma and its Indians. *Pioneer Days in the Early Southwest,* published in 1926, was the first of more than a dozen excellent books. Grant Foreman died in 1953.

The unexpected acquisition of Louisiana Territory in 1803 added a vast and largely unknown region to the fledgling United States. The area had four major waterways—the Mississippi, Missouri, Arkansas, and Red rivers—which were well-known to French and Spanish fur traders. But to Americans the country beyond the Mississippi was a mysterious wilderness.

Although some in Congress opposed ratification of the Louisiana Purchase for fear that a rival government might arise in the West, President Thomas Jefferson promptly took steps to learn the extent and characteristics of the new land that had cost the United States a mere fifteen million dollars. He sent Captains Meriwether Lewis and William Clark on their memorable trek up the Missouri and across the mountains to the Pacific. He ordered Lieutenant Zebulon Montgomery Pike to the head of the Mississippi, and on his return sent him to explore the Arkansas River and then travel south to the source of the Red River and descend it. But Spanish troops from New Mexico arrested Pike and his party for trespass and took them to Chihuahua.

The name Arkansas was a corruption of Akansea, the Illinois Indians' name for the Quapaws, a Siouan tribe whose village was near the Mississippi in present Arkansas. The Arkansas River was navigable for six hundred miles from its mouth to the Three Forks, where the Verdigris and Grand rivers entered it near modern Muskogee, Oklahoma. In the era when river navigation played so vital a role, the Three Forks area maintained an importance second to none west of the Mississippi, an importance long since forgotten. This region, which became Arkansas Territory in 1819 and which included the present state of Oklahoma, was the old Southwest that Grant Foreman wrote about. The capital was briefly at the Arkansas Post that Henri de Tonti established in 1686 when searching for La Salle. In 1821 the legislature moved it to the town "at the Little Rock."

The first military post in the region was Fort Smith, built in 1817 on the Arkansas River to protect whites and Cherokees, who had moved there earlier, from Osage raiders. In 1841 it became headquarters for General Zachary Taylor, commander of the Second Military Department, and it gained notoriety in 1849 as an assembly point for caravans of gold-seekers heading for California.

In 1824 a post was needed nearer the Arkansas Osages, who still harassed the Cherokees, so Fort Gibson was built in the Three Forks area, and Fort Smith was temporarily abandoned. Fort Gibson's position at the center of the five frontier forts—Snelling and Leavenworth to the north and Towson and Jesup to the south—made it the most important. In 1832 it had ten companies of infantry and three of rangers, nearly as many troops as the other four combined.

For some unfortunate reason, Fort Gibson was built below the hill where it was relocated during the Civil War. It was surrounded by a canebrake, where stagnant water harbored mosquitoes and malaria germs. As a result, many men were always on the sick list, and frequent pleas to move the post to a more salubrious site met no success. The number of youthful soldiers who died of disease is appalling. From its founding through 1835, 561 soldiers and nine officers died there. It isn't surprising that many officers resigned and enlisted men deserted, in spite of the brutal punishment they faced if recaptured.

Fort Gibson was supplied by river steamers towing keel boats. A yearly consignment to the post included several thousand gallons of good whiskey, 400 barrels of pork, 800 barrels of flour, 360 bushels of beans, 1600 pounds of hard soap, 3500 pounds of tallow candles, 1500 bushels of salt, and 1400 gallons of vinegar. Fresh meat, corn, and vegetables were obtained locally when available.

Many of the men who figured prominently in this opening period of the old Southwest had long been forgotten when Grant Foreman rescued them from oblivion. The most influential and respected family name was Chouteau. In the 1760s half-brothers Pierre and Auguste Chouteau had moved from New Orleans to St. Louis, where they engaged in the fur trade, especially with the Osage tribe in what is now western Missouri. In 1802, when Spanish authorities gave Manuel Lisa exclusive rights to the Osage trade, Pierre persuaded three thousand Osages—about half the tribe—to move to the Three Forks area, where they became the Arkansas Osages.

Of the many able Chouteaus who were active in the region, the most noteworthy was Pierre's son A. P., known as "Colonel" Chouteau. For a time he traded with Indians at the head of the Arkansas and Platte rivers. In 1815 his men were attacked by a large Pawnee war party near the site of modern Dodge City, but held them off. One governor of New Mexico agreed that Americans could trade there, but in 1816, when Colonel Chouteau took thirty thousand dollars worth of goods to Santa Fe, the new governor arrested him and confiscated his property. Chouteau apparently had several trading posts, including one at his baronial estate near present Salina, Oklahoma. His two-story, double log house was even whitewashed, and he and his Osage wife

Rosalie enjoyed such luxuries as were available—they even had a teacher for their many children.

Chouteau had a multitude of retainers—blacks, Indians, and mixed-bloods. Washington Irving, who accompanied a small party there in 1832, was astonished at the great numbers of dogs, chickens, turkeys, ducks, geese, and horses—there was even a race track. Rosalie and her sister Masina served the party a sumptuous meal that included venison, roast beef, turkey, bread, cakes, wild honey, and coffee. Later black retainers drove a herd of excellent horses past the house for the guests to admire.

The Chouteaus, especially the Colonel, were regularly called on for assistance on the numerous occasions when treaties or agreements were negotiated with the Osages or other tribes in order to make land available for the thousands of eastern Indians the government was urging to emigrate beyond the Mississippi. As early as 1808, part of the Cherokees requested permission to move where they could subsist by hunting, and in the next few years moved to the Arkansas River country. In 1813 Major William L. Lovely was named their agent. He complained bitterly of the whites' wasteful slaughter of the buffalo just for their tallow and bears for their oil, leaving the meat, which could have fed many Indians, to rot.

The frequent Osage raids on the Cherokees induced Lovely to persuade Chief Clermont's band to cede seven million acres on the north side of the Arkansas River in exchange for the government assuming the Cherokees' claims against the Osages. The huge tract, known as Lovely's Purchase, was too attractive to whites for the Cherokees to retain, and another treaty moved them farther west. In this treaty the government included five hundred dollars for George Guess, or Sequoyah, for inventing the Cherokee alphabet, and a thousand dollars for the purchase of a printing press and type.

Colonel Chouteau was still negotiating for the government when he fell ill and died at Fort Gibson on December

25, 1838, a few months after the death of his friend the Osage chief Clermont. As Chouteau was heavily in debt, creditors seized his assets, leaving his family destitute, but eventually the claims were satisfactorily adjusted.

Although Sam Houston's activities after he resigned as governor of Tennessee have often been dismissed as a drunken orgy, he was quite active as a trader and in taking the part of Indians against their agents. Because he was a friend of President Andrew Jackson, his interventions were effective. Although he refused any official position, Houston was persistent in offering suggestions to and criticisms of the Indian Service, which were neither welcomed nor appreciated.

Soon after his arrival at Fort Gibson in 1829, rumors spread that Houston had designs on Texas. He cultivated the friendship of the Creeks as well as the Cherokees, and he apparently was behind his Creek friend Benjamin Hawkins' efforts to secure land for the rest of the tribe in East Texas, where many Cherokees had settled earlier. The rumor that Houston intended to employ Cherokee and Creek warriors in the conquest of Texas and in creating an empire for himself reached President Jackson, who wrote him a sharp letter on the subject of his *illegal* enterprise." In February 1833 Houston wrote Jackson from Texas to explain why he considered the time ripe for the United States to acquire Texas and to say that he intended to live there.

A most admirable old gentleman and public official was Montford Stokes, who had served under Commodore Stephen Decatur in the Continental Navy, and who resigned as governor of North Carolina to head an important two-year commission in Arkansas Territory. The commissioners were to examine the country set apart for the emigrating tribes, adjust differences between them over boundaries and locations, report on proper places for locating the tribes, compose differences with the hostiles, and to report on the manner in which the emigration of Indians was conducted and to make recommendations for improvements.

The secretary of war instructed the commissioners to consult regularly with Colonel Chouteau. Stokes and Chouteau became firm friends, but the other two commissioners, Henry L. Ellsworth and the Reverend John Schermerhorn, refused to comply—Chouteau had criticized and opposed their shabby attempt to move the Osages onto a worthless tract because they considered it a good bargain for the government.

Governor Stokes served on another commission that negotiated with the Comanches, Kiowas, and others at Fort Gibson. In 1836 he became agent for the Cherokees and Senecas; he died in March 1842 at the age of eighty-two, after a lifetime of dedicated service.

In 1833 an expedition was sent from Fort Gibson to impress the prairie tribes with the military power of the United States, but it lost one ranger captured and later killed by the Indians, leaving them more scornful than impressed. That same year Congress authorized the formation of a regiment of dragoons for service in the West. Major Henry Dodge was named colonel of the new unit, Stephen Watts Kearny was major, and Jefferson Davis was first lieutenant. The dragoons seemed doomed to constant frustration, for they got off to a bad start and their fortunes declined steadily thereafter. The first five companies had to march from Jefferson Barracks in November before their uniforms arrived, and they suffered severely from the cold on the way to Fort Gibson, where they were housed in tents. Their winter uniforms were on the steamer *Little Rock,* which struck a submerged rock and sank just above the village of Little Rock. The uniforms were eventually salvaged, but in a damaged state.

Floods the previous summer had swept away cornfields and stored corn, and the dragoons' mounts suffered severely from hunger. Most of the recruits were unfamiliar with guns and horses, and since half of them had to guard the horse herd each day, their training was far from satisfactory. During the winter five more companies were recruited and sent to Jefferson Barracks on their way to Fort Gibson.

Whoever designed the dragoon uniforms was thinking of the parade ground rather than the campaign trail over sweltering prairies. The dark blue coats were double-breasted with two rows of ten gilt buttons and yellow cuffs and collars. The blue-gray trousers had two yellow stripes down the outside seams. The caps were like the infantry's, with silver eagles and gilt stars in front and a drooping tassel of white horsehair on top. Ankle boots and yellow spurs completed the outfit, except for double-breasted greatcoats and capes for winter.

After unfortunate delays, the ill-prepared dragoons belatedly marched in mid-June 1834 for a two-month expedition on the plains in the hottest part of the summer. Again the purpose was to impress the wild tribes with the nation's military might. General Henry Leavenworth was in command, and when they sighted buffalo, he was foremost among the officers struck by the buffalo madness that impelled Americans to kill the huge beasts at every opportunity for "sport." Aware that this was foolish and injurious to the horses, Leavenworth ordered no more buffalo chasing. But the next time more were sighted, he was the first to dash after them. This time his horse fell and he was fatally injured.

Men fell ill every day and had to be left behind with others to care for them, and the regiment shrunk steadily. One night a broken-down horse that had been abandoned dutifully caught up with the troops. A nervous sentry, hearing a strange sound, shot it, stampeding the others, so the next day was spent combing the prairies for them. A supply of horseshoes hadn't arrived before they marched, so many horses were now sorefooted.

They finally reached a big Comanche camp near the Wichita Mountains, but the regiment was now down to less than two hundred men fit for duty. The Comanches they had come to impress found them more to be pitied than feared. After visiting the Comanches, Kiowas, and Wich-

itas, and persuading the Indians to send chiefs and head-
men to Fort Gibson, the dragoons headed for home.

The return trip was even more difficult. The numerous
invalids were carried in litters or jolting wagons; those unable to travel were left with others to tend them, and many
continued to die each day. The heat was intense, the grass
was dried up, and the horses were famished. Often the only
water they could find was in buffalo wallows, from which
they had to eject the occupants before desperately gulping
down the putrid water. After they finally reached Fort Gibson, eight or ten men continued to die each day for some
weeks, and there weren't enough healthy ones to tend the
sick. The artist George Catlin, who accompanied the expedition, was gravely ill but recovered.

The costly expedition, which was much criticized in the
East, was deemed a success because it had finally made contact with the Comanches, Kiowas, and others and persuaded them to send delegations to Fort Gibson for a three-
day powwow with the Osages, Cherokees, Creeks, and
Choctaws in early September. Colonel Dodge presided, but
he had no authority to negotiate treaties. Foreman nev-
ertheless acknowledged this as the most important Indian
conference ever held in the Southwest, for it paved the way
for subsequent treaties and agreements essential to the government's plan to transplant sixty thousand members of the
Five Civilized Tribes from east of the Mississippi, and for
the security of settlers and travelers. The treaties that ensued weren't always observed by either side, but the Fort
Gibson conference was the beginning and basis upon which
the government's program was ultimately carried out.

Pioneer Days
in the Early Southwest

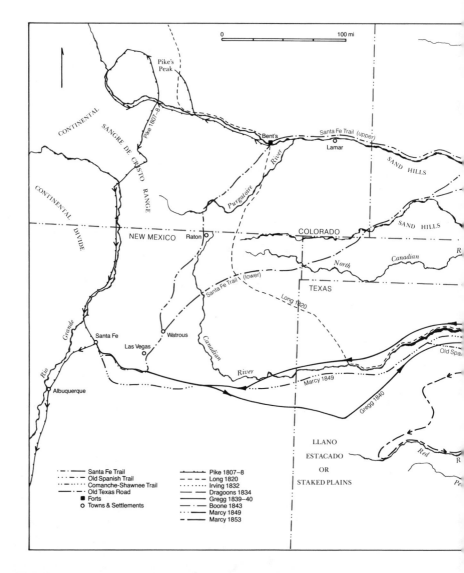

MAP SHOWING ROUTES OF EARLY EXPLORATIONS AND
EXPEDITIONS IN THE SOUTHWEST ALONG THE ARKANSAS,
CANADIAN, AND RED RIVERS AND THEIR TRIBUTARIES.

(Based on original map compiled by Grant Foreman and T. P. Clonts.)

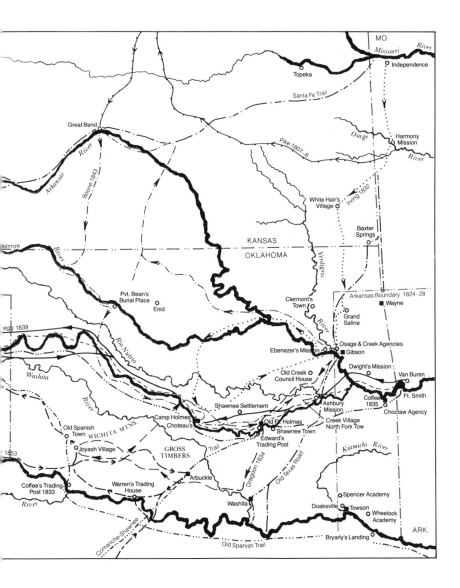

Early Explorations of Louisiana Territory

Three miles northeast of Muskogee the Verdigris and Grand rivers half a mile apart, discharge their waters into the Arkansas, which thus augmented, flows in a southeasterly direction to the Mississippi, six hundred miles distant by the course of the stream. This junction of the three rivers, establishing the head of navigation, became known in early times as the Three Forks, or more commonly, as the mouth of the Verdigris. In the days when river navigation played such a tremendously important part in the life of this western country, the mouth of the Verdigris maintained for many years an importance that long since has passed away and been forgotten. As a trading center and theatre of military and more peaceful operations in the winning of this country, it was second to none west of the Mississippi.

From the mouth of the Verdigris, in its day the farthest thrust of the pioneer, the conquest of a large part of the Southwest was achieved. The story of this campaign covering a period of nearly fifty years, has never been written, though it contains much of romance that even in the form of isolated or related incidents, it is possible to record. The Louisiana Purchase itself was romance. In 1803 President Jefferson directed Monroe and Livingston to negotiate for the purchase of New Orleans for the United States, and they brought home title to an empire, practically a donation from France.

From the day in April, 1682, when La Salle stood at the mouth of the Mississippi and proclaimed the great western country drained by that river to belong to France, until 1762, when she ceded it to Spain, France made no adequate effort to utilize or even to explore that great empire. The earliest explorers of the southwest were Spaniards. The first known visitors were De Soto who crossed the Mississippi in 1540, and Coronado who came from the south the next year. Schoolcraft traces the march of De Soto to the mouth of the Verdigris. He says [1] that after De Soto crossed the Mississippi with his army "he passed an uninhabited region for five days, west, over the remaining elevations of the Ozark chain, and came to fertile prairies beyond, inhabited by Indians called Quipana, Pani, or Pawnee. A few days' further march brought him to the banks of the Arkansas, near the Neosho, which appears to have been about the present site of Fort Gibson. Here, in a fruitful country of meadows, he wintered. Next spring he marched down the north banks of the Arkansas, to a point opposite the present Fort Smith, where he crossed in a boat, previously prepared. He then descended the south bank of the river to Anilco (Little Rock), where the army crossed to the north bank, partly on rafts, and reached the mouth of the Arkansas where he died." It was within the next year that Coronado entered the western part of Oklahoma from the southwest and proceeded to a point within what is now Kansas.[2]

The limits of the Spanish and French dominions were not clearly defined and between them there was a

---

[1] Schoolcraft, Henry R., LL.D. *Information Respecting the History, Condition, and Prospects of the Indian Tribes of the United States*, vol. iii, 50.

[2] Bancroft, Hubert Howe. *Works of Hubert Howe Bancroft, History of the North Mexican States*, vol. xv, 85.

vast expanse of unknown country over which the Indians hunted and fought for supremacy that afterward
became the American Southwest.   While both nations
had contributed to the nomenclature of the natural
features of this region and thus recorded the transient
presence of their trappers and traders, neither built
any settlements upon it.   On the eastern fringe, along
the Mississippi the French had established Arkansas
Post,³ destined to figure in the history of the southwest

---

³ "Arkansas Post perpetuates the name of the oldest establishment of
whites in the lower Mississippi valley.   The present village is on the N.
bank of the Arkansaw r., in the county and State of Arkansas, 73 m. S.E. of
Little Rock, the capital.   Though never a locality of much importance, its
place in history is secure and permanent.   Early in the year 1685, Henri
de Tonti, the famous trusty lieutenant of La Salle, was reinstated in command of Fort St. Louis of the Illinois, with titles of captain and governor,
by order of the French king Louis XIV.   Tonti learned that La Salle was
in trouble somewhere in New Spain (Texas), and organized an expedition
for his relief.   On Feb. 16th, 1686, he left Fort St. Louis, with 30 Frenchmen and 5 Indians, descended the Illinois and Miss. rivers to the Gulf,
and scoured the coast for miles, but saw no sign of his great chief.   He
wrote a letter for La Salle, which he committed to the care of a chief of
the Quinipissas for delivery, should opportunity offer, and retraced his
way up the Miss. r. to the mouth of the Arkansaw, which latter river he
ascended to the village of the Arkensa Indians.   There, on lands which La
Salle had already granted him, he stationed six of his men, who volunteered
to remain in hopes of hearing from the distant commander.   This was the
origin of the Poste aux Arkansas.   La Salle was murdered by the traitor
Duhaut, one of several ruffians among his own men who conspired to his
foul assassination, some say on one of the tributaries of the Brazos, at a
spot which has been supposed to be perhaps 40-50 m. N. of present town
of Washington, Tex.; the date is Mar. 19th or 20th, 1687.   Seven of the
survivors of La Salle's ill-starred colony at Fort St. Louis of Texas, reached
Arkansas Post after a journey computed at the time to have been 250
leagues, in the summer of 1687, and found Couture and De Launay, two
of the six whom Tonti had stationed there the year before.   (See Wallace,
Hist. Ill. and La., etc., 1893.)   This Tonti (or Tonty), b. about 1650, died
at Mobile, 1704, was the son of Lorenzo Tonti, who devised the Tontine
scheme or policy of life insurance.   Arkansas Post was the scene of La-
clede's death, June 20th, 1778.   The place was taken by the Unionists from
the Confederates, Jan. 11th, 1863." – Coues, Elliott. *The expeditions of
Zebulon Montgomery Pike,* vol. 11, 560 n. 21.

    The Act of Congress of March 2, 1819, creating the territory of Arkan-
saw, established the capital at the "post of the Arkansaw", where it con-

and pass away; Sainte Genevieve, Saint Charles, Saint Louis and other early settlements. On the south and west the Spaniards were found at Natchitoches and San Antonio de Bexar, Santa Fe and Taos and along ancient Spanish trails that connected them.

Desultory efforts at exploration and conquest of this great region were made by both nations. The French Government issued a patent to Antoine de Crozat in 1712, granting him "the commerce of the country of Louisiana." After five years, despairing of anything to be gained by its possession, de Crozat surrendered his patent and abandoned his colony. The same year a grant was made by the French Government to John Law, of the Mississippi Commerce Company, to be exploited in the ill-fated Mississippi Bubble. The Mississippi Company undertook to establish barrier settlements to maintain the territorial claims of France and to arrest the progress of the Spaniards. Bernard de la Harpe in 1719 with a body of troops ascended Red River to the Caddo villages where he built a fort called Saint Louis de Carlorette on the right bank of that river. He then pursued his discoveries to the Arkansas River where he visited an Indian village three miles in extent, containing upwards of four thousand persons. It was situated about one hundred twenty miles southwest of the Osage.

Early in the eighteenth century the French ascended the Arkansas to its source and for nearly eighty years navigated that river, the Canadian and other tributaries as far as the Spanish possessions in the pursuit of trade and furs. At an early day a company of French traders ascended Arkansas River and established a

tinued until 1821, when by the legislature it was removed to "the town at the Little Rock."

trading post in the mountains south of the headwaters of that stream. There they trafficked with the Indians and with the Spaniards of Mexico until the Spanish merchants of Santa Fe feeling the stress of competition, procured their imprisonment and seizure of their effects on the charge that the Frenchmen were trespassing on Spanish territory. Ultimately however it was decided at Havana that they were within the boundaries of Louisiana and the prisoners were released and their goods restored to them.

At the same time the Spaniards were making similar ventures from the west across this unknown land. A company under Captain Villasur left Santa Fe in 1719 and marched northeast in quest of the Pawnee villages, but lost their way and unluckily arrived among the Missouri, whose destruction they meditated. Ignorant of their mistake as the latter spoke the Pawnee language, they disclosed their plans without reserve and requested the coöperation of the Missouri. The latter attacked the Spaniards in the night while they slept in fancied security and killed all of them except the priest who escaped on his horse.[4] The boldness of the Spaniards in penetrating six hundred miles from Santa Fe into an unknown country apprised the French of their danger. The latter therefore dispatched De Burgmont with a considerable force who took possession of an island in the Missouri River some distance above the Osage on which he built Fort Orleans.[5]

Finally wearying of the ownership of a territory that had occasioned great trouble and expense and offered little hope of profit, and that exposed her to costly

---

[4] This massacre is said to have taken place in what is now Saline County, Missouri.

[5] Stoddard, Major Amos. *Sketches, Historical and Descriptive of Louisiana,* 39, 41, 45, 147.

reprisals at the hands of England, France ceded to
Spain that part of Louisiana lying west of the Mississippi.   During the thirty-eight years that Spain owned
Louisiana, frequent irritations arose between Spain and
the American Colonies over the use of the Mississippi
River through Spanish territory.   On October 1, 1800,
Spain secretly ceded Louisiana back to France so that
the United States did not hear of it for nearly two
years; but, learning of the transaction in which we had
such deep concern, American indignation manifested
itself by threats of war against France and negotiations
were opened with the latter which led to the purchase
of Louisiana by the United States.   In 1803, again to
rid France of the territory she was unable to use and to
prevent England taking it from her, Napoleon sold
Louisiana to the United States for less than fifteen
million dollars, a sum that is returned in a few days
to the owners of oil wells in that territory.

In contrast with the futile policy, or lack of policy,
of France and Spain, were the vigorous steps at once
inaugurated by the United States, in spite of short-
sighted opposition of members of Congress, many of
whom opposed the ratification of the purchase of
Louisiana on the ground that it was so remote from the
populated part of the United States that its possession
threatened dismemberment of the Union by the setting
up of another government in the West.   Even before
the Louisiana Purchase was consummated, Thomas
Jefferson was planning an inquiry into the extent and
character of that great region, and the next year after
the purchase was made his plans were so far matured
that he was able to send Captain Meriwether Lewis
and Captain William Clark on their memorable voyage up the Missouri River in the performance of an

achievement without parallel in the history of our country.

The Louisiana Purchase was served by four great natural highways; the Mississippi, Missouri, Arkansas, and Red rivers, that at once lent themselves to the scheme of exploration launched by Jefferson.

Before Lewis and Clark returned from their expedition, Lieutenant Zebulon M. Pike [6] had ascended to the headwaters of the Mississippi to explore and report on that region of newly acquired territory, which he accomplished in eight months and twenty days. The next year, in 1806, Pike was sent on an expedition to explore the headwaters of the Arkansas, with directions to travel south from that region to the headwaters of Red River and, returning down that stream, to report on the southwestern boundary of our purchase.

Relations between Spain and the United States were then serious, and the troops of the two governments came near hostilities on the frontiers of Texas and the Orleans territory. News of Pike's preparation was conveyed to Nacogdoches and from there to Chihuahua. The Spaniards then ordered out an expedition to halt the American explorers and to explore the country between New Mexico and the Missouri.

From Santa Fe the Spanish invasion departed under the command of Lieutenant Don Facundo Malgares. It consisted of six hundred mounted troops with over two thousand horses and mules carrying ammunition and supplies for six months. They descended Red

[6] Zebulon Montgomery Pike was born in Lamberton, New Jersey, January 5, 1779. Passing through various grades in the army he was commissioned Brigadier-general March 12, 1813. Early in that year he was appointed adjutant and Inspector-general of the army on the northern frontier. He was killed in an attack upon York, Upper Canada, April 27, 1813.

River two hundred thirty-three leagues, where they held a council with the Comanche Indians, then struck off northeast to the Arkansas where Lieutenant Malgares left two hundred forty of his men with the lame and tired horses, while he proceeded to the Pawnee republic. Here he was met by the chiefs and warriors of the Grand Pawnee with whom he held councils and presented them with medals and flags in token of Spanish sovereignty. Malagres took as prisoners all the American traders he found among the Indians.

Pike soon afterward visited the Pawnee villages and induced the chiefs to take down the Spanish flags and substitute those of the United States.[7] He then proceeded up the Arkansas and was successful in gaining the sources and then departed southward upon what was unquestionably Spanish territory now within the limits of southern Colorado; here he was taken prisoner by the Spaniards and carried to Santa Fe and under the command of Lieutenant Malgares he was conveyed from Santa Fe to Chihuahua; his papers were seized and he was taken to Natchitoches where he was released July 1, 1807.

Under Pike's command upon this expedition was James B. Wilkinson,[8] first-lieutenant of the Second Regiment of Infantry, who separated from Pike on the upper reaches of the Arkansas River within the present limits of Kansas, and under orders of his chief descended that river to its mouth. Wilkinson had five men with him, and at the beginning of their descent

---

[7] Coues, Elliott. *The Expeditions of Zebulon Montgomery Pike,* vol. ii, 415.

[8] James B. Wilkinson, the son of General James Wilkinson, was born in Maryland; he was commissioned first-lieutenant in the army September 30, 1803, and captain October 8, 1808. He died September 7, 1813. Wilkinson's account of his expedition is contained in Coues, Elliott, *op. cit.,* vol. ii, 538-561.

they cut a small cottonwood tree from which they fashioned a canoe with great difficulty; this being insufficient, they formed a second with four buffalo skins and two elk skins; this held three men beside himself and one Osage. In his wooden canoe were one soldier, one Osage and their baggage. One other soldier walked along the shore.

From their departure on the twenty-seventh of October, their journey was a succession of discouraging difficulties and hardships, occasioned by the cold, rain, and snow, and frequent lack of food. On December 27, they passed the mouths of the Verdigris and Grand rivers, where Wilkinson first noted the quantities of cane with which the fertile river bottom was covered beyond that point. Two days later they passed the falls now known as Webbers Falls, near the mouth of the Canadian, then "a fall of nearly seven feet perpendicular", and now only a ripple over submerged rocks.

Lieutenant Wilkinson reached Arkansas Post January 9 and New Orleans March 1; immediately thereafter another expedition was planned to explore the Arkansas River from the mouth to its source and the country beyond. It was in charge of William Dunbar and Thomas Freeman and was to be accompanied by an escort of thirty-five men under the command of Lieutenant Wilkinson assisted by Lieutenant Thomas A. Smith. May 20, 1807, General Wilkinson at New Orleans wrote to Captain Pike,[9] then about to reach Natchitoches at the end of his captivity in Mexico. He told Pike that the exploring party was then in motion on the Arkansas and the escort in two boats would reach Natchez in a week or ten days, and would then proceed with all possible dispatch. Pike was

---

[9] Coues, Elliott, *op. cit.*, vol. ii, 827.

directed to send to the exploring party on the Arkansas all the information gained by him which he thought essential to the enterprise.   General Wilkinson added that the party expected to camp for the winter near the Arkansas Osage at the mouth of the Verdigris.   However, as appears from Pike's letter [10] of July 5, 1807, the expedition was suspended for reasons which he does not disclose; but one may assume that further exploration in the west was embarrassed by the charges freely made that Wilkinson's orders to Pike to explore Arkansas and Red rivers were but a subterfuge for carrying into effect Wilkinson's share of the conspiracy he was charged with having entered into with Aaron Burr for the conquest and exploitation of the Spanish Southwest.

President Jefferson laid before Congress February 19, 1806, the interesting report of Lewis and Clark and of Doctor John Sibley on his travels up Red River as high as the Ouichita, now in Arkansas, in 1803-1804 [11] and a report of a Red River expedition in 1804 by Dunbar and his exploration of the hot springs, now in that state.[12]

A second expedition was undertaken in 1806 by Thomas Freeman, Captain Sparks, Lieutenant Humphrey, and Doctor Custis and a force of twenty-four men in two flat-bottomed barges and a pirogue.   They passed the Great Raft with difficulty, but were arrested and driven back by the Spaniards after they had ascended Red River six hundred miles.[13]   Doctor

[10] Coues, Elliott, *op. cit.*, vol. ii, 835.

[11] *American State Papers*, "Indian Affairs" vol. i, 705.

[12] Dunbar's interesting journal of that expedition was deposited with the American Philosophical Society in 1817 and was published in *Documents Relating to the Purchase and Exploration of Louisiana.* (New York, 1904).

[13] Thwaites, R. G., editor, *Early Western Travels*, vol. xvii, 66ff; American Historical Association *Annual Report for 1904*, 168 ff.

Sibley furnished a report[14] made to him by his assistant, a Frenchman named Francis Grappe, concerning a trip he made in 1803 up Red River from Natchitoches to Washita River now in the Chickasaw Nation.

When the cession of Louisiana was made, the ceded territory was at first divided into two parts. The district on the west bank of the Mississippi, lying south of latitude thirty-three, or what is now the state of Louisiana, was called the territory of Orleans; and the remaining portion, comprising a vast and unknown extent of country between the Mississippi and the Pacific Ocean was at the same time constituted the district of Louisiana and placed under the government of Indiana Territory. In March, 1805, it was denominated the territory of Louisiana.

The district of Louisiana under the same boundaries in 1812 was constituted a territorial government under the name of the territory of Missouri, which remained so until March, 1819, when the southern part of the territory was cut off and from it was created the territory of "Arkansaw." Arkansaw Territory extended from the Mississippi River westward to the Spanish possessions and was about six hundred miles long, including approximately the present area of Arkansas and Oklahoma.

At the time of the Louisiana Purchase there had begun the growth of the influence of the family of Chouteau which was destined to affect profoundly the development of this southwestern country. Auguste Chouteau and Pierre Chouteau[15] were half-brothers who came to Saint Louis from New Orleans. Pierre

---

[14] *American State Papers,* "Indian Affairs" vol. i, 729.

[15] Pierre and Auguste Chouteau negotiated for the United States a large number of treaties with the Indian tribes in the early years after the Louisiana Purchase.

Chouteau who was born in New Orleans and arrived in Saint Louis in 1764, was the father of Colonel A. P. Chouteau born in 1786, Pierre Chouteau Jr. born 1789, Paul Ligueste Chouteau born 1792, and a number of other sons.   Pierre Chouteau was engaged in the fur trade out of Saint Louis in the early days, operating largely on the Missouri River.   For twenty years he had traded with the Osage Indians who lived on the Missouri in the western part of the present limits of the state of that name.   Manuel Lisa,[16] a Spanish trader of Saint Louis, and other traders in 1802 secured from the authorities then in power the exclusive license to trade with the Osage Indians,[17] and thereby deprived Pierre Chouteau of this business.   Chouteau was resourceful, and having great influence with the Osage, induced half of that tribe, or nearly three thousand individuals, to remove from the Missouri River to the vicinity of the Three Forks, or the mouth of the Verdigris River, which was the head of navigation, and offered the best facilities for shipping supplies to the Indians and for carrying furs from the Indian country to markets in Saint Louis and New Orleans.   The presence of large salt springs in the vicinity was an

[16] Manuel Lisa, a Spaniard, was born in Louisiana in 1776.   He made several voyages from New Orleans up the Mississippi River in connection with the Indian trade and located in Saint Louis in 1799; and engaged at first in the Osage trade of which he obtained a monopoly from the Spanish government. Lisa made his first voyage up Missouri River in 1807, and from that time exercised a commanding influence in the fur trade out of Saint Louis.   He died in that city August 12, 1820.

[17] In 1802 the exclusive privilege of trading with the Osage was given by the Spanish authorities to Manuel Lisa, Charles Sanguinet, Francis M. Beniot, and Gregoire Sarpy.   The next year at the instance of Sarpy the grant was revoked and given to him, without notice to the other grantees. After the Louisiana Purchase was consummated, Sarpy filed a claim against the government for damages on account of the loss of this monopoly.   In 1814 the Committee of Claims of the House of Representatives reported against his claim. – *American State Papers*, "Claims" vol. i, 432.

added inducement to settlement there. Chouteau had selected for chief of this portion of the tribe an influential Osage named Cashesegra, or Big Track; but while he was the nominal head, Clermont, also known as the Builder of Towns, was the greatest warrior and leader, and their principal town on the Verdigris was called Clermont's or Clermo's Town.[18]

President Jefferson, in February 1806, submitted to Congress a statistical report made to him by Captain Meriwether Lewis in 1805, concerning the Indians west of the Mississippi. Speaking of the Osage, Captain Lewis said: [19]

"About three years since, nearly one-half of this nation, headed by their chief, *Big Track,* emigrated to the three forks of the Arkansas, near which, and on its north side, they established a village, where they now reside."

Answering the President's inquiry as to the place where it would be mutually advantageous to set up a trading establishment with these Indians, Captain Lewis designated the Three Forks of Arkansas River. In the account of the Lewis and Clark Expedition, they record that on May 31, 1804, they were encamped near the mouth of the Osage River, not far from where Jefferson City, Missouri, now is: [20]

". . . In the afternoon a boat came down from the Grand Osage river, bringing a letter from a person sent to the Osage nation on the Arkansas river, which mentioned that the letter announcing the cession of Louisiana was committed to the flames – that the Indians would not believe that the Americans were

---

[18] Near the site of the present town of Claremore, Oklahoma.

[19] *American State Papers,* "Indian Affairs" vol. i, 708.

[20] Hosmer, James R. *History of the Lewis and Clark Expedition,* vol. i, 8.

owners of that country, and disregarded St. Louis and its supplies."

The incident of Pierre Chouteau bringing the Osage down to the mouth of the Verdigris was mentioned by Lieutenant Wilkinson and by Major Pike [21] in their accounts of their explorations of the Arkansas River in 1806, and by Major Stephen H. Long in 1820.

The great influence of Chouteau with the Osage and his enterprise in leading two or three thousand of this tribe from their old home to the mouth of the Verdigris where they established themselves convenient to navigation; and the resultant location of a trading post, a mission, an army post, and Indian agencies in the neighborhood, affected enormously the importance and development of that vicinity and its influence over the surrounding country.   And the name of Chouteau, now scarcely remembered in the annals of the Southwest, was probably more potent in the destinies of that section of country than any other.   It will be seen that the Three Forks was planned by nature, and was early recognized and selected by white explorers as the focal point for enterprise in the midst of a vast extent of unexplored country, which was in time to extend its influence to the winning of the great Southwest. President Jefferson's message at this early day introduced the vital element of transportation into the destiny of that country, and fixed upon a point and route that survived in that employment until the coming of the railroad.

In the first message of President Jefferson after the Louisiana Purchase, he committed the administration to the policy of confirming to the Indian inhabitants of that country, their right of occupancy and self-

---

[21] Coues, Elliot, *op. cit.*, vol. ii, 529, 557.

government, to establishing friendly and commercial relations with them, and to ascertaining the geography of the country acquired. It soon became a favorite policy with the government to present to Indians living east of the Mississippi the advantages of moving westward to the Louisiana Purchase; and within the first few years after that acquisition many treaties were entered into with eastern tribes providing for their removal.

A delegation of Cherokee chiefs in May, 1808, requested President Jefferson to permit part of the tribe to remove west of the Mississippi where they could pursue the lives of hunters. The President gave the necessary permission but in order to effect the desired removal it was necessary to acquire the title to the land from the Osage Indians who claimed dominion over the country west of the Mississippi between the Arkansas and Missouri rivers where the Cherokee wished to locate. This was accomplished by treaty entered into at Saint Louis in 1808 and 1809.[22]

While this treaty was not ratified until April 28, 1810, President Jefferson on January 9, 1809, authorized the Cherokee to send exploring parties to the country ceded by the Osage to examine that on the waters of the White and Arkansas rivers. The report of the explorers being favorable, emigrating parties were soon on the march to Arkansas with the active assistance of government; and within a few years there were several thousand Cherokee living in the vicinity of White and Arkansas rivers.

William L. Lovely,[23] who had been serving as assis-

---

[22] *American State Papers*, "Indian Affairs" vol. i, 765. Kappler, Charles J. compiler and editor. *Indian Affairs, Laws and Treaties*, vol. ii, 69.

[23] "Major Lovely at the commencement of the War of the Revolution received a Commiſsion in the Virginia line of the regular Army and con-

tant to Colonel Return J. Meigs, Cherokee Indian Agent in Tennessee, was directed in 1813 to take up his station with the Cherokee in Arkansas. Directly upon his arrival he reported [24] to Governor Clark. He complained bitterly of the havoc wrought by white people on the game of the country which belonged to the Indians. He said that they killed the buffalo in great numbers for the tallow, and left to decay the carcasses that might have sustained the Indians. Bears were killed in the same ruthless manner for the oil they yielded.

Lovely wrote [25] to his friend Colonel Meigs, May 29, 1815, ". . . You will perceive amongst the papers enclosed to you for the Secretary of War, a copy of a letter from some gentlemen to whom I have given positive permission to establish a salt work near the Osage village. A work of this kind is essentially necessary to the good of the Indians and others of this country, having to give $30.00 often per barrel. I wish you therefore to write to Governor Clark and the Secretary of War on the subject." In all probability this was the famous salt works near which Union Mission was located.

Lovely reported [26] to Governor Clark in 1816 that

tinued in that line to the end of that war. At the capture of Burgoyne he belonged to a select Corps under Command of then Colonel Morgan. During his life he continued an undeviating friend to his adopted Country. About the commencement of the American revolution he came from Dublin where he had acquired the information & the manners of a gentleman. He lived some time in the family of Mr. Madison the father of the late President." – Colonel Return J. Meigs to the Acting Secretary of War June 2, 1817, Indian Office, Retired Classified Files, *1817 Cherokee Agency*.

[24] Lovely to General Clark, Governor of Missouri Territory, August 9, 1814, *ibid., 1814, Cherokee Agency on Arkansas*.

[25] Lovely to Meigs, *ibid., 1815, Cherokee Agency on the Arkansas*.

[26] Lovely to Clark, January 20, 1816, *ibid., 1816, Cherokee Agency on the Arkansas*.

robberies and murders committed by the Osage were about to force the Cherokee to war. He secured the attendance of the chiefs of Clermont's band in July 1816, at the mouth of the Verdigris,[27] where he attempted to adjust the difficulties of the Osage with the Cherokee and whites. Lovely proposed to the Osage that the government would pay all claims held against them by the Cherokee and white people for robberies and other depredations, if the Osage would relinquish to the United States the great tract of land lying on the north side of Arkansas River, bounded on the west by the falls of the Verdigris and on the north by a line running thence to the upper saline on Six Bull (Grand) River, and from there east to White River and the Cherokee settlements. This proposition was assented to by the Osage and their agreement was signed July 9, 1816, by Clermont and other Osage chiefs.[28] This great tract of over seven million acres became known as Lovely's Purchase, and was later the subject of acrimonious contention between the people of Arkansas and the Cherokee Indians.

But the apparent adjustment between the tribes was only temporary. In August 1817, Tallantusky and other Cherokee chiefs in the west wrote to Governor Clark [29] that for nine years they had been trying to make friends with the Osage, but to no purpose; that they had been trying to raise crops for their families but the Osage had stolen all their horses so that they were

---

[27] Nuttall says: [Thwaites, *op. cit.*, vol. xiii, 236] "The low hills contiguous to the falls of this river [Verdigris] and on which there exist several aboriginal mounds, were chosen by the Cherokees and Osages to hold their council, and to form a treaty of reciprocal amity as neighbors."

[28] U.S. House, *Documents*, 20th congress, first session, no. 263, Letter from Secretary of War concerning settlement of Lovely's Purchase, 38.

[29] Niles Register (Baltimore), vol. xiii, 74.

reduced to working the land with their bare hands; they had promised the President not to spill the blood of the Osage if they could help it, but that now the rivers were running with the blood of the Cherokee, they had determined to proceed against their enemies.

The news came from Saint Louis [30] that a "formidable coalition had been effected consisting of Cherokee, Choctaw, Shawnee, and Delaware from east of the Mississippi, and Caddoes, Coshatte, Tankawa, Comanche, and Cherokee west, for a combined assault on the Osage. The Coshatte, Tankawa, and Caddoes on Red River and the Cherokees of the Arkansas complained that the Osage were perpetually sending strong war parties into their country, killing small hunting bands of their people and driving off their horses." The report came from a man from New Orleans who said that he traveled part of the distance between Ouichita and Arkansas rivers with a large party going to join the confederate troops who had with them six field pieces with several whites and half breeds who learned the use of artillery under General Jackson during the recent war.

While this account of the preparations for battle was probably overdrawn, the contemplated attack was actually made by a large force. Say's report of Captain Bell's exploration of Arkansas River contains an account of the engagement that ensued when the invading army reached Clermont's town. [31] He says the attacking force amounted to six hundred and included Cherokee, Delaware, Shawnee, Quapaw, and eleven white men. They sent word to the Osage that they were a small party of chiefs and old men coming

[30] Niles Register (Baltimore), vol. xiii, 80.
[31] Thwaites, *op. cit.*, vol. xvii, 20.

to discuss peace with them, and requested Clermont to meet them at an appointed place near their town. Clermont was away from home with the warriors of the band on a hunting expedition, and an old man was appointed to act in his stead.   On his arrival at the proposed council ground the Osage found himself surrounded by hostile forces who immediately killed him. The design of this act of perfidy, says Say, was to effect the destruction of Clermont, the bravest and most powerful of the Osage.   The invaders then attacked the defenseless town in which remained only old men, women, and children, who offered but little resistance. A scene of outrage and bloodshed ensued, in which the eleven white men were said to have acted a conspicuous part.   They fired the village, destroyed the corn and other provisions of which the Osage had raised a plentiful crop, killed and took prisoners fifty or sixty of the inhabitants.   In Nuttall's more highly colored account he says: [32]

"The Cherokees, now forgetting the claims of civilization, fell upon the old and decrepit, upon the women and innocent children, and by their own account destroyed not less than 90 individuals, and carried away a number of prisoners.   A white man who accompanied them (named Chisholm), with a diabolical cruelty that ought to have been punished with death, dashed out the brains of a helpless infant, torn from the arms of its butchered mother.   Satiated with a horrid vengeance, the Cherokees returned with exultation to bear the tidings of their own infamy and atrocity."

---

[32] Thwaites, *op. cit.*, vol. xiii, 192.

Establishment of Fort Smith in 1817

The white population in Arkansas in 1817 had increased to several thousand, whose protection, as well as that of the Cherokee people living in that territory, from the continued hostilities of the Osage, required the establishment of a military post at the western border dividing the white settlements from the Osage. From Saint Louis came further news of threatened hostilities by the Osage near Clermont's Town, and a report [33] that Major William Bradford with a detachment of United States riflemen, and accompanied by Major Long, topographical engineer, had left that city for the purpose of establishing a military post on the Arkansas near the Osage boundary.

Major Stephen H. Long, at "Post of Ozark fifty miles up the Arkansas," reported [34] that he was ordered on a mission to the Forks of the Arkansas thence across country by land to Red River; thence to return by land to Saint Louis. "On the Arkansaw near the place where the Osage line strikes this river, I am to select a position for a military post to be under the command of Major Bradford, who is now at this place with his company, destined for that command. This business I am in hopes to accomplish by the first of December."

The point chosen by Long and Bradford for a military post was at the junction of the Poteau and Arkansas

[33] Niles Register, (Baltimore) vol. xiii, 176.

[34] Long to Brig. Gen. Joseph G. Swift, Oct. 15, 1817, U.S. War Department. *Army Engineers Department, Miscellaneous papers* File "A" L. 48.

rivers called by the French, Belle Point, and after
some years known as Fort Smith, after General Thomas
A. Smith.[35]   On this expedition, Long ascended as high
as the falls of the Verdigris, and made an observation
of the longitude and latitude at that point, as well as
at the mouth of the Verdigris four miles below.   On
May 12, 1818, Major Long made a formal report[36]
to his chief, Brigadier-general Thomas A. Smith, concerning the eligibility of certain places for military
purposes, visited by him in 1817.   In the course of his
remarks he stated that Arkansas River was navigable
at all stages of water for keel boats or barges of from
fifteen to twenty tons burden, from its mouth to The
Forks, a distance of six hundred miles.   The average
daily progress of such boats in ascending the river was
fifteen miles, requiring forty-two days to ascend the
whole of the above distance, or thirty-four days to
Belle Point, one hundred and thirty miles [sic] below
The Forks.   During very high water, or when contrary
winds prevailed, more time was required.   Long recommended two posts in the Southwest, one on Red
River above the American settlements, and "The other
on the Arkansaw, either at Belle Point or higher up,
should we extend the limits of our territory in that
direction by extinguishing the Osage claims."   He suggested that two companies of infantry be stationed at
Belle Point and one on Red River.

The Osage were induced to enter into another treaty
by which they ceded to the United States the country
north of the Arkansas, from their old boundary line

---

[35] Thomas A. Smith was born in Virginia and entered the Army from
Georgia; became Brigadier-general January 24, 1814; resigned from the
Army November 10, 1818, and died the next month.

[36] War Department, *Reports to Corps of Engineers July 3, 1812, to Oct.
4, 1823*, p. 278.

to the Three Forks, with a width of sixty miles, which included a large body of very fine land. This treaty was executed September 25, 1818,[37] in Saint Louis, but was not proclaimed until January 7, 1819. The Osage had accumulated a large number of claims against themselves by depredations on white people and the Cherokee; and being without the means of making restitution, they ceded this tract of land to satisfy the demands. The treaty was made by the Great and Little Osage and conveyed much the same land as that conveyed by the Arkansas Osage to Lovely, except that in the cession of 1818 the north boundary extended from the falls of the Verdigris east to the Osage line, whereas in the Lovely Purchase the line went farther north, "from the Falls to the Upper Saline on Six Bull and then east to Clark's line on White River."

In Governor Clark's letter of transmittal he said,[38] "The Osages have determined to unite themselves in one village, and have requested that Mr. Peter Chouteau may be re-appointed their agent. Mr. Chouteau has certainly more influence with that nation than any other person; and if the agency should be re-established (which I would strongly recommend), it would perhaps be well to gratify their wishes."

A treaty [39] proclaimed January 5, 1818, had been negotiated by William Clark and Auguste Chouteau for the United States and the Quapaw, by which the latter, for the sum of four thousand dollars and an annuity of about one thousand dollars in goods, ceded to the United States practically all that territory lying

[37] Kappler *op. cit.,* vol. ii, 116.
[38] *American State Papers,* "Indian Affairs" vol. ii, 179.
[39] Kappler, *op. cit.,* vol. ii, 112.

beween Red River and the Arkansas and Canadian and
extending west from the Mississippi to the Spanish
possessions.

A treaty [40] was concluded July 8, 1817, between the
United States, represented by General Andrew Jackson and others, and the Cherokee Nation east of the
Mississippi River and the Cherokee of Arkansas, represented by their deputies, John D. Chisholm and
James Rogers. Referring to the inducements given
by President Jefferson to those who wished to remove
west of the Mississippi River, and to measures taken
by the Cherokee to carry out their agreement, the
government bound itself to give the Cherokee people
on the Arkansas and White rivers as much land, acre
for acre, as they left in the east, and provided that all
citizens of the United States should be removed from
the land to be surveyed for them, except Mrs. Percis
Lovely, the widow of Major Lovely who had died in
February 1817.[41]

President Monroe in 1818 addressed Tallantusky
as chief, and the Cherokee east of the Mississippi, telling them he thought it best for all of them to remove
to Arkansas pursuant to the treay of 1817; he said it
was his wish that they should have no limits to the
west, so that they would have good mill-seats, plenty
of game, and not be surrounded by white people. As
the emigrants would not have food for the first year, he
agreed to furnish them as much corn as they needed,

---

[40] Kappler, *op. cit.*, vol. ii, 96.

[41] John C. Calhoun, Secretary of War, on September 9, 1818, issued
orders to Captain William Bradford at Belle Point, Arkansas, directing
him to remove from Lovely's Purchase all white persons except Mrs. P.
Lovely, who was to be allowed to remain where she was living during her
natural life. – U.S. House, *Document,* 20th congress, first session, no. 263,
Letter from Secretary of War concerning settlement of Lovely's Purchase,
p. 6.

and Governor McMinn of Tennessee was directed to furnish them with rifles to secure their game.[42]

The English naturalist, Thomas Nuttall, reached Fort Smith in 1819, on the expedition which he described in his journal.[43] Soon after his arrival there he accompanied Major Bradford to the mouth of the Kiamichi, to remove from the Choctaw country a number of white settlers who were unlawfully located there.[44] They found a considerable settlement on Gates Creek near Kiamichi River. Nuttall, in his quest for botanical specimens, got lost and he did not arrive at Fort Smith for nearly a month after Major Bradford's return. After some time spent in and about the garrison, on July 6, he ascended Arkansas River in the boat of Mr. Bogy (called by him "Bougie"), for his trading establishment at the mouth of the Verdigris. Their first camp was at Skin Bayou, and on the morning of the tenth they "passed the mouth of the rivulet or brook, called by the French, Salaiseau, from some hunters having here killed a quantity of bison and salted the beef for traffic." [45]

On the eleventh, they passed the outlet of the Canadian, and four miles farther the Illinois. "A few miles from its mouth, its banks present salt springs similar to those of Grand River, and scarcely less productive." At that place two of the hunters killed a fat bison. Four miles farther they came to Webbers

---

[42] Several hundred families of Cherokee emigrated to Arkansas during 1818 and 1819, including the Chief John Jolly, whom Samuel Houston called his Indian father.

[43] Thwaites, *op. cit.,* vol. xiii.

[44] In June 1819, General Andrew Jackson ordered Captain Bradford at Fort Smith to remove all white persons found west of a line drawn from the sources of the Kiamichi to the Poteau and compel all such settlers to return to the east side of that line. — *American State Papers,* "Indian Affairs" vol. ii, 557.

[45] Thwaites, *op. cit.,* vol. xiii, 231.

Falls, which Nuttall described as a cascade of two or
three feet perpendicular fall. In 1807, Lieutenant
Wilkinson found it a fall seven feet high. Nuttall's
party spent several hours trying to get their boat past
the falls, and finally were obliged to abandon the
effort until the next day, the thirteenth, when the
wind assisted them in passing up. No boat, he said,
drawing more than eighteen inches of water could pass
the falls at that season without unloading.

On the fourteenth, they passed the mouth of the
Grand River, "Six Bulls as it is called by the French
hunters," and entered the Verdigris where "M. Bougie
and Mr. Prior had their trading houses." On their
arrival he asked Pryor to walk with him about the
neighborhood, and the naturalist gives us his first impression of his surroundings.

They visited the falls of the Verdigris about three
miles above the mouth. Nuttall made a prediction
which is interesting in view of the subsequent building
of the city of Muskogee near by.[46] "If the confluence
of the Verdigris, Arkansa, and Grand rivers, shall
ever become of importance as a settlement, which the
great and irresistable tide of western emigration promises, a town will probably be founded here at the junction of these streams; and this obstruction in the navigation of the Verdigris, as well as the rapids of Grand
River, will afford good and convenient situations for
mills, a matter of no small importance in the list of
civilized comforts."

On the seventeenth, Nuttall went with two men in
a canoe up Grand River for a visit to the salt works
near the site of the subsequently located Union Mission. On the eighteenth, they arrived at the home of a

---

[46] Thwaites, *op. cit.,* vol. xiii, 235.

Mr. Slover, a hunter who had a good farm on a fine elevation two miles below the Saline. The next day he walked with Mr. Slover to "see the salt works, now indeed lying idle, and nearly deserted in consequence of the murder of Mr. Campbell by Erhart, his late partner, and two accomplices in their employ. Melancholy as were the reflections naturally arising from this horrid circumstance, I could not but congratulate myself on having escaped, perhaps a similar fate. At the Cadron,[47] I had made application to Childers, one of these remorseless villains, as a woodsman and hunter, to accompany me for hire, only about a month before he had shot and barbarously scalped Mr. Campbell, for the purpose of obtaining his little property, and in spite of the friendship which he had uniformly received from the deceased."[48]

Nuttall left the trading post on August 11, with a hunter named Lee, for a land journey up the Arkansas and Cimarron. This river was called by Nuttall Salt River or the First Red Fork of the Arkansas. Some old maps called it the Semerone of the Traders; others, the Negracka or Red Fork. Nuttall was taken desperately ill on the prairies and after weeks of incredible hardship and suffering, barely escaping death from fever and the Indians, he succeeded in again reaching the Verdigris trading post; here he remained for a

[47] "The site of Cadron settlement was the mouth of Cadron Creek, thirty-eight miles above Little Rock, in Faulkner County. In 1820 it was made the seat of justice for Pulaski County against the wishes of Governor James Miller, who favored Pyeattstown, his own residence. In time Cadron fell into decay, and it has now disappeared from the map." – Thwaites, *op. cit.,* vol. xiii, 156, n.

[48] Erhart and Childers were captured and taken to Arkansas Post where they were imprisoned while awaiting trial, but in a few days made their escape. Flint, Timothy. *Recollections of the Last Ten Years in the Valley of the Mississippi,* 270.

week to recover some of his strength, and then returned to Fort Smith, a journey of five days by boat.

Major Stephen H. Long [49] was sent in 1819 [50] in charge of an expedition to the Rocky Mountains to explore the head waters of Arkansas and Red rivers. The party included a zoologist, botanist, geographer, landscape painter, and naturalist. They went as far as the Rocky Mountains, and Major Long, with some of the party, went south to what he supposed was one of the tributaries of Red River, but which in fact was Canadian River. He followed it to its junction with the Arkansas, and then for the first time learned his mistake.[51] Part of the Long party under orders from their chief descended Arkansas River under Captain Bell. On the fifth day of September, 1820, Bell arrived at the trading establishment of Mr. Hugh Glenn, about a mile above the mouth of the Verdigris. Leaving Glenn's place, a short ride brought them to "The Neosho, or Grand River, better known to hunters by the singular designation of the Six Bulls."

[49] Stephen Harriman Long, born in New Hampshire; became second lieutenant of engineers December 12, 1814; brevet major of topographical engineers April 29, 1816; major July 7, 1828 and colonel September 9, 1861; retired June 1, 1863; died September 4, 1864.

[50] The treaty of February 22, 1819, with Spain had just been entered into by which Red River was established as the boundary line between that country and the United States. It was not proclaimed until February 22, 1821. Spain had contended that the Arkansas River should be taken as the boundary. So little was known at that time of the country between those rivers now comprising most of the state of Oklahoma, that it was characterized as worthless and unfit for cultivation; during the negotiations between the two countries, the Spanish representative wrote to Mr. Adams, Secretary of State, "It must be indifferent to them [the United States] to accept the Arkansas instead of the Red River as the boundary. This opinion is strengthened by the well-known fact that the intermediate space between these two rivers is so much impregnated with nitre as scarcely to be susceptible of improvement." – "United States v. State of Texas." United States Supreme Court *Reports,* vol. clxi, 25.

[51] Thwaites, *op. cit.,* vol. xvi, 180.

At Glenn's house they found two soldiers who had deserted from Fort Smith, whom Bell took in charge and compelled to travel with him to the post. After crossing Grand River, probably about where Fort Gibson was later located, they had great difficulty in penetrating the canebrake, but after a considerable time emerged upon the prairie of Bayou Manard. Continuing their journey they arrived at Bean's salt works on the Illinois River. Mark Bean had commenced operations in the spring of 1820, and had already a neat farmhouse with a considerable stock of cattle, hogs, and poultry, and several acres of Indian corn. Near the spring he had erected a good log house and a shed for the furnace; but his kettles which were purchased of the owners of the abandoned Neosho establishment, were not yet fixed. "On the side of a large well, which he had sunk to collect the salt water, and perhaps two feet from the surface of the soil, he pointed out the remains of a stratum of charcoal of inconsiderable extent, through which they had penetrated, and which to a by-stander was a certain proof that these springs had been formerly worked by the Indians."

Continuing his journey, on September 9, 1820, he arrived at Fort Smith, which he described as having a commanding position in every direction, sixty feet above the level of the river. "Next to the water, its figure is two sides of a square, on soil twenty feet deep, under which is rock about forty feet deep, whose base is washed by the united waters of the Portean and Arkansaw. The plan of the Fort, yet unfinished, is a square of one hundred and thirty-two feet, with two blockhouses at opposite angles, to be surrounded by a ditch. The sides next to the land and two blockhouses are completed." [52]   Pursuing his course down the river, Captain Bell described the homes of the Cherokee, whom he found considerably advanced in civilization. Their country was productive and contained plantations in a good state of cultivation, bearing cotton, corn, sweet potatoes, beans, and pumpkins.

At this time the western country was attracting the attention of the missionary societies in the East, and plans were made to establish missionary outposts among the western Indians of Arkansas. Harmony Mission was established among the Osage of the Missouri River; Union Mission among the Arkansas Osage, and Dwight Mission [53] in the Cherokee country in Arkansas. In the summer of 1819, Reverend Mr. Epaphras Chapman of Connecticut and Mr. Vinall, as agents for the United Foreign Missionary Society, went west to explore the country and determine on sites for missions. While ascending Arkansas River Mr. Vinall was taken sick, and died at Fort Smith; [54] Mr. Chapman continued, and in company with Nathaniel

[52] Morse, Rev. Jedidiah. *A Report to the Secretary of War on Indian Affairs*, App. 254; extract from Captain Bell's Journal. Nuttall (Thwaites, *op. cit.*, vol. xiii, 201) described the garrison on April 24, 1819, as "consisting of two blockhouses and lines of cabins or barracks for the accomodation of 70 men whom it contains."

[53] The station was named in honor of Timothy Dwight, the president of Yale College, and a pioneer organizer of the mission board. Thwaites, *op. cit.*, vol. xiii, 182, n. "In June 1820, the two branches of the Family destined for this distant station, having proceeded by different routes, met on the spot destined for their future residence, and scene of labor in civilizing and evangelizing the Indians. . . The first tree was felled on the 25th of August." Morse, Rev. Jedidiah, D.D. *op. cit.*, app. 214, 215. See also the pungent account of Dwight Mission in 1823 in General Thomas James, *Three Years Among the Indians and Mexicans*, 238, ff.

[54] Nuttall remained at Fort Smith until October 16, 1819, recovering from his serious illness. He mentions [Thwaites, *op. cit.*, vol. xiii, 279] that among his associates in affliction were numbered two missionaries who had intended to proceed to the Osage, among whom was Mr. Vinall, called by him "Viner", who, "after the attacks of a lingering fever, paid the debt of nature."

Pryor visited the Arkansas Osage and selected a site for Union Mission on land near Grand River, which was given to them by the Osage.

Credentials were issued by the War Department May 3, 1820, to Vaill and Chapman,[55] authorizing them to establish a mission among the Osage; and on November 15, 1820, Reverend Mr. Chapman, Mr. Requa, Mr. Redfield, and three others reached the place on Grand River selected the year before by Mr. Chapman as the site for Union Mission, and began the erection of the buildings. Tal-lai, the Osage chief, gave them a cordial welcome and a history of his family and events in the nation since Mr. Chapman was there the year before.[56]

The site, five miles northeast of Mazie, Mayes County, Oklahoma, is about forty-five miles by water up Grand River, and twenty-five miles by land from its junction with the Arkansas. The early arrivals had completed the erection of five log cabins by the month of March, the cabins being under one roof, eighty feet long by eighteen wide. It was early in 1820, the missionaries organized in New York for their adventure into this wild and unknown country.[57] They left New York in April, arrived in Philadelphia on April 22, and sermons were preached in all the churches

---

[55] On May 8, 1820, the Government paid Mr. "Ephraim" Chapman as agent of the United Foreign Missionary Society of New York, seven hundred dollars, on account of the buildings to be erected for a school at Union Mission. – *American State Papers,* "Indian Affairs" vol. ii, 272.

[56] Morse, Rev. Jedidiah, *op. cit.,* app. 217, ff.

[57] The Mission consisted of the following: Reverend William F. Vaill, wife and four children, North Guilford, Connecticut; Reverend Epaphras Chapman and wife, East Haddon, Connecticut; Doctor Marcus Palmer, Greenwich, Connecticut; Mr. Stephen Fuller, East Haddon, Connecticut; Mr. Abraham Redfield, Orange County, New York; Mr. Alexander Woodruff, Newark, New Jersey; Mr. John M. Spaulding, Coldchester, Connecticut; George and William Requa, Winchester, New York; Miss Clarissa Johnston, Coldchester, New York; Miss Susan Lines, Redding, Connecticut;

of the city where collections amounting to two thousand dollars were donated to the mission. The same day they left for Pittsburg on their long journey to their post, which they did not reach for nearly ten months.

Reverend Mr. Vaill was the principal of the Mission, two of the men were carpenters, three were husbandmen, one was the blacksmith, and one a school teacher. In June 1820, in two comfortable keel boats the missionaries arrived at Arkansas Post, fifty miles up Arkansas River where they remained until July 3, when they resumed their river journey. Traveling in the heat of July,[58] many of the members of the party, unused to the climate, were taken sick, and nearly all of the men who managed the boats were ill after the first sixty or seventy miles above Arkansas Post. One of the boatmen named Gach, of Baltimore, died; and within thirty miles of Little Rock, Miss Dollie E. White, aged twenty-three of Danbury, Connecticut, died and was buried near the bank of the river at that place. At Little Rock, the whole party left the boats to remain until cooler weather; Chapman, Redfield, Requa and three others continued in the fall to the site of the mission to erect a few log houses before winter. The remainder of the party did not resume their journey until the twelfth of December. Proceeding on their weary way, they reached their post on the eighteenth day of February, 1821, where they found a few buildings completed and others under construction; and here, three hundred miles from Little Rock,

Miss Mary Foster, New York City; Miss Dollie E. White, Danbury, Connecticut; Miss Eliza Cleaver, Litchfield, Connecticut; Miss Phoebe Beach, Newburgh, New York; from New York *Advertiser*, copied in Arkansas *Gazette*, (Arkansas Post) July 8, 1820, p. 2, col. 4.

[58] Arkansas *Gazette* (Arkansas Post), July 29, 1820, p. 3, col. 1.

the nearest post office, the mission family made their stand, the farthest missionary outpost.

Mr. Vaill made his first annual report [59] to the Secretary of War on October 30, 1821. He described the buildings as erected on a moderate eminence, about a mile from the river, and an equal distance from a valuable saline, at which a quantity of salt was manufactured for the settlements below. Grand River, they reported, was navigable about half the year. The Mission tract of land of about one thousand acres of prairie was enclosed on two sides by a bend of the river and bounded on the other sides by hills. The Mission was established under great difficulties. The Osage and Cherokee were at war with each other, and the former were fearful of allowing their children to leave their homes to attend the Mission school. There were but seven children in attendance in 1822, twelve in 1823 and twenty in 1824; but they maintained an extensive establishment including a large number of buildings, shops, barns, cribs, cattle, fields; and there was a combined grist-mill and sawmill the motive power of which was furnished by eighteen oxen worked in shifts of six at one time upon the treadwheel.

In the spring of 1824, Mr. William C. Requa and Mr. E. Chapman of the Mission removed their families to a point across Grand River and four miles above the Mission, which they named Hopefield. Here by precept and example they taught a small colony of Osage to maintain themselves by farming. Hopefield being included in the Cherokee country by the Treaty of 1828, the Osage were compelled to leave there the next winter. It was afterward re-established and

---

[59] Vaill to Calhoun, Oct. 30, 1821, Indian Office, Retired Classified Files, *1821, Osage, Union, Arkansas Territory.*

called New Hopefield on Grand River at the mouth
of Cabin Creek in the northern part of what is now
Mayes county, Oklahoma.   These Indian settlers were
compelled to endure the menace and scorn of their
tribesmen; they were called field-makers and missionaries, withering taunts expressing ribald mirth and
derision.   The patience and perseverance of the good
missionaries held them to their tasks, and those members of the Osage tribe called Requa's band for years
maintained a position for industry, sobriety and comfort that set them quite apart from the remainder of the
tribe.

When the missionaries arrived at their station on
Grand River, they furnished interesting descriptions
of the beautiful country about them, probably the first
detailed description ever written concerning that particular section.   In the fall of 1819, after Mr. Chapman decided on the beautiful timber-fringed prairie
on Grand River as a location for the Mission, he went
to Clermont's Town for a conference.   The town was
situated on Verdigris River about twenty-five miles
west of the proposed site of the Mission.   Mr. Chapman wrote,[60] March 18, 1820 of many interesting features of the section they were about to occupy – the
navigable stream at hand, the fertile soil, the timber
near by, the Osage whom they were to labor for – but
not the least important was the salt spring a mile away,
which they planned to work that year.   Later in the
year he wrote: "On the 10th November 1820, we examined the celebrated Saline, on Illinois river, and the
apparatus just erected for making salt.   This place
had evidently been before occupied by Indians, or
others, for the like purpose."

[60] Morse, Rev. Jedidiah, *op. cit.,* App. 227.

Expeditions of Fowler and James to Santa Fe, 1821

When Pike returned from his western expedition and related his experiences in Santa Fe and other places among the Spaniards, his accounts excited great interest in the east, which resulted in further exploits. In 1812, an expedition was undertaken [61] by Robert McKnight, James Baird, Samuel Chambers, Peter Baum, Benjamin Shrive, Alfred Allen, Michael Mc-Donald, William Mines, and Thomas Cook, all citizens of Missouri Territory; they were arrested by the Spaniards, charged with being in Spanish territory without a passport, and thrown into the calabazos of Chihuahua, where they were kept for nine years. In 1821, two of them escaped, and coming down Canadian and Arkansas rivers met Hugh Glenn, owner of a trading house at the mouth of the Verdigris, and told him of the wonders of Santa Fe. Inspired by the accounts of these travelers, Glenn engaged in an enterprise with Major Jacob Fowler and Captain Pryor for an expedition from the Verdigris to Santa Fe. [62]

The members of the McKnight party who had escaped from the Spaniards, continued their journey to Saint Louis, where they repeated their romantic tale to John McKnight, a brother of Robert McKnight who was still a prisoner with the Spaniards, and to

[61] *American State Papers,* "Foreign Relations" vol. iv, 208.

[62] For Fowler's picturesque account of their experiences see Coues, Elliott, *The Journal of Jacob Fowler.*

others. As a result of their account, McKnight and General Thomas James organized an expedition to go from Saint Louis to Santa Fe. James's purpose was to trade with the Indians, and John McKnight went to see his brother and procure his release, if possible. The two expeditions got under way the same summer, and both went by way of the Arkansas as high as the Verdigris, which at that time was recognized as the Santa Fe route.

While James's party left Saint Louis on May 10, 1821, Fowler, leaving Fort Smith September 6 of that year, seems to have been in advance. From Fort Smith, Fowler traversed the rich Arkansas bottom covered with timber and cane, until he came to a creek which he calls the Tallecaw,[63] and locates ten miles below Illinois River. At the latter stream he stopped at Bean's salt works, which Captain Bell visited and described the year before.[64] Fowler said the works consisted of one small well with a few kettles. About fifty-five gallons of water made a bushel of salt, and the spring furnished sufficient water to keep the works going three days a week. Bean and Sanders had a license from the Governor of Arkansas to operate the works, and sold the salt for one dollar a bushel.

After passing over the mountain and subsequent prairie land, they traversed eight miles of bottom land covered with cane and timber, and came to Grand River or Six Bulls; this they forded and continued to

[63] Probably intended for Tahlequah, but called by Long [Thwaites, *op. cit.*, vol. xvi, 287] Bayou Viande, meaning Meat Bayou, and since corrupted into Vian, and by some map makers, Vine Creek.

[64] During the Civil War these works, known as Mackey's Salt Works furnished salt for the contending armies until they were destroyed by one side to prevent them falling into the hands of the enemy. In the lean days of reconstruction the huge broken kettles each weighing over half a ton were patched up and salt was again made there.

the Verdigris, where they stopped at the trading house of Colonel Hugh Glenn, about a mile above the mouth of the river. They remained there, engaged in outfitting their expedition, until September 25. Five of their hunters deserted them there, but while that event dispirited some of the men, they departed under the command of Colonel Glenn, with twenty men whom Fowler names as folows:[65] Colonel Hugh Glenn in command; Major Jacob Fowler, Robert Fowler, his brother, Nathaniel Pryor, Baptiste Roy, interpreter, Baptiste Peno, George Douglas, Bone, Barbo, Louis Dawson, Taylor, Richard Walters, Eli Ward, Jesse Van Bibber, Slover, Simpson, Dudley Maxwell, Findley, Baptiste Moran, and Paul, Fowler's negro slave. They went north through the heavily timbered bottom land, between the Grand and the Verdigris, and out on to the prairie. Colonel Glenn left them and went by way of the Union Mission, established the year before on Grand River. On the twenty-ninth, they were overtaken by Glenn and soon reached Clermont's Town. Here they met James and some of his party, who came overland from Arkansas River to the Osage village to exchange some of their goods for horses.

Fowler and his party ascended the Arkansas to the Rocky Mountains. While camped at the mouth of Purgatory River, in what is now eastern Colorado, Lewis Dawson, one of the party, was killed in camp by a grizzly bear. In the latter part of November they were encamped in what is now Otero County, Colorado, for a month, surrounded by the lodges of thousands of Arapaho, Kiowa, and other Indians, where they were engaged in trapping and trading with the Indians for horses much needed by the party. On

[65] Coues, Elliott, *op. cit.,* 4.

Christmas day, 1821, they removed their camp to a point higher up, where they were accompanied by the Arapaho in such numbers that Fowler notes they consumed one hundred buffaloes daily. They camped on the site of what is now Pueblo, Colorado. This was on what was known as the war trail of the Indian tribes, and was so much frequented by large numbers of roving Indians that for protection Fowler's party were obliged to build a log house, first on the south side of the river and then across the river on the American side.[66] They built also a log corral for their horses, and the time of the men was about equally divided between trapping for beaver, hunting for deer and buffalo meat for food, and guarding their horses and personal effects against predatory Indians. On January 2, Glenn and a few of his companions left the party with a number of Spaniards for Taos. On the thirtieth of that month, Fowler and the remainder of the party left the Arkansas and joined Glenn at Taos on the eighth of February. From then until near the time they joined James on the return east, Fowler and several of his party were engaged in trapping beaver in what is now southern Colorado.

James secured a passport signed March 6, by John Q. Adams, Secretary of State, vised by the Spanish minister Don Francisco Dionisso Vives, and his party left Saint Louis May 10, 1821,[67] in a keel boat, with James in command; with him were John McKnight, John G. James, David Kirker, William Shearer, Alexander Howard, Benjamin Potter, John Ivey, and Francois Malsaw, a Spaniard. Two others joined

---

[66] Probably the first house inhabited by white men on the site of the city of Pueblo.

[67] Douglas, Walter B., editor. *Three Years Among the Indians and Mexicans,* by General Thomas James, 98.

after starting, Frederick Hector at the mouth of the Ohio and James Wilson in the Cherokee country. They made their journey down the Mississippi and up the Arkansas River in their boat, with ten thousand dollars worth of biscuits, whiskey, flour, lead, powder, and other merchandise. At Little Rock, James procured from Robert Crittenden,[68] acting governor, a license to trade with the Indians on Arkansas River, and the party proceeded on its way to Fort Smith. There they stopped for a few days and visited with Major Bradford,[69] who examined their license before they crossed the line into the Indian country. James took occasion in his journal to express their appreciation of the kindness and hospitality of Major Bradford, or Old Billy Bradford, as he calls him. They passed the Grand and the Verdigris and proceeded up the river as far as the depth of the water would permit, and succeeded in reaching a point about thirty miles above Salt Fork or as it was since known, the Red Fork or the

[68] Robert Crittenden of Frankfort, Kentucky, entered the Army in the war against England at the age of sixteen and on May 30, 1814, was made an ensign; honorably discharged June 15, 1815. Studied law with his brother John J. Crittenden of Frankfort, and on March 3, 1819, at the age of twenty-two was appointed secretary of the newly created territory of Arkansas. Acted as governor of the territory for the most of his term.

[69] William Bradford, born in Virginia, was appointed (March 12, 1812) from Kentucky as captain in the Seventeenth Infantry in the war against England and became major in the Twenty-first Infantry. Appointed captain of the Seventh Infantry June 1, 1821, major October 6, 1822, and resigned May 1, 1824. Upon the establishment of Cantonment Smith at Belle Point in 1817, Major Bradford was placed in charge and continued at this post until superseded by Colonel Arbuckle in 1822. Then transferred to Natchitoches. After his resignation from the Army he became sutler to the post at Fort Towson where he died on October 20, 1826, at the age of fifty-five. At the time of his death he was Brigadier-general of militia of the territory of Arkansas. In the War of 1812 and in the war with the Indians, where he served under General Jackson, he had seen much service and carried with him to his death a severe and painful wound received in battle, that caused him great inconvenience.

Cimarron, a short distance above where Tulsa now is.

Unable to ascend higher, and as the season was then late and rains unlikely to increase the depth of the water, they dropped down the river a few miles to an Osage trail; and from here James sent three men to Clermont's Town, where the Fowler expedition had preceded him. James's purpose was to trade some of his goods to the Osage for horses before striking across the country for Santa Fe. In five or six days his men, in company with Captain Pryor and forty Osage, returned from Clermont's Town to the Arkansas, where James had remained with his boat. He described Pryor [70] as a sergeant in Lewis and Clark's Expedition, and a captain at the Battle of New Orleans. "On the reduction of the army after the war, he was discharged to make way for some parlor soldier and sunshine patriot, and turned out in his old age upon the 'world's wide common.' I found him here among the Osages, with whom he had taken refuge from his country's ingratitude, and was living as one of their tribe, where he may yet be, unless death has discharged the debt his country owed him."

James took some goods from the cargo, and with McKnight, his brother, Captain Pryor and the Osage, returned to their village which they reached in two days. Here they found Major Bradford whom they left at Fort Smith, and Colonel Hugh Glenn and his party of twenty men on their way to Santa Fe. They found also Captain Barbour, an Indian trader formerly of Pittsburg, who had come up from New Orleans, and in partnership with George Brand, had set up a trading establishment at the mouth of the Verdigris. There were also present several Pawnee

[70] Douglas, Walter B., *op. cit.*, 108.

Indians from the Platte who had come to discuss with the Osage a treaty of peace.

James proposed to Glenn that the two parties travel together, but Glenn opposed the suggestion. James bought twenty-three horses from the Osage, and agreed with Barbour to cache his heaviest and least portable goods which Barbour was to take the following spring down to his store at the mouth of the Verdigris, sell and account for the proceeds to James when he returned from Santa Fe. Returning to his boat, James cached or buried all his flour, whiskey, lead, hardware, and other heavy goods on an island in the river. He showed the place to Captain Pryor when he came up the next day with a party of Osage going out on their fall hunt. These arrangements made, James loaded the horses that he had bought, and struck off across the country in a southwest direction toward Santa Fe. For the first two days of the journey, Pryor and the Indians accompanied James's party.

James ascended the Cimarron for some time, and then, crossing over to the Canadian, ascended that stream; after being captured and robbed by the Comanche and miraculously escaping with his life, he reached Santa Fe the first day of December, 1821, and rented a house where he opened up a trading store, while his companions engaged in trapping for beaver on the surrounding mountain streams. Of the first proceeds of his trading venture, he advanced two hundred dollars to John McKnight for the expense of his journey to Durango, sixteen hundred miles to the south, to see his brother Robert. They both returned in April. After spending six months in Santa Fe, James with his party started on their return to the United States by way of Taos, where, on June first, they were joined by the party under Glenn and Fowler, numbering about sixty men. On the way east they met two Santa Fe trading parties [71] from Boone's Lick neighborhood, Missouri; one under Colonel Benjamin Cooper with fifteen persons, and the other with Captain William Becknell with twenty-one men. James, Fowler, and Glenn proceeded by way of Arkansas River and Fort Clark on the Missouri, and after many hardships and adventures reached Saint Louis in July; Fowler proceeded to his home in Covington, Kentucky, and James to his in Monroe County, Illinois. Two of the men of Glenn's party reached Union Mission July 6 almost starved, having been without food for four days.

In the succeeding fall, James and the two McKnights organized another trading venture among the Comanche Indians. [72] John and Robert McKnight left Saint Louis with fifty-five hundred dollars worth of goods in a keel boat by way of the Mississippi and Arkansas for the mouth of the Canadian; there they awaited the arrival of James, who went overland with a party of twelve men and five loaded packhorses. James's party walked all the way from Saint Louis, and in the latter part of February, 1823, arrived at the mouth of Illinois River on the north side of the Arkansas, five miles above the Canadian. McKnight's

---

[71] "During the same year, Captain Becknell, of Missouri, with four trusty companions, went out to Santa Fe by the far western prairie route. This intrepid little band started from the vicinity of Franklin . . . The favorable reports brought by the enterprising Captain, stimulated others to embark in the trade; and early in the following May, Colonel Cooper and sons, from the same neighborhood, accompanied by several others (their whole number about fifteen), set out with four or five thousand dollars worth of goods, which they transported upon pack horses." – Thwaites, *op. cit.,* vol. xix, 177. This was said to be the commencement of the Sante Fe trade.

[72] Douglas, Walter B., *op. cit.,* 190, ff.

party had been camped there six weeks, their boat being securely tied up by the ice.

James then went to the mouth of the Verdigris to see Barbour about the goods he had left with the latter to sell for him. Barbour told him that the flour was found to be damaged when removed from the cache, but he was just starting for New Orleans in James's keel boat with furs and peltry he expected to sell in that market, and with the proceeds he promised to pay James for his goods on his return. James then returned to the mouth of the Illinois, and the ice having broken up and released their boat, they began the ascent of the Canadian; five days were consumed in reaching the mouth of the North Fork; and soon after, near the site of the present town of Eufaula, further passage of their boat was arrested by rapids and shallow water. They then made their boat fast to trees with strong ropes, put their bear and deer skins in it, and buried their heaviest hardware in the ground, where it may yet be, as James never returned to the place of concealment. They then made three pirogues into which they placed their remaining goods, except such as could be packed on their horses.

With pirogues and horses they ascended the Canadian to a point above the Cross Timbers, and as they saw evidence of Indians about them, they commenced the building of a fort, as well for defense as for a trading post. Before the fort was completed, four of the men, including John McKnight, left in a southerly direction to invite the Comanche Indians to come and trade with them. A sudden rise in the river induced James to abandon their half-finished fort and ascend the river a hundred miles higher, where another trading post was built. John McKnight never returned however, as he was killed by the Comanche Indians.

After many interesting experiences with the Indians, and hair-breadth escapes well told in James's book, the party descended the Canadian. Passing through the Cross Timbers, James left the party with the boats and went overland to the mouth of the Verdigris to see Barbour who, he learned, had died on the trip to New Orleans in James's keel boat, and James was unable to secure pay for his goods or his boat. James obtained a canoe at the trading post, and with his companions descended the Arkansas to the mouth of the Canadian to meet the remainder of his party who had descended with the boats, and who were waiting at the salt works on the Illinois. This was the summer of 1824; though James does not give the month, the season may be assumed from the fact that many of his horses were dying daily from the hordes of flies that infested the country.[73] To avoid them, they had been forced to travel only by night and sleep by day. When he took an account of his property at the mouth of the Illinois, he found that out of three hundred twenty-three horses and mules he had purchased of the Indians and started home with, he had lost by flies and stampedes two hundred fifty-three, leaving only seventy in his possession. But in the two or three days before they were ready to take their departure from the Illinois, many more of them became sick and died, so that he left them all there together with his pirogue loaded with skins and robes, in charge of Adams and Denison. The expedition was a most unfortunate one for James, who lost all the money he had invested in it, and returned home on foot, poorer than when he left.

---

[73] Early travelers in the southwest often told of the myriads of flies that killed horses and cattle and frequently made travel in the day time impossible.

Establishment of Fort Gibson in 1824

By Act of Congress of March 2, 1819, Arkansas Territory was established July 4, embracing substantially all of what are now the states of Arkansas and Oklahoma; though the civil government of Arkansas Territory was limited to that section lying east of the Osage line, divided into counties, and embracing approximately the present state of Arkansas. That west of the Osage line was the Indian country, and in later years became known as Indian Territory. James Miller [74] of New Hampshire was appointed the first Governor of Arkansas Territory, and among the duties of his office was that of supervision of the Indians within his jurisdiction.

After the battle at Clermont's Town an effort was made to induce the warring tribes to enter into a treaty of peace. This was accomplished in October 1818, [75] in Saint Louis, in the presence of William Clark, the Governor of Missouri Territory. Directly after Governor Miller assumed his duties as executive, he was required to intervene between the Osage and Cherokee

---

[74] James Miller was born in Peterboro, N. H., April 25, 1776; entered the army as major in 1808, became Lieutenant-colonel in 1810, and colonel in 1814. Distinguished in the battle of Niagara Falls for which he was brevetted Brigadier-general and on November 4, 1814, by resolution of Congress received a gold medal. Resigned from the Army June 1, 1819, to become the first governor of Arkansas. On December 26, 1819, Governor Miller reached the Territory on a keel boat from Saint Louis and assumed his duties as governor. He served until the latter part of 1824 when he was appointed collector of customs of the Port of Salem, Massachusetts, which post he held until 1849. He died at Temple, N. H., July 7, 1851.

[75] *American State Papers*, "Indian Affairs" vol. ii, 172.

in an effort to prevent imminent hostilities growing out of the killing of a number of Cherokee hunters by a band of Osage under Mad Buffalo.   In April 1820, Governor Miller departed from the seat of government at Arkansas Post, on his mission to the Cherokee and Osage.   He was gone two months, and prevented – temporarily at least – the threatened renewal of warfare by the Cherokee.   He went first to the Cherokee settlements, where he sought to dissuade the members of that tribe from further hostilities by his promise that he would endeavor to secure from the Osage the murderers of their hunters.   Accompanied by several Cherokee chiefs, he then ascended Arkansas River to the mouth of the Verdigris and visited the Osage town. He then induced representatives of both tribes to agree to meet at Fort Smith on the first of the next October, and return all prisoners and stolen horses.

The conference held at Fort Smith in October, however, did not restore peace.   During the following December a band of Osage attacked a number of Cherokee hunters on the Poteau near Fort Smith.   Four hundred Osage warriors accompanied by some of their Sauk and Fox allies made a hostile demonstration in May 1821,[76] against Fort Smith, then protected by only seventy men.   They were on their way against the Cherokee, and in an insolent manner demanded ammunition, which was refused by the officers of the post. They threatened to attack the garrison, but being warned by the officers in command not to approach, and menaced by the cannon of the post, sullenly retired; and on their departure they killed three peaceful Quapaw, robbed several white families on Poteau and

[76] Arkansas *Gazette* (Arkansas Post), May 12, 1821, p. 3, col. 2.   Niles Register (Baltimore), vol. xx, 298.

Lee's creek, and carried off all the horses they could find. Soon after this occurrence a war party under Walter Webber killed a Frenchman named Joseph Revoir,[77] living fifteen miles above Union Mission, whose offense was that he, like many other Frenchmen, was living with the Osage, with whom the Cherokee said they would not make peace "as long as the Arkansas River runs."

The continued insolence of the Osage, reprisals and turbulence by that tribe and the Cherokee, uneasiness of the missionary establishments and other white people, led to a change in the military policy of the Goverment; and in the summer of 1821 orders were given that the Seventh Infantry should be removed from Fort Scott and Bay of Saint Louis, and employed for the purpose of giving greater security to white people west of the Mississippi, of maintaining peace between the Indians, and of protecting trading expeditions to Santa Fe. Four companies of that regiment were assigned to increase the force at Fort Smith and six were sent to Natchitoches. In November of that year, two hundred fifty soldiers of the Seventh Regiment, under Colonel Matthew Arbuckle,[78] arrived at

---

[77] Arkansas *Gazette* (Arkansas Post), July 14, 1821, p. 3, col. 1.

[78] Matthew Arbuckle was born in Greenbrier County, Virginia in 1776. He became second-lieutenant in the Third Infantry on March 3, 1799; as Lieutenant-colonel he was transferred to the Seventh Infantry April 10, 1817, and saw much service in the south in the Seminole War; colonel March 16, 1820, and brevet Brigadier-general March 16, 1830, for ten years faithful service in one grade; he died at Fort Smith June 11, 1851.

The name of the veteran Arbuckle was conferred upon four distinct army establishments in Indian Territory. The encampment of the Ranger companies of Captains Boone and Ford during the winter of 1832 and 1833 was located one and one-half miles below Fort Gibson and on the opposite side of the river and was called Camp Arbuckle. A second Camp Arbuckle was established on Arkansas River at the mouth of the Cimarron, June 24, 1834.

Another Camp Arbuckle was established on the right bank and one mile

the mouth of Arkansas River from New Orleans, on their way to Fort Smith, but having to wait for keel boats for their passage up the river, did not reach their destination until the twenty-sixth of February, 1822.[79] The remainder of the regiment left New Orleans on the sixth of November, 1821, under Lieutenant-colonel Zachary Taylor for the military post at Natchitoches on Red River.

When Colonel Arbuckle came to Fort Smith he superseded Major William Bradford, who had been in command there since 1817, and who went to Natchitoches; and from a small force of seventy men the garrison assumed a new importance which it maintained for two years, until it was removed farther up the river. The troops at Fort Smith had been compelled to subsist themselves, and Colonel Arbuckle found there a farm of eighty acres cultivated by the soldiers, with one hundred head of cattle, four hundred hogs and one thousand bushels of corn from

from Canadian River August 22, 1850, by Company D, Fifth Infantry, Captain R. B. Marcy, four officers and forty-eight men to protect from Indians travelers enroute to California. Store houses and huts were erected so that by December 1, the command were all under roof but the War Department did not approve the site and ordered it removed south near Washita River. On April 17, 1851, camp was struck and the command moved to a point on Wild Horse Creek.

The permanent Fort Arbuckle established April 19, 1851, on Wild Horse Creek near Washita River was at first built of logs to accomodate four companies and June 25, 1851, by general order number thirty-four the Adjutant-general named it Fort Arbuckle for General Arbuckle who had died the eleventh of that month. The Fort was abandoned February 13, 1858, and reoccupied June 20, 1858. It was then occupied until May 5, 1861, when it was seized by the confederates. (Reservation Division Adjutant-general's office, Outline Index, Military Forts and Stations, "A" page 376.)

[79] Arkansas *Gazette* (Little Rock), April 2, 1822, p. 3, col. 1. The Arkansas *Gazette,* the first number of which was published at Arkansas Post Nov. 20, 1819, was removed to Little Rock where the first issue appeared Dec. 29, 1821.

the preceding year. The soldiers were not only obliged to raise from the soil the grain and vegetables they and their stock consumed, and supplement their larder with buffalo meat, but they were required to build their own houses.

The steamboat Robert Thompson from Pittsburg, arrived at Fort Smith in March or early April, 1822,[80] with a large keel boat in tow, loaded with provisions for the garrison. This was probably the first steamboat to reach Fort Smith.[81] Prior to that time supplies had been brought from Saint Louis in keel boats propelled by man power and sail. The detachment of the Seventh Infantry that Colonel Taylor had taken up to Natchitoches was removed in July farther up Red River near its junction with the Kiamichi, where in May, 1824, a post was established on a higher and healthier site and called Fort Towson.[82]

The treaty effected at Saint Louis between the Cherokee and Osage in 1818, had not resulted in the peace that had been hoped for. With the establishment of the relatively large military force at Fort Smith in

---

[80] Arkansas *Gazette*, (Little Rock), April 9, 1822, p. 3, col. 1.

[81] In May the Robert Thompson made her second trip to Fort Smith towing a deeply laden keel boat and a sixty-five-foot half-loaded flat boat.

[82] Fort Towson was named for Nathan Towson, Paymaster General. Soon after it was established soldiers and officers became involved in differences with the white settlers near by to the extent of resisting the civil authority of the Territory of Arkansas which was claimed to extend to the adjoining part of what is now Texas. In the summer of 1829 the garrison was abandoned, the five yoke of oxen and two ox wagons were sold, and the troops and effects were removed on four flat-bottom boats down Red River to Cantonment Jesup near Natchitoches. Scarcely had they left when persons in the neighborhood fired and burned all the buildings of the garrison. About a year and a half later four companies of the Third Infantry under Major S. W. Kearny ascended Red River again to the mouth of the Kiamichi, and established another on the site of the old post, which on May 1, 1831, was designated Camp Phoenix; November 20, 1831, it was officially named Cantonment Towson, and February 8, 1832, Fort Towson.

1822, renewed efforts were made to remove the con-
tentions between those tribes and compel them to cease
their warfare.   These efforts resulted in a new treaty
of peace [83] between the Osage and Cherokee at Fort
Smith on the ninth day of August, 1822.   It was executed in the presence of "James Miller as Governor
of the Arkansas Territory, commander in chief of the
militia and Superintendent of Indian affairs," and
Colonel Matthew Arbuckle commanding the United
States troops in the territory.

The treaty provided that the Cherokee were to
return by the twentieth of the next month seventeen
Osage prisoners still in their possession, conditioned
that those who preferred to live with their captors
might do so.   It provided also that members of each
tribe might pass from one nation to the other on the
north side of the Arkansas, killing only such game as
might be necessary to sustain life while traveling, but
without the right to establish hunting camps in the
land of the other tribe.   The Osage granted to the
Cherokee the right in common with themselves to hunt
on the lands south of Arkansas River.

The treaty contained a formal declaration of peace
and termination of the long war that had raged between
the tribes.   The execution of the treaty with the form-
alities that accompanied it, and the menace of the
military arm of the Government to encourage its ob-
servance, brought relief and joy to the meagre white
population along Arkansas River and particularly to
the Mission School at Union, where the new turn of
events presaged an increase in the attendance of Indian
children.   But while the war was over, the turbulent

---

[83] Indian Office, Retired Classified Files, *folio drawer,* manuscript copy of
treaty.

Osage continued to make trouble, and the troops under Colonel Arbuckle, operating out of Fort Smith, were constantly employed in policing the country. Hostilities and acts of violence at the hands of the Osage were frequent. Major Curtis Wilborn was killed on November 17, 1823, while hunting on Blue River, and the Osage were held responsible, but they refused to deliver up Mad Buffalo and others who were charged with the murder. It was reported in January, 1824, that the Osage, Cherokee, Kickapoo, and Delaware met at the mouth of the Verdigris and indulged in a dance which was characterized as a demonstration against the whites. Union and Harmony missions were disturbed, the white settlers along the Arkansas were becoming nervous and were raising volunteers.

It is not surprising then that in April, 1824, Colonel Arbuckle received orders [84] for the immediate removal of the troops from Fort Smith to the mouth of the Verdigris, where a new military establishment was to be erected near the Arkansas Osage, who would thus be under stricter surveillance of the troops. The site of the new garrison was said to be about eighty miles above Fort Smith, fifty miles below the Osage village, and at the proposed western boundary of Arkansas Territory, and the new move was believed to guarantee security to the western frontier.

When the troops arrived at their western destination in April, it was decided to locate the post on the east bank of Grand River three miles from the mouth, three or four miles from the Verdigris, and an equal distance

[84] War Department, Adjutant-general's office, *General Orders* No. 20, March 6, 1824. In the Senate discussion of the proposed change, in February 1824, it was considered that the new post would afford protection to traders between Missouri and Santa Fe. – *American State Papers,* "Indian Affairs", vol. ii, 456.

from Chouteau's trading house.   The post was named
Cantonment Gibson, in honor of the then commanding
General of subsistence, George Gibson.   Soon after
the arrival of the troops from Fort Smith, another
detachment of two hundred men from New Orleans
arrived at Cantonment Gibson.   The troops were
quartered in tents and were immediately set to the task
of erecting log cabins for the reception of public property; their own quarters were to be constructed later.
By January, 1825, it was reported that works of defense
and quarters for the soldiers were rapidly progressing,
and that the latter were so far completed as to afford
snug and comfortable accomodations for the officers
and men attached to the garrison.

Congress passed an act May 26, 1824, locating the
western boundary of Arkansas Territory forty miles
west of where it had been, so that it included in Arkansas, Fort Gibson and all of Lovely's Purchase.   The
line began forty miles west of the southwest corner of
Missouri, and ran south to Red River.[85]   It crossed the
Arkansas and Verdigris near their confluence, and today would intersect the city of Muskogee.

Immediately after the passage of the act removing
the boundary line farther west, the General Assembly
of Arkansas on June 3, 1824, addressed a memorial[86]
to the President, praying that he countermand the order

[85] While this Arkansas line was moved east in 1828 (Kappler, *op. cit.,*
vol. ii, 206) to approximately where it now is, the western line established
in 1824 was preserved and employed as the dividing line between the
Cherokee and Creek Nations in their treaty of 1833 (Kappler, *op. cit.,*
vol. ii, 287), extending north and south a few miles east of where Wagoner,
Oklahoma, now is.

[86] The correspondence involved in the controversy over Lovely's Purchase was attached to a letter from the Secretary of War responsive to
a resolution of the House of Representatives and published in U. S.
House, *Documents* 20th congress, first session, no. 263.

prohibiting white settlers on Lovely's Purchase, and asking him to permit its occupation; "the salubrity of the climate and fertility of the soil which distinguish this beautiful and interesting section of our country" presented strong inducements to emigrants who were rapidly settling it.

This request was strongly resented by the Cherokee, who claimed the use, if not the title, to Lovely's Purchase, as an outlet westerly to the hunting grounds. The General Assembly adopted another memorial the next year on the subject, adding mention of the rich saline and mineral ores included within the forbidden land; but the Government promptly denied their requests on the ground of its duty to the Cherokee; this tract extended from the Cherokee land at the junction of the White and Arkansas rivers westwardly to the Falls of the Verdigris, and when surveyed by the Government was found to contain seven million three hundred ninety-two thousand acres.

The Government reaffirmed its intention of preserving this country for the Cherokee as an outlet to their western hunting grounds, qualified only by the reservation to the Government of the right to lease the salt springs included in the tract. Notwithstanding the position of the Government, in October, 1827, the Arkansas General Assembly presented to the President another and more forceful memorial, renewing their demands for Lovely's Purchase, and without waiting for permission, on October 16, 1827, included the western part of the tract in a new county called Lovely County,[87] and proceeded to issue a commission to Ben-

[87] Lovely county embraced what are now Sequoyah, Adair, Ottawa, Delaware, and Cherokee, and parts of Muskogee, Wagoner, Mayes, and Craig counties, Oklahoma.

jamin Weaver, October 23, 1827, as Justice of the Peace
for Lovely County, for two years. The seat of government of the county was fixed at a place on the west
side of Sallisaw Creek thirteen miles above its mouth.
Here a number of log buildings were put up and the
place was called Nicksville. After the Cherokee treaty
of 1828 was enacted the Cherokee, Colonel Walter
Webber selected the place as the seat of his mercantile
establishment. Webber in turn sold the improvements
to the commissioners for Foreign Missions as the site
for Dwight Mission which removed from Arkansas
with the Cherokee and opened its school here the first
of May 1830.[88] White people had been settling in the
so-called Lovely county in such numbers that the government finally yielded to them. The correspond:nce
on the subject terminated in an extended communication by the Cherokee, dated February 28, 1828, in
defense of their rights. In reading this as well as the
other documents on the subject, one is impressed with
their dignity, moderation, diction, and cogent reasoning
compared with which the arguments of the people of
Arkansas made but a poor showing.

Accordingly, the Government entered into a new
treaty with the Cherokee in May, 1828, by which the
latter exchanged their lands on Arkansas and White
rivers for seven million acres west of the Osage line, on
which they were later permanently located and which
became the last home of the Cherokee. This was
bounded on the east by the western boundary of Arkansas, which was by the treaty of 1828, moved back east
to where it was formerly located, and thus Lovely

---

[88] Cephas Washburn to Jeremiah Evarts, September 1, 1830, Board for
Foreign Missions, Boston, Manuscript Library, vol. 73, no. 2. For the
Cherokee Treaty of 1828, see Kappler, *op. cit.*, vol. ii, 206.

County was extinguished and became only a memory.

The new home of the Cherokee included the western part of Lovely's Purchase, but a reservation was made to the United States of a tract of land two miles by six in extent on the east side of Grand River, for the military force established at Fort Gibson. The treaty contained a number of interesting provisions: Five hundred dollars was provided for the remarkable Cherokee, George Guess, or Sequoyah, for the great benefits he had conferred upon his people by his invention of an alphabet, and one thousand dollars was to be given the tribe to purchase a printing press and type, which would soon be employed in printing in their own language. In exchange for a saline which Sequoyah was operating in Arkansas, he was to be allowed the use of one on Lee's Creek in the new country.

To induce the Cherokee east of the Mississippi to remove to the new home provided for them, it was agreed to give each head of a family who would so remove, a rifle, a kettle, and five pounds of tobacco, besides a blanket to each member of the family. Under this treaty, the Arkansas Cherokee soon began removing westward to their new home.

Before this treaty could be made, it had been necessary, in 1825, for the United States to enter into a new treaty [89] with the Osage, by which the latter ceded all the lands lying within or west of Arkansas Territory. This treaty, however, made provision for reservations

---

[89] Kappler, *op. cit.*, vol. ii, 153. This treaty was made in Saint Louis June 2. On August 10 of that summer, another treaty [Kappler, *op. cit.*, vol. ii, 174] with the Osage was entered into at Council Grove on the Santa Fe trail, pursuant to an act of Congress of March 3, 1825, providing for making a road "from the Western frontier of Missouri to the confines of New Mexico." By the treaty the Osage agreed to this road being marked through their country and promised not to molest the travelers going to Santa Fe.

on Grand River of one section each to a number of half-breed Osage, all bearing French names. The Chouteau reservations, being afterward included in the Cherokee domain, became the subject of controversy and were later extinguished.

However, the Creeks were the first to arrive in any number in the new country that was to be the home of the Five Civilized Tribes. They came in the shadow of tragedy that was the forerunner of others, marking the removal of thousands who followed them. In 1825, General William McIntosh, a prominent member of the Creek Tribe, had been induced by the authorities of Georgia to sign a treaty [90] ceding the lands of the Creek Nation and agreeing to the removal of the tribe west of the Mississippi. The more conservative members of the tribe opposed this measure, and sentenced McIntosh to death for his act, which was claimed to be in violation of the laws and against the will of a large majority of the tribe. The sentence was executed by a body of Okfuskee warriors who surrounded McIntosh's house and shot him and his son-in-law, Colonel Samuel Hawkins, as they tried to escape.[91]

The signing of the treaty so enraged the great majority of the Creeks, and the killing of McIntosh created such bitter feeling among his friends, that the latter determined to separate from the other members of the tribe and migrate to the country west of the Mississippi. This was authorized by the Government by a new treaty [92] of January 24, 1826, and provision was made by the Government to remove the Indians.

[90] Kappler, *op. cit.*, vol. ii, 151.
[91] *American State Papers*, "Indian Affairs" vol. ii, 768.
[92] Kappler, *op. cit.*, vol. ii, 188.

Colonel David Brearley,[93] who had been an agent to the Arkansas Cherokee, was appointed May 13, 1826, agent to the McIntosh Creeks; and in April, 1827, Brearley came up the Arkansas with an exploring party of Creeks, who selected as their future home the country lying continguous to the mouth of the Verdigris. Brearley selected and purchased for an agency some of the buildings of Colonel A. P. Chouteau, used as a trading post, on the east side and about three miles above the mouth of the Verdigris. By November, Brearley had a number of the McIntosh party enrolled for the journey, and the twenty-fifth of that month they arrived at Tuscumbia; in February, 1828, Brearley ascended Arkansas and Verdigris rivers in the steamboat Facility, with two keel boats in tow, having on board the vessels seven hundred eighty men, women, and children, who were landed at the Creek Agency. The Facility, probably the first steamboat to ascend the Verdigris, returned to New Orleans with a cargo of hides, furs, cotton, and five hundred barrels of pecans taken on at the Verdigris trading houses and points lower down the Arkansas.[94]

Colonel Arbuckle, ever solicitous for the peace of the country, proposed a conference at the agency between the Osage and the newly-arrived Creeks, who were the first strangers from the east to come so far west to locate upon the land formerly claimed by the

---

[93] David Brearly was born in New Jersey and became captain of the Light Dragoons May 3, 1808. With the Seventh Infantry he saw active service in the Seminole War; while colonel of that regiment he resigned from the Army, on March 16, 1820, and in the following June the President appointed him agent for the Western Cherokee in place of Reuben Lewis former agent, brother of Meriwether Lewis, who had resigned, and in September he began his duties in Arkansas. In 1833 he was appointed postmaster at Dardennelles, Arkansas, where he died in 1837.

[94] Arkansas *Gazette* (Little Rock), February 13, 1828, p. 3, col. 1.

Osage. Clermont extended a welcome from his tribe, and mutual expressions of good will gave the appearance at least of an auspicious beginning for the new home.

Brearley returned in November with five hundred more Creeks, who joined the first arrivals in their settlement on the point of land between Arkansas and Verdigris rivers. Here, they were convenient to the agency and their rations, and under the protection of Fort Gibson; then it was not considered safe for them to venture to settle in the more remote districts where they would be in danger of attack by the western more warlike tribes including even their neighbors, the Osage, who could not be trusted. In the following August, five hundred more Creeks arrived and joined those who had preceded them.[95]

[95] Soon after the removal of the McIntosh Creeks in 1829 a school was established in this settlement. "A school, which the [Baptist] convention commenced in 1823, on the Chattahooche river, among the Creeks in Georgia, was transferred in 1830, upon the removal of the tribe, to a point about 20 miles above Fort Gibson on the Arkansas. The board has authorized the erection of buildings for the school and for the families attached to the mission. The station is under the care of the Rev. David Lewis, assisted by John Davis, an educated native, by whom the school has been regularly kept, but the number of pupils has not been reported." – U.S. House. *Executive Documents*, 22d congress, second session, no. 2, *Report of Secretary of War of November, 1832*, p. 170. In 1832, Reverend Isaac McCoy arrived at this place where missionary labors had been conducted since October 1829 by John Davis [McCoy, Isaac. *Annual Register of Indian Affairs*, May 1837, No. iii, 19]. Here, [in a grove, near the Falls of Verdigris River] he said "On the 9th of September, I constituted the Muskogee Baptist Church, consisting of Mr. Lewis and wife, Mr. Davis and three black men, [named Quash, Bob, and Ned] who were slaves to the Creeks . . . This was the first Baptist church formed in the Indian Territory . . . The first act of the church after organizing, was to order a written license, as a preacher, to Mr. Davis, the Creek missionary, and I was directed to prepare the same." – McCoy, Reverend Isaac, *History of Baptist Indian Missions*, 451. The next year other buildings were erected; a Sunday School was started and the establishment was called Ebenezer. It was three miles north of Arkansas River and four miles west of the Verdigris [Wyeth, Walter N. D.D. *Isaac McCoy, Early Indian Missions*, 193].

Earliest Known Traders on Arkansas River

With the help of contemporary records it is possible to identify some of the early traders at the Mouth of the Verdigris. Even before the Louisiana Purchase, hardy French adventurers ascended the Arkansas in their little boats, hunting, trapping, and trading with the Indians, and recorded their presence if not their identity in the nomenclature of the adjacent country and streams, now sadly corrupted by their English-speaking successors.[96]

[96] Many tributaries of Arkansas River originally bore French names. There was the Fourche La Feve named for a French family [Thwaites, *op. cit.*, vol. xiii, 156]; the Petit Jean or Little John, named for a Frenchman of small stature who was killed on its banks by the Indians [Thwaites, *op. cit.*, vol. xiii, 171]; Vache Grasse Creek – these and others bearing French names were noted by Nuttall within the present limits of Arkansas. Lee's Creek emptying in the Arkansas near Fort Smith was called river au Milleau by Lieutenant Wilkinson in 1807. The Poteau flows into the Arkansas at Fort Smith; the word being French for Post, may have been given to the river by some unhistoric French station [Thwaites, *op. cit.*, vol. xiii, 199 n]. The Sallisaw was named by the French the Salaison, from meat having been salted there, and from that the transition was easy to Salaiseau and then to the present rendering [Thwaites, *op. cit.*, vol. xiii, 231]. Vian Creek was originally Bayou Viande. But consider the sad case of the creek bearing the name of Dardenne a prominent early French family mentioned by Nuttall [Thwaites, *op. cit.*, vol. viii, 136], living on the north side of Arkansas River below where is now Pine Bluff. Map makers afterwards shortened this name to Derden, and now, alas, it has descended to the appellation of Dirty Creek. It debouches into the Arkansas about twenty miles below Muskogee. One of the main forks of Grand River was at an early day called Pomme de terre River. Cache creek, of course, is French, as likewise is Verdigris.

The tributaries of the Arkansas from the west testify to their Spanish origin. While the Arkansas bore that name throughout its length it was often called by the early trappers Pawnee River above the Three Forks. The first fork of the Arkansas noted by Pike, was called by the French, Riviere Purgatoire and by the Spaniards, Rio Purgatorio and Rio de Las

One of the first of the French traders up the Arkansas whose name has been recorded was Joseph Bogy, an early resident of the old French town, Arkansas Post,

Animas. The English speaking successors have changed this pronunciation and now this creek in eastern Colorado from Purgatoire has become Picket-wire.

Cimarron, the name of the tributary entering the Arkansas from the west, also formerly called Red Fork, is a Spanish-American word meaning something wild, runaway, or unreclaimed [Coues, *Expeditions of* Zebulon M. Pike, vol. ii, 438, n]. It was sometimes known as the "Semerone of the Traders." " 'Canadian,' as applied to the main fork of the Arkansas has no more to do with the Dominion of Canada in history or politics than it has in geography, and many have wondered how this river came to be called the Canadian. The word is from the Spanish Rio Cañada, or Rio Cañadiano, through such form as Rio Cañadian, whence directly 'Canadian' r., meaning 'Canon' r., and referring to the way in which the stream is boxed up or shut in by precipitous walls near its headwaters." – Coues, *op. cit.,* vol. ii, 558 n, 17. The North Fork of Canadian River was by the early trappers and traders called Rio Nutria a Spanish name meaning Otter River. It was also called Rio Rojo, and Rio Roxo, Spanish for red river. One of its tributaries was called Rio Mora, a Spanish word meaning mulberry. Red River was called by the Spanish Rio Roxo and Rio Colorado. False Washita was called also Rio Negro, Spanish for black river. Brazos river of Texas was named by the Spaniards " 'el Rio de los Brazos de Dios,' River of the Arms of God, which seemed neither blasphemous nor sacrilegious to the admirable fanatics who so solemly theographized geography in their excursions for the salvation of souls," – Coues, *op. cit.,* vol. ii, 706, n. 13.

The influence of the French on the Indian tribes of the Arkansas valley was important. They intermarried freely with the Quapaw and Osage and not only named many individual Indians of those tribes but gave the Osage tribe its name. Osage is the corruption by the French of Wazhazhe, their own name (Handbook of American Indians, vol. ii, 156). Cheveu Blanc or White Hair and Pahuska are the several names of one of the most celebrated Osage chiefs. Belle Oisseau – Beautiful Bird, of course was named by the French. The name of the chief Clermont also is French. The name Akansea, adopted by the French, is what the Quapaw were called by the Illinois Indians and is the origin of our Arkansas or Arkansaw [Coues, *op. cit.,* vol. ii, 559, n. 20] [Thwaites, *op. cit.,* vol. xiii, 117]. The Quapaw tribe is now the only remnant of the Arkansea. A band of Illinois Indians lived with the Akansea on Arkansas River [Handbook of American Indians, vol. ii, 335] and they or French trappers from the Illinois country probably were responsible for the naming of the Illinois rivers emptying into the Arkansas, one in the present limits of the state of that name and the other in Oklahoma. Little Rock was called La Petite Rochelle by the French, to distinguish it from the larger rocky promontory two miles farther up the river [Thwaites, *op. cit.,* vol. viii, 146].

from which point he traded with the Osage Indians in the vicinity of the Three Forks. On one of his expeditions he had ascended the Arkansas with a boatload of merchandise, to trade to the Osage near the mouth of the Verdigris. There on the seventh of January, 1807, he was attacked and robbed of all his goods by a large band of Choctaw Indians under the famous chief, Pushmataha.[97] When charged with the offense, Pushmataha admitted it and justified the robbery on the ground that they were at war with the Osage, against whom they were proceeding at the time; and that as Bogy was trading with their enemies, he was a proper subject for reprisal. Bogy laid a claim before the Government for nine thousand dollars damages against the Choctaw, based on the protection guaranteed by his trader's license. This claim was pending until after 1835, before it was allowed. Among the interesting papers in connection with the claim, is Bogy's report of having met on his ascent of the Arkansas Lieutenant Wilkinson, who had recently parted from Captain Pike. "But sir, suppose the same Indians (the Choctaws), who fell upon me and plundered my property, had fallen in with Lieutenant Wilkinson, whom I met a few days before, and not far from the place of depredation, (who had parted on the Arkansas with my then brave friend, but now lamented Pike), while he was coming down the river, with but few men, destitute of everything, and whom I furnished with such provisions and ammunitions as it was in my power, suppose the same Indians, I say, had fallen upon him, plundered him and his men . . . would the Government have interfered in their behalf?"[98]

[97] For an account of Pushmataha, see U.S. Bureau of Ethnology, *Bulletin* 30, Handbook of American Indians, part ii, 329, 330.

[98] U.S. Senate, *Documents*, 24th congress, first session, no. 23. Petition

Bogy continued to trade at the mouth of the Verdigris for many years; Nuttall traveled from Fort Smith to the Verdigris in Bogy's boat, and on July 14, 1819, entered "The Verdigris, where Mr. Bougie and Mr. Prior had their trading houses." When Nuttall returned to the mouth of the Verdigris, desperately sick from his prairie expedition, he remained a week under the hospitable roof of Mr. Bogy at the trading post, while he gained sufficient strength to descend the Arkansas.[99]

In the summer of 1812 a trading party under the leadership of Alexander McFarland left Cadron on the Arkansas to trade with the Indians on upper Red River for their horses and mules.[100] Though they endeavored to avoid the Osage Indians, the latter entered their camp near the Wichita villages, August 13, and killed McFarland while his companions were absent. Subsequently, in 1813, a claim was filed with the government by the widow, Lydia McFarland, for the loss of her husband and his property. In 1814 depositions were given by John Lemmons, who was with McFarland's party, by William Ingles, Robert Kuyrkendall and Benjamin Murphy. The latter three stated that in October 1812 they were at the mouth of the Verdigris, where the Osage had collected to trade and there were present the band of Osage who had just returned from Red River bearing with them some of the property taken from McFarland. The Cherokee Chief Tallantusky was there in quest of merchandise he had confided to McFarland for trade to the western Indians. Recognizing in the possession of the Osage some of his

of Joseph Bogy praying for compensation for spoliation by Choctaw Indians while on trading expedition on Arkansas River.

[99] Thwaites, op. cit., vol. xiii, 277.

[100] Indian office, Old Files. Special case 191.

property including two short swords, he demanded their possession and the Osage gave them up and through Ingles as interpreter admitted to Tallantusky that they had killed and robbed McFarland. From this it appears that there were traders at the mouth of the Verdigris as early as 1812.

One of the early arrivals to establish a trading house at the mouth of the Verdigris was Captain Barbour, who came from New Orleans and entered into partnership with George W. Brand, who, being married to to a Cherokee woman, exercised the privileges of a member of the tribe. Long before the Cherokee were removed from their home on Arkansas River in the present state of Arkansas to their final location, Brand and Barbour built at the Falls of the Verdigris an extensive trading establishment consisting of ten or twelve houses, cleared thirty acres of land, and established a ferry at the same place. In the journal of his expedition, Nuttall speaks of meeting Barbour in January 1820, and traveling on the Arkansas in "the boat of Mr. Barber, a merchant of New Orleans."

Colonel A. P. Chouteau became the owner of the trading establishment of Brand and Barbour at an early day,[101] and continued so until 1827, when he sold some of his buildings to Colonel David Brearley, to be used as the Creek Agency, the earliest agency to be established within the present limits of Oklahoma.[102]

---

[101] The purchase was probably made just prior to the time of Barbour's descent to New Orleans and his death, which occurred early in 1823.

[102] The Creek Agency "is situated immediately on the eastern bank of the Verdigris three of four miles from its mouth." – U.S. House, *Reports,* 20th congress, second session, no. 87. Report of Committee on Indian Affairs, 41. In 1827 Major McClelland, Choctaw Agent occupied some of the government buildings at Fort Smith, that had been left in charge of Nicks and Rogers. They were located on land claimed by the Choctaw, (Arbuckle to Jesup, February 26, 1827, Quartermaster's Depot, Old Files).

After the treaty of 1828 with the Cherokee conveyed to
that tribe the land on which the Creek Agency was
located, the Cherokee insisted on its removal, and
Brand demanded possession of the improvements.
After his death, his heirs pressed their claim for
damages for the use of the improvements; and in 1837
the Committee on Indian Affairs of the Senate reported
that Brand was entitled to the buildings, field, and falls
of the Verdigris, and recommended a bill to compensate the heirs for their use by the Government at the
rate of five hundred dollars annually.[103]

One of the most romantic figures connected with the
trading settlement at the mouth of the Verdigris was
Nathaniel Pryor, a veteran of the War of 1812, and a
sergeant with the memorable Lewis and Clark Expedition to the mouth of the Columbia in 1804, in which he
had a creditable part.   Almost continuously after that
service, he was engaged in trading with the Indians
except when he answered the call of his country during
the war with England.   Soon after the war he ascended
the Mississippi and Arkansas to Arkansas Post, from
which point, with a partner, Samuel B. Richards, he
engaged in trading with the Indians up Arkansas River.
Shortly after the organization of Arkansas Territory,
a license was issued by the governor, November 29,
1819,[104] "to Nathaniel Pryor, to trade with the Osage
Nation of Indians, as well as to ascend the river Arkansas with one trading boat to the Six Bull or Verdigree,
together with all hands that may appertain thereto."

Pryor built a trading store about one and one-half

---

[103] U.S. Senate, *Documents,* 24th congress, second session, no. 47, Report
of Senate Committee on Indian Affairs on petition of George W. Brand
with Senate Bill no. 91.

[104] Vashon to Cass, April 30, 1832 (enclosure) Indian Office *1832 Cherokee West Agency.*

miles above the mouth of Verdigris River, and with an Osage wife lived ten years in the vicinity until his death. He had great influence with the Osage Indians, with whom he was an active trader. He was held in the highest esteem by the white officials and others who subsequently came to Fort Gibson, and who repeatedly urged upon the War Department the wisdom of appointing Pryor to a responsible position in connection with the Indian service, for which, by his long experience and standing with the Indians, he was preëminently qualified. Indifferent to these considerations, official Washington permitted his talents to go all but unnoticed. Though Pryor was industrious and honest, he was equally unfortunate in his private business. He held the friendship of those who knew him, and became one of the dominating figures of the little colony at the mouth of the Verdigris, exerting its influence over the entire Southwest.

Another well-known trader at the mouth of the Verdigris at this period was Hugh Glenn, who headed the Fowler expedition in 1821, the first to go from there to Santa Fe. Colonel Hugh Love was also a trader in this frontier settlement.

As an active trader and man of influence among the Indians, A. P. Chouteau was the outstanding figure of all those in business at the mouth of the Verdigris. Chouteau had for several years traded with the Indians on the headwaters of the Arkansas and Platte rivers, but abandoned the hazards of that field in 1817. In September, 1815, Colonel Chouteau and Julius De Mun, with forty-five men, engaged in a trading expedition to the Arapaho Indians at the head waters of Arkansas River. They were having a successful winter when in February De Mun with two companions returned to Saint Louis for additional supplies. In July he started back, proceeding up Missouri River by boat to join Chouteau at the mouth of Kansas River. The latter, in coming east, had been attacked by two hundred Pawnee [105] Indians at a place since called Chouteau's Island, near the present site of Fort Dodge, Kansas, but he arrived at the appointed place with his furs; these he and De Mun sent down the river to Saint Louis, and again turned their faces to the Rocky Mountains. In their absence, a friendly governor at Santa Fe had been succeeded by one hostile to Americans. Disregarding the permission granted by his predecessor for the Americans to enter the Spanish territory, the governor caused the arrest of Chouteau and De Mun with their men, as they were about to leave the Arkansas for the Crow Indian country on Columbia River. They were thrown in prison at Santa Fe, where they were confined for forty-eight days, part of the time in irons; their lives were threatened, and they were subjected to other indignities; the final and most poignant of all was compelling Chouteau and De Mun to kneel to hear a lieutenant read the sentence pronounced by the governor, and then "forced likewise to kiss the unjust and iniquitous sentence, that deprived harmless and inoffensive men of all they possessed – of the fruits of two years' labor and perils," as reported by them to our Government.[106] This sentence of the governor gave them their liberty, but confiscated all their property, valued at over thirty thousand dollars.

[105] "A Mr. Chouteau and party had been attacked by 150 Pawnees. He had one man killed and four wounded; but he defeated the Savages, killed seven and wounded several others and brought in 44 packs of beaver, that is about 4,400 pounds." _ Niles Register (Baltimore) October 19, 1816, vol. xi, 127.

[106] *American State Papers*, "Foreign Relations" vol. iv, 211.

A claim for this loss was made by the United States, but it was not paid for over thirty years – long after Chouteau's death.[107]

Some years after this incident, in answering a letter from the Secretary of War, inquiring about trading conditions in the west, Colonel Chouteau wrote from the Verdigris:[108]

"Shortly after the war I went upon a trading expedition on the head of the Arkansas and was taken by the Spaniards. When I was near Santa Fe, I was invited by them to visit their place. Convinced of my own innocence and believing the invitation to be an act of hospitality, I unhesitatingly accepted what I believed was intended as a mark of respect. Immediately upon my arrival in town I was arrested, thrown into prison, charged with revolutionary designs, my property confiscated, and after having undergone an examination in which my life was endangered, I was discharged without any compensation for my property which had been taken by violence.

"On my return home I was determined to abandon a trade that was attended with so much risk until the time when the United States Government would extend its protection to those citizens who embarked their capital and risked their lives in a trade that ultimately must produce advantages to the citizens of the United States, and in a political point of view cement the bonds of friendship between the governments of the United States and Mexico."

The Indian trade at the Verdigris was conducted

[107] From the files of the Saint Louis, Missouri, County Court. *In the matter of the Estate of August P. Chouteau deceased,* John B. Sarpy, administrator. Payment was made about 1850.

[108] Chouteau to Secretary of War, Nov. 12, 1831, Indian Office, Retired Classified Files, *1831 Miscellaneous.*

for the sake of the furs, skins, and bear oil the Indians brought to the trading post. Wild bees were abundant, and honey and beeswax found a ready market. Wild horses, buffalo, elk, and deer ranged the prairies, and beaver, bear, wolves, otter, fox, wildcats, panthers, turkeys, ducks, and swans were found in vast numbers. The Indians brought to the Verdigris the fruits of the chase and the trap, to exchange for the earrings, strouds, twists of tobacco, pipes, rope, vermillion, axes, knives, beads, cheap jewelry, and bright-colored cloth, which constituted the medium of exchange.

Chouteau had another trading house at the Saline on Grand River, near where Salina, Oklahoma, now is, where he built up a comfortable country seat which was visited and described by Washington Irving in 1832.[109] The Saline was distant from the mouth of the Verdigris about thirty-five miles overland and sixty by canoe.

From the trading house at the mouth of the Verdigris in 1823 and 1824 Chouteau wrote in French a number of letters to his cousin, P. Milicour Papin, at the Saline,[110] relating to the business in which several members of the family were engaged, and which he supervised so efficiently from the "Ver di Gris"; gave directions in several quarters, warned Milicour against Mr. Guilless who is going to call at "La Saline"; "he is a good fellow, but one must be wary of him for he has some merchandise," and might beguile the Osage Indians into bartering to him the peltry that Chouteau hopes to ship to New Orleans that winter. However,

---

[109] Trent, William P. and George S. Hellman. *The Journals of Washington Irving,* The Bibliophile Society, vol. iii, 131.

[110] Missouri Historical Society, Saint Louis, Missouri, "Pierre Chouteau Collection." Translated by Mrs. N. H. Beauregard, Archivist.

"treat him well for he is one of Menard's [111] men, and that means a great deal to me." It is the eleventh of December, 1823, and Chouteau deplores the fact that the Indians have done less hunting that season than formerly; however, he hopes to secure forty to sixty more packs before very cold weather sets in. And he tells with some relish how his friend Clermont, the Osage chief, ordered some of "Les Loups" not to hunt on Osage lands. After expressing his appreciation for the news from "La Saline", he warns Milicour not to sleep too much during the day, or the business will not prosper.

He wrote to Milicour, January 3, 1824, that he has just had a letter from his brother Ligueste, who is among the Little Osage on the headwaters of Osage River, many miles north of the Arkansas Osage. He has little faith in the business sagacity of Ligueste, who reports that he has made ninety-two packs with the Little Osage without informing him how many pelts each pack contains. He warns Milicour of the presence of another white trader poaching on the Osage farther north, and commands his cousin to send for the Indians at once to bring in their peltries before their competitor appears among them, or make himself responsible for the value of the furs that are lost.

[111]Pierre Menard was born October 7, 1766, at San Antoine, Quebec, came to Vincennes in 1788, and Kaskaskia in 1790. He was Lieutenant-governor of Illinois in 1818, and died in 1844. He was an active fur trader dealing with the Indians, and was one of the partners in the Missouri Fur Company which included A. P. Chouteau and his father Pierre Chouteau. A. P. Chouteau shipped from the mouth of the Verdigris seven hundred twenty-six deer skins belonging to Menard. Bayou Menard a small stream flowing into the Arkansas below Fort Gibson was so named prior to 1820 when it was mentioned in the account of Long's Expedition [Thwaites, *op. cit.*, vol. xvi, 285]. The mountain south of this stream was called Menard Mountain.

The fur trader had his losses to recoup too – "should Campbell come by here, we must try to make him trade off, by means of the Indians, all of our defective skins as well as our imperfect cats." The mouth of the Verdigris was the emporium of the Southwest; merchandise that came up-stream by keel boat from New Orleans and Saint Louis was distributed from here. Chouteau was sending to Ligueste "150 twists of tobacco, 10 pounds of vermillion and 13 of Rase-dez"; and to Milicour went a small chest with some Christmas gifts which he was requested to share "with Madam Rivar and my old woman." Beside directing Milicour to take good care of the boat, he was told to make his preparation to go to Chihuahua on a two months' trip in the summer.

Again, on January 12, he wrote a long letter of advice and directions about the business; information concerning pelts acquired and owing to the house; Milicour must do all in his power to keep the Osage of Pahuska's or White Hair's town from coming down to the mouth of the Verdigris; "tell them that you are expecting me [at the Saline] any day; I must tell you, however, that it is quite impossible that I go. Much of our credit has not been turned in, and the affairs between the Osages and the Government,[112] not having been settled, prevents my leaving, for fear something should turn up, which some one else would not be able to settle; I do not remember whether I told you about Goche; he gave me 50 pelts for his credit, and since that he has had a cotton cloth with three stripes, which is worth 16 pelts. The Indians like it, but they are too poor to buy it. Next Monday at the latest, I shall send my men to the Saline. Work has been

[112] Which were soon to cause the establishment of Fort Gibson.

started on the small barge, but unfortunately, from present appearances, we shall not need it for December."

However, on the second day of April, the large barge left down-stream with a cargo of thirty-eight thousand seven hundred fifty-seven pounds of furs and skins; the shipment included three hundred eighty-seven packs and fifty-seven pounds, made up of three hundred female bear skins, one hundred sixty bear cubs, three hundred eighty-seven beavers, sixty-seven otters, seven hundred twenty cats, ninety-five "Pinchon" and fox, and three hundred sixty-four packages of deer skins, which included seven hundred twenty-six deer skins belonging to Mr. Menard. This information is contained in a letter written at "Ver de Gris" on April 4. It contained the news also of the drowning of Mr. Philbrook, the Osage sub-agent. He had been at Bean's salt works on the Illinois, and was returning to his post when, attempting to cross Grand River near the mouth, he was drowned. Young Pryor came by the place a few days later, and discovering Philbrook's horse, bridle, saddle bag and "cloque", learned the sad story of his death.

Two days later Chouteau wrote Milicour again. He was accompanying the valuable cargo of peltry, but would be unable to go all the way to New Orleans with the boat. The troops from Fort Smith were on their way to the mouth of the Verdigris, where they were to establish a new army post, and Chouteau felt the necessity of returning soon. The Indians were troublesome, and were likely to become involved with the troops that were about to be located near them. To maintain his influence with the Osage, he must be near at hand to advise them if the proximity of the soldiers threatens them with difficulties. Also there was the business to be had of securing provisions for the troops. He was disappointed that Ligueste had not sent his furs down Grand River in time to accompany the shipment to New Orleans. He directs Milicour to arrange his bear pelts in packs of twenty each, and to send them down at once, as they must be in New Orleans by May first, or they will lose money on the shipment. The packs must be marked so he can tell the female from the male bear pelts. "I send you four battle-axes with which to procure oil; you may trade one axe for one font of oil and even something extra thrown in." Chouteau was interested in live stock, and later had a race-track at the Saline. He warns Milicour not to let any of the visitors at the Saline beat or run his horses too hard, and when taking horses for transporting furs not to use the plow-horses.[113]

---

[113] In December, 1831, George Vashon, Cherokee Agent, issued licenses to traders in the Cherokee country including A. P. Chouteau near the Falls of the Verdigris and on the east side of the river; Hugh Love at the same place, but on the opposite side of the river. Eli Jacobs was his clerk. Thompson & Drenen at the Point, between the Neosho and the Verdigris; Jesse B. Turley also at this Point, and A. P. Chouteau on the Neosho near Grand Saline. Seaborne Hill was later located at the mouth of the Verdigris. Benjamin Hawkins, who was married to a Cherokee woman, was a trader in that nation and a friend of Sam Houston's. Sixty barrels of whiskey delivered to Hawkins on the Verdigris by the steamboat Elke in 1832, caused a grand jury inquisition at Little Rock. Hill was killed at Fort Gibson in July, 1844, by Captain Dawson and a man named Baylor. – Fort Gibson *Letter Book* no. 17, p. 140.

Washington Irving at Fort Gibson, 1832

The McIntosh Creeks had been located along Arkansas River near the Verdigris on fertile timbered land which they began at once to clear, cultivate, and transform into productive farms. The treaty of 1828 with the Cherokee gave the latter a great tract of land on both sides of Arkansas River embracing that on which the Creeks were located. This was accomplished by a blunder of the Government officials, in the language of the Secretary of War, [114] "when we had not a correct knowledge of the location of the Creek Indians nor of the features of the country." This situation produced much unhappiness and contention between the people of the two tribes. The Indians had other grievances, and the Creeks took the lead in calling the attention of the officials to their needs by the preparation of a memorial in which they complained of frequent attacks upon them by bands of wild Indians from the south and west of their location. They asked the Government to appoint a commission to meet with them for the redress of their wrongs, and to call a council of the different tribes for the adoption of measures to establish peace and security in their new home.

The Creek memorial and a long report by the Secretary of War on February 16, 1832, were transmitted to Congress by President Jackson,[115] who recommended

[114] U.S. House, *Executive Documents,* 22d congress, first session, no. 116, President's Message submitting the memorial of the Creek Indians.

[115] *Ibid,* Message of President Jackson.

that three commissioners be appointed as requested
in the memorial, and recommended by the Secretary.
It appeared from the report of the Secretary of War
that there were then west of the Mississippi twenty-five
hundred Creeks, six thousand Choctaw, thirty-five
hundred Cherokee and three thousand Delaware.

The President's recommendation was enacted into
law by Act of Congress of July 14, 1832, providing for
the appointment of three commissioners to examine the
country west of the Mississippi set apart for the emigrating Indians; to help adjust difficulties between
them concerning their boundaries and locations; to
report on proper places for locating emigrating tribes;
to compose difficulties with hostile Indians; and to
report on the manner in which emigration of Indians
had been conducted and recommend improvements.
The commissioners with headquarters at Fort Gibson
were to hold office for two years, and twenty thousand
dollars was provided to carry the act into effect.

Commissions issued on the date of the act,[116] to Mont-
ford Stokes,[117] Governor of North Carolina, Governor
William Carroll of Tennessee, and Roberts Vaux of
Pennsylvania, as commissioners under the act.   Gov-

[116] Cass to Carroll, Stokes and Vaux, July 14, 1832, Indian Office *Letter
Book,* no. 9, p. 32ff.

[117] Montford Stokes was born in Wilkes County, North Carolina in
1760. Entered the merchant service when very young and left it in 1776
to enlist in the Continental Navy under Commodore Stephen Decatur.
Captured by the British before he had served a year and held on a prison
ship in New York harbor. After the war Stokes returned to North Carolina, and from 1786 to 1790 he was assistant clerk of the State Senate,
where he was very popular. Elected to United States Senate but declined.
In 1816 he was again elected senator, this time in place of James Turner
who had resigned, and he took his seat in the Senate on December 16, 1816;
at the expiration of his term, reelected and served until March 3, 1823.
Served as state senator from 1826 to 1829 and from then as state representative. He was elected governor of his state in 1830 and served until

ernor Stokes accepted, but the others declined, Vaux
for the reason that as he belonged to the religious order
of Friends, he could not consistently assume the obliga-
tions implied by the military attachment which was to
attend the commission.   Reverend John F. Schermerhorn of Utica, New York, who had been a persistent
applicant for appointment on the commission, was
passed over until several others had declined it, when
he was appointed along with Henry L. Ellsworth of
Hartford, Connecticut.   Colonel S. C. Stambaugh [118]
was appointed Secretary at five dollars a day.   On the
date of the act, a letter [119] was addressed by the Secretary of War to Colonel A. P. Chouteau, requesting
him to coöperate with the commission and give it the
benefit of his extensive acquaintance and friendship
with the Indians, and at the same time he wrote the
Commissioners to consult freely with Chouteau and
avail themselves of his information about the Indians.
Captain William Armstrong[120] had been appointed on

he resigned to accept the appointment given him by Andrew Jackson as
commissioner to the Indians west of the Mississippi River which brought
him to Fort Gibson.

Stokes was trustee of the University of North Carolina from 1805 to
1838 and for part of the time was president of the board.   In 1830 he was
president of the board of visitors to West Point.   He was the father of
several children one of whom, Major Montford S. Stokes served with
distinction in the war with Mexico.   Governor Stokes fought a duel at
Mason's old field near Salisbury with General Jesse D. Pierson and was
severely wounded.

[118] Stambaugh was editor of the Pennsylvania Reporter published at
Harrisburg, when he was appointed Indian agent at Green Bay in 1830.

[119] Cass to Chouteau, July 14, 1832, Indian Office, *Letter Book,* no. 9,
p. 42 ff.

[120] William Armstrong of Nashville, Tennessee, on the death of his
brother Major Francis W. Armstrong succeeded him as Choctaw agent
and acting superintendent for the Western Territory.   December 26, 1843,
Captain Armstrong was confirmed by the Senate as superintendent of Indian
Affairs for the Western Territory, which office he held until his death
at Doaksville, near Fort Towson, June 12, 1847.

July 2, 1832, superintendent for the removal of the Choctaw.[121]

During the Black Hawk War in Illinois, Congress passed an act, July 15, 1832, providing for a battalion of mounted rangers, to be composed of six companies of approximately one hundred volunteer officers and privates to each company, to serve for one year. Captain Jesse Bean of Tennessee raised a company in Arkansas, and made his rendezvous at Batesville the last of August,[122] taking up his march to Fort Gibson where he arrived September 14, and where his company, the first of the rangers at that post, was to attend the commissioners upon such duties as should be required of them. Bean was soon to meet one of the world's greatest writers, whose coming to Fort Gibson was the result of a series of happenings that were then taking place in the east.

Mr. Ellsworth was the first of the commissioners to prepare for departure to Fort Gibson. He was planning to go by way of the Arkansas, but after learning from the Secretary of War that Colonel A. P. Chouteau was at Saint Louis, concluded to meet him there and return with him to Fort Gibson by way of the Missouri and Independence. He left Hartford August 20, by way of Lake Erie and the Ohio River, hoping by this northern route to avoid the cholera that was then raging further south.

Washington Irving sailed from Havre for New

---

[121] On July 29, 1832, an act of Congress provided for the appointment by the President, by and with the consent of the Senate of a commissioner of Indian Affairs to act under the Secretary of War.

[122] Arkansas *Gazette*, (Little Rock), August 8, 1832, p. 3, col. 2. Joseph Pentecost was first-lieutenant, Robert King second-lieutenant, and George Caldwell, third-lieutenant. They were delayed on the road by an epidemic of measles but arrived at Fort Gibson September 14, 1832. They were immediately mustered into the service and on October 6, departed for the

York in the summer of 1832. On the same boat were
Charles Joseph Latrobe, an Englishman, and Count
de Portales of Switzerland, whom he had met in
Europe. The three became friends and made several
sight-seeing trips together after their arrival in New
York. While traveling on Lake Erie, they met Ellsworth whom Irving described [123] as a very gentlemanly
and amiable person, and an excellent traveling companion. And well he might think so, for in an excess
of amiability Ellsworth invited the three of them to
accompany him to Fort Gibson. They were delighted
to accept the invitation, and were enthusiastic over the
prospect of visiting this far western outpost of which
the east was then hearing so much. And the "idea of
travelling on horseback through the forests and
prairies, camping in tents at nights, and hunting deer,
buffaloes, and wild turkeys," Irving wrote to his sister,
strongly fascinated them. They arrived at Cincinnati
September first, embarked on a boat there the third,
changed at Louisville the next day, and arrived at Saint
Louis on the eleventh. While there preparing for the
overland journey, Irving went to Jefferson Barracks
to see the prisoner Black Hawk, whom he described as
an old man, upwards of seventy, emaciated and enfeebled by the sufferings he has experienced, and by a
touch of cholera. They also drove out to see Governor
Clark, " a fine, healthy, robust man, tall, about fifty,
hair getting gray."

Providing themselves with horses and a covered
wagon for transporting their equipment, they purchased
from the American Fur Company tents, bear skins,

west on the expedition that was joined by Washington Irving (Arbuckle
to Jones, Adjutant-general, September 15, 1832, 167 A. 1832).

[123] Irving, Pierre M., *The Life and Letters of Washington Irving*, vol.
iii, 34.

blankets, and other personal effects, and left Saint Louis on the fifteenth. Traveling on the north side of the Missouri to Franklin, they crossed the river above Boone's Lick. As they neared Lexington they "met the long train of trappers, which annually crosses the great western desert toward New Mexico, returning from the Rocky Mountains and Santa Fe; their mules laden with skins for which they had dared that long and perilous pilgrimage. They were about seventy in number; men worn with toil and travel, bearing in their garb and on their persons evident marks of the adventurous passage of those immense prairies which lie to the westward. Seven of their number had fallen in combat with the Indians on their return." [124]

After nine days on horseback they reached Independence, then a straggling village five years old. But it was three days before the arrival of Ellsworth and a companion who had essayed the journey by steamboat which had grounded one hundred miles below Independence and forced the passengers to seek other methods of locomotion. The party consisting of Ellsworth, Latrobe, General Clark,[125] Irving, Chouteau, Portales, and Doctor O'Dwyer set off on the twenty-sixth. Some of them traveled in a dearborn wagon

---

[124] Latrobe, Charles Joseph. *The Rambler in North America*, vol. i, 103.

[125] William Clark, the brother of George Rogers Clark, who conquered the Northwest during the Revolutionary War, and the associate of Meriwether Lewis on the famous transcontinental expedition of 1803-06, was born in Virginia in 1770. He entered the army in 1792, and shared in several western campaigns, notably that of Wayne in 1794-95. In 1796 he left the service on account of ill health, and became a hunter and trapper. After the expedition to the Pacific coast, Clark was stationed at Saint Louis as Indian Agent and Brigadier-general of Militia. In 1813 he became governor of the Missouri Territory, which at first included Arkansas. Upon the admission of Missouri to statehood, he was appointed superintendent of Indian Affairs, and remained at Saint Louis in this capacity until his death in 1838. — Thwaites, *op. cit.*, vol. xiii, 134, n.

and others on horseback. They camped in the open except the nights spent at Harmony and Union missions and at Chouteau's house. Their journey of twelve days to Fort Gibson was a succession of novel and interesting experiences.

Because of his many qualifications, by common consent Colonel Chouteau was looked to as the leader, and he was generally in the van; and the whole party was indebted to his courtesy and extensive information on every subject connected with the country and its inhabitants, for much of their comfort and entertainment. Among the Osage, whose principal trader he was, he possessed great influence; he had hunted, feasted, fought for and with them, and was considered by them as a chief and a brother. From him the travelers took their first lessons in hunting, camping and backwoodsman's craft, accomplishments that had endowed him with the good health indicated by a fine physique and ruddy countenance.

They stopped at Colonel Chouteau's house near the Grand Saline on Grand River. It was an imposing establishment in the midst of the wilderness where Chouteau lived with his Osage wife, Rosalie, by whom he had an interesting family of children. Surrounded by a retinue of colored and Indian retainers, he was the feudal lord of this whole country. A shrewd Indian trader, of dominating personality and great influence with the Indians, he lived a care-free life with all the luxury obtainable in the wilderness. His was a double log house with a large passage through the center from which a stairway ascended to the second story and the whole was covered with whitewash. A piazza extended across the front, with buffalo and bear skins draped over the railing, while one end was loaded with har-

ness, where dogs and cats were sleeping together. One
room, the treasure house of the establishment, contained
his guns, rifles and traps.

In a large yard in front of the house a number of
Indians were roasting venison under a tree; negroes,
half-breeds, and squaws welcomed the distinguished
visitors; negro girls ran about giggling, while others
took and tethered the horses. Numerous dogs and
pigs, hens flying and cackling, turkeys, geese, and
ducks, all fat and happy, sounded a noisy welcome,
making the scene one of animation and color.

They passed to their supper through the open hall-
way where Indians sat on the floor. And such a supper! Venison steak, roast beef, fricasseed wild turkey,
bread, cake, wild honey, and coffee served by Masina,
the half-breed sister of Rosalie, as curious Indians
peered at them through the window. Chouteau was
a lover of horses, and his establishment included a race-
track a quarter of a mile from his house, on a level
piece of prairie. And for the entertainment of his
guests, his negro retainers rode and drove by the house
a great number of horses. Chouteau's children, together with those of his neighbor, John Rogers, were
taught by Mr. B. H. Smith, a white man who wore a
calico surcoat cut on Indian lines.

They visited the saline near the house of Mr. Rogers,
set in the midst of a locust grove. On a hill above the
house, where a Pawnee village formerly stood, they
observed the holes in which the Pawnee cached their
effects when they left on their hunting trips. They
left the saline on the seventh, stopped over night at
Union Mission, and arrived at the Creek Agency on
the Verdigris the next day. Stopping long enough at
the Agency to leave with General Campbell, the Creek
Agent, the baggage of Latrobe and Portales, and pass-

ing through woods and canebrakes, they soon saw across Grand River the white fortifications and block-houses of Fort Gibson. Crossing in a scow, they arrived at the gate of the post where they were admitted by a neat looking sergeant, and passing by culprits in a pillory and others riding the wooden horse, they soon arrived at the log house of Colonel Arbuckle, whose guests they became.

The day after their arrival at Fort Gibson, Ellsworth reported to the Secretary of War and informed him of Irving's presence with him. One of the first persons he met there was Samuel Houston. Ellsworth learned on his arrival that Colonel Arbuckle had no information concerning the coming of the commissioners, but knowing of the policy of the Government, had decided to send Captain Bean with his newly recruited company of rangers on a tour to the southwest to give the troops something to do, and incidentally overawe the wild Indians of that region with this new arm of the service. They had been gone but two days when Ellsworth and Irving arrived, and the former decided to join them, thinking that the best way to employ his time while waiting for the other commissioners. At his request, Colonel Arbuckle sent two Creek Indians to overtake the rangers, who were advancing up Arkansas River, and direct them to wait for the commissioner and Irving. Ellsworth wished to explore the country lying between the Canadian and Cimarron rivers, with a view to the location in that section of some of the tribes from the east.

While Latrobe wrote his impressions of this expedition, Irving's account [126] is more graphic and detailed. Latrobe and Portales had planned to part from Irving

---

[126] Irving, Washington. *A Tour on the Prairies.* Hudson Edition, The Crayon Miscellany.

at the Creek Agency and accompany the Osage on their buffalo hunt; but finding the Osage already gone, the commissioner was kind enough to invite them to go with him and the rangers, which they were glad to do.

Colonel Arbuckle detailed Lieutenant Joseph Pentecost of the rangers, in command of fourteen men of that company, as an escort for Ellsworth and his friends until they should overtake Captain Bean in command of the remainder of the company. On the morning of the tenth, accompanied to the Agency by Colonel Arbuckle and Governor Houston, Ellsworth and Irving left Fort Gibson, crossing Grand River in front of the post, and proceeded to the ford of the Verdigris just below the falls, where the Creek Agency was located. Crossing the Verdigris, they made their way to the Osage Agency, which consisted of a few log houses on the bank of the river, and presented a motley frontier scene. There they found Lieutenant Pentecost and his escort awaiting their arrival. The law under which the rangers were recruited made no provision for furnishing them anything but food and ammunition; the nature of their service being of the roughest, uniforms were dispensed with. Each provided his own horse, rifle and clothing. So it was a weird looking crew that greeted the sight of Irving and Ellsworth on the bank of the Verdigris.[127] "Some in frock-coats made of green blankets; others in leathern hunting-shirts, but the most part in marvellously ill-cut garments, much the worse for wear, and evidently put on for rugged service.

"Near by these was a group of Osage; stately fellows; stern and simple in garb and aspect. They wore no ornaments; their dress consisted merely of blankets,

---

[127] Irving, Washington. *Op. cit.*, 28.

leggings, and moccasins.   Their heads were bare; their hair was cropped close excepting a bristling ridge on the top, like the crest of a helmet, with a long scalp lock hanging behind."

And there were Creeks also; dressed in calico hunting-shirts of various brilliant colors, decorated with bright fringes, and belted with broad girdles, embroidered with beads; with leggings of dressed deer skin, or of green or scarlet cloth with embroidered knee-bands and tassels; their moccasins were fancifully wrought and ornamented, and they wore gaudy handkerchiefs tastefully bound around their heads.

And there were many others in this striking picture on the bank of the Verdigris.   Trappers, hunters, half-breeds, creoles, negroes of every hue.   The whole little settlement was in a bustle; the blacksmith's shop was a scene of preparation; a strapping negro was shoeing a horse; two half-breeds were making iron spoons in which to melt lead for bullets.   An old trapper in leathern hunting frock and moccasins, had placed his rifle against a work bench, while he superintended the operation, and gossipped about his hunting exploits; several large dogs were lounging in and out of the shop, or sleeping in the sunshine.

It was two o'clock when the notes of the bugle sounding through the great pecan and walnut trees lining the Verdigris River gave the signal for departure, and the cavalcade [128] took up its march through the country recently settled by the McIntosh Creek Indians on the north side of Arkansas River; "thridding lofty forests, and entangling thickets, and passing by Indian wigwams and negro huts, until toward dusk we arrived

[128] They were accompanied by a captive Wichita woman, probably living with the Osage, whom they intended to use as an interpreter.

at a frontier farm-house, owned by a settler of the name of Berryhill." Passing northwest in the general direction now pursued by the Missouri, Kansas and Texas Railroad from Muskogee to Tulsa, it was three or four days before they overtook the larger body of rangers; after joining them they continued about thirty miles above where Tulsa is now located, and crossed Arkansas River above its confluence with the Cimarron, called by Irving the Red Fork. They ascended the Cimarron about eighty miles, then crossed it, and struggling through the Cross Timbers, arrived at the Canadian near the site of Oklahoma City.[129]

After a month of adventure, hardships, and privations graphically described by Irving, their horses so nearly exhausted that the travelers were compelled to walk and lead them, they returned and arrived on the ninth day of November at noon, at a clearing on the bank of the Arkansas six miles above the Verdigris, and reached Creek Agency about sundown. The luxury of corn bread, sugar, salt, and log houses to sleep in was most alluring and the horses revelled in a return to a diet of corn and cane. Ellsworth and Irving left the agency the next morning for Fort Gibson, where they resumed their quarters with Colonel Arbuckle; Latrobe and Portales remained on the Verdigris.

[129] Colonel Arbuckle had ordered Bean (Arbuckle to Jones, Adjutant-general's office 184 A. 1832), to ascend Little Red (Cimarron) River, sixty miles and then to proceed due south to Red River, thence down that stream to the mouth of the Washita then northeast to the waters of L'eau Bleu (Blue River) which he was to ascend to the western borders of the Cross Timbers thence north to North Fork of Canadian, and northeast to Fort Gibson. But the hardships of the undertaking prevented their compassing more than half the task set for them; and after reaching a point near where is now Oklahoma City and engaging in the buffalo hunt described by Irving they abandoned further progress toward the south and turned their steps toward Fort Gibson.

Indian Alarm on the Cimarron River

At the post, Irving sketched a picture [130] of several bachelors languishing for the smile of Mrs. Nicks,[131] a plump buxom dame, the young widow of General John Nicks, the late sutler at the fort, who, at the age of fifty married her, had amassed a fortune of twenty thousand dollars and, recently dying, had multiplied the allurement of his wife. General Clark and Colonel Arbuckle both aspired to her favor. A lawyer named Lewis, with the militia title of Major had just made his appearance at the fort as aspirant, and occasioned some jealousy among the military men who all united against the intrusion of the visitor. The widow was serenaded by the "horrible drover's voice of the quartermaster, that broke the sleep of men, women, and dogs throughout the fortress."

The evening of their return, the steamboat Little Rock arrived at Fort Gibson, and Irving took passage on her for the return trip. At two o'clock the next day he boarded the boat at Fort Gibson, and as Colonel Arbuckle and the other officers bade him goodbye, the steamer slipped down the river to the Arkansas and turned up the Verdigris to the agency and trading post, to take on a cargo of freight. While waiting there he took tea with Latrobe and Portales who were to remain two weeks longer. There he noted Creek Indians crossing the river in canoes and leading their horses, while other Indians were lying about the banks. And

---

[130] Trent, William P. and George S. Hellman., *op. cit.*, vol. iii, 169.

[131] On January 1, 1832, the day after the death of General Nicks, Colonel Arbuckle appointed his widow, Sally, sutler at the post (Adjutant-general's office, Old Records Division 5 N. 32, order no. 2), until she could dispose of the ten thousand dollars worth of goods left by her husband. And thus she probably became the first business woman within what is now Oklahoma. She was married December 3, 1835, to Robert S. Gibson, a merchant and postmaster at Fort Gibson to which post he had succeeded General Nicks.

after he came aboard again the boat dropped down a mile below the agency, where she tied up in the still, deep water under the great trees that almost touched across the river; and from there he watched the night come and the gleam of sky along the water between the lines of trees that fringed each bank gave way to the light of the moon rising among the trees. There was a large consignment of merchandise to unload, and furs, peltry, pecans and other produce to take on, and it was six o'clock in the morning before the boat got under way. And as in the early light they headed into the beautiful dawn, they passed fires on the banks around which Indians were moving; a canoe was fastened to a bush near by; streaming flocks of wild ducks passed over them, and pigeons in clouds rising from the sand-bars where they went to drink and pick up gravel. Other clouds of pigeons were flying over the trees. Passing down the Arkansas River, they stopped to land Mr. Brown, a Creek Indian and trader, at his place opposite the mouth of the Illinois. Crossing the river, they landed for wood, while passengers went ashore to shoot pigeons. Their boat arrived at Little Rock on the thirteenth, and left the next day for the mouth of the Arkansas.

Latrobe and Portales remained at the agency on the Verdigris and employed their time shooting the prairie chickens that came in countless thousands from all points of the compass to sleep at a favored spot on the prairie. A shot from the gun caused them to rise in thousands, and the sound of their wings could be heard for a great distance. After rising, for about half an hour they would crowd scattered trees on the edge of the prairie by hundreds at a time. On the twenty-third of November, Latrobe and Portales departed in a thirty-five-foot canoe for their six hundred-mile voyage to the mouth of the Arkansas, with two ex-soldiers to manipulate the boat.

Captain Bean's company of rangers went into quarters in a rich and retired nook on Grand River, about six miles above Fort Gibson, where they built themselves huts for the winter. In December, two more companies of rangers arrived at Fort Gibson, and went into similar quarters nearer to the fort, called Camp Arbuckle. One of these companies was under Captain Nathan Boone, a son of Daniel Boone, and the other was commanded by Captain Lemuel Ford. These companies brought the number of troops at Fort Gibson to eight hundred.

When Ellsworth returned to Fort Gibson his associates on the commission had not reached there, and it was December before Reverend J. T. Schermerhorn arrived on the steamboat Spy, and Colonel S. C. Stambaugh, Secretary, came on the steamboat Volant. In the early part of February, 1833, Governor Stokes arrived on the steamboat Arkansas, a new boat of one hundred twenty tons.

While Ellsworth was waiting for his associates, he reported to the Secretary of War.[132] He wrote that availing himself of an unexpected steamboat, Mr. Irving had secured passage and left immediately for Washington on his way to New York. "He assured me he will call and see you and inform you generally of some matters of interest respecting this country."

On his arrival at Fort Gibson, the secretary of the commission not having arrived, Ellsworth offered the position temporarily to Mr. Irving. Irving declined

---

[132] Ellsworth to Cass, November 18, 1832. Indian Office, Retired Classified Files, *1832 Western Superintendency.*

the appointment as it would detain him from his literary pursuits; but although he probably would not accept the pay of secretary in full, Ellsworth said, "he will accept and receive I trust enough to cover his expenses which are more in consequence of losing a horse which he purchased for the occasion." Ellsworth purchased for the Government from Mr. Irving his saddle and stirrups, bridle, pair of mackinaw blankets, a large bear skin and an Indian mat, for the sum of thirty dollars. This act of ready accommodation formed part of the basis for charges that were afterward made against Ellsworth. Five thousand Choctaw were crossing Arkansas on their way to their new home in the West, and Ellsworth reported that cholera had broken out among them in the vicinity of Little Rock. But he was able to report that the Cherokee had twenty-five thousand and the Creeks fifty thousand bushels of surplus corn that would be available for feeding the emigrant Indians.

Peace Attempts with Western Prairie Indians, 1833

What was known as the Treaty of Dancing Rabbit Creek was entered into in Mississippi with the Choctaw Indians September 27, 1830;[133] pursuant to the terms of the treaty, in 1832 the movement of the Choctaw to their new home between the Canadian and Red rivers was under way but they were in danger from incursions of the Comanche and Pani Picts[134] or Wichita, and the Kiowa tribe, who came east as far as the Washita and Blue rivers; these Indians had also evinced a hostile attitude toward white citizens and had attacked and plundered Santa Fe traders, trappers, and other unprotected travelers.

A party of twelve traders had left Santa Fe in December, 1832, under Judge Carr of Saint Louis for their homes in Missouri. Their baggage and about ten thousand dollars in specie were packed upon mules. They were descending the Canadian River when, near the present town of Lathrop in the Panhandle of Texas, they were attacked by an overwhelming force of Comanche and Kiowa Indians. Two of the men, one named Pratt, and the other Mitchell, were killed; and after a siege of thirty-six hours the survivors made their

---

133 Kappler, *op. cit.,* vol. ii, 221.

134 Called by early French traders Pani Pique – tattooed Pawnee, and known to the Kiowa and Comanche by names meaning Tattooed Faces. [U.S. Bureau of Ethnology, *Handbook of American Indians,* part ii, 947.] The French called them Panis, and the Spaniards, Towiaches according to Sibley.– *American State Papers* "Indian Affairs" vol. i, 723.

escape at night on foot, leaving all their property in possession of the Indians. The party became separated and after incredible hardship and suffering five of them made their way to the Creek settlements on the Arkansas and to Fort Gibson where they found succor. Of the other five only two survived. The money secured by the Indians was the first they had ever seen.[135]

Colonel Arbuckle on May 6, ordered [136] a military force to Red River with instructions to ascend the Blue and Washita, and scour the country between North Fork of the Canadian and Red rivers where white soldiers had never been seen. They were ordered to drive to the west any Comanche or Wichita Indians found there and if possible, to induce some of their chiefs to come to Fort Gibson for a conference where they might be impressed by the power of the United States in order to give security to the emigrating Indians.

This force left Fort Gibson May 7, 1833, and made their first camp just across Arkansas River. It was composed of two select companies of the Seventh Infantry and the three companies of rangers in charge of Lieutenant-colonel Many [137] of the infantry. The

---

[135] For Gregg's interesting account of this attack, see Thwaites *op. cit.,* vol. xx, 133 ff. It is described also in U.S. Bureau of Ethnology, *Annual Report for 1895-96,* Part i, 254 ff, where it is said that the Kiowa commemorated the event on their calendar as the "Winter they captured the money", and the occasion on which their chief Black-wolf was killed.

[136] Arbuckle to Many, May 6, 1833, Adjutant-general's office, Old Files Division, 90 A. 1833.

[137] James B. Many was born in Delaware and entered the army from that state as first-lieutenant in the Second Artillery and Engineers on June 4, 1798. As Lieutenant-colonel of the Seventh Infantry he came to Fort Gibson in 1824 where he saw many years of service and was at one time in command. June 1, 1831, Many was brevetted colonel for ten years faithful service in one grade; he died February 23, 1852. Many was frequently mentioned by Pike in connection with his exploration of the upper Mississippi in 1806.

rangers were commanded by Captains Boone, Ford, and Bean. On June 2, when they were nearing Red River between Washita and Blue rivers, approximately in the southern part of what is now Pontotoc County, Oklahoma, one of the rangers named George B. Abbay was surprised by a band of Indians and carried off. The whole expedition under Colonel Many joined in the pursuit of the Indians estimated by Captain Boone to number one hundred fifty to two hundred, who crossed the Washita and left a trail of horses, buffalo robes, saddles, bows and arrows, but made their escape with the prisoner. The troops continued the pursuit for twelve days in a westerly direction, but were forced to abandon it when they arrived near where is now Fort Sill, as their food had given out and they had passed beyond the buffalo range. The men were so worn out and ill from the hardship of the effort to rescue their companion, that Many was forced to abandon the object of the expedition and return to Fort Gibson, where they arrived early in July.[138] Abbay was subsequently killed by his captors south of Red River, but before his fate was known he was the subject of considerable correspondence concerned with plans to effect his recovery. The anxiety and grief of his parents are manifest in the pathetic letter of his father:[139]

"Mount Paraira, Ralls County State of Missouri, March 25ᵗʰ 1834; Dear Sir; It is with pain I have to addrefs you with this letter. My son George Abbay

---

[138] Many to Arbuckle July 4, 1833, Adjutant-general's office, *Old Files*, 90 A. 1833. George B. Abbay, born in Woodward County, Kentucky, enlisted at Cave Spring, Missouri, at the age of thirty years, August 4, 1832, for one year in Captain Nathan Boone's company of mounted rangers.

[139] Jonathan Abbay to Secretary of War, March 25, 1834, Indian Office, Retired Classified Files *1834 Upper Missouri*.

was taken a Prisoner on the 2nd of June last by the Pawnee Peak Indians and is still a prisoner with them, and they will not give him up. I have used every means in my power to Obtain him by Ransom or other wise but all in Vain, he was One of the Mounted Rangers in Capt. Nathan Boons Company. If the Captain has or has not reported him I should like to know of you from your Office, Will you condecend so far as to write to me, on that subject, and let me know what has, & can be done to Obtain my Son. I wish the President with yourself to send on a special mefsage to Col. Dodge of the Mounted Dragoons at Fort Gibson with an appointment to him & his command to go on to the Pawnees Peak Towns & Release my son. He has now been a Prisonier for nine or Ten Months. And I hope the simpathy of your heart and that of United States President (General Jackson) will not let a loving Father & tender Mother go down with sorrow to their grave for the lofs of their son. Should you disapprove of my plans, you will please to addopt any other in your wisdom that you may think best to obtain him. And I will go with them (if permitted) & will have my son or they shall walk over my body a dead corps, although I am now sixty five years of age. Please to answer this letter as soon as any thing can be done. And I hope to Remain. Dear Sir, Your most obt. Jonathan Abbay. Sen. NB The Osage Friendly Indians & the Pawnee Peak Indians have had a Fight about my son but they could not obtain my Son. And in the Battle the Osage Indians took from the Pawnee Peaks twenty of their Chiefs. If I was able I would buy one or two of their Chiefs from the Osages, & would go on home with them & make an exchange for my son. I am Sir, truly yours, J. Abbay sen."

In March, 1834, Sam Houston, then in Washington wrote a long letter to the Secretary of War giving his views about the Indians who were supposed to have captured Abbay and the possibilities of effecting his recovery. Governor Stokes's commission also was called on for information on the subject.

The expedition in 1833 was a failure. Instead of bringing home hostages of the western tribes to impress with the prowess of the white men, they had lost a prisoner to the Indians. Because of the fact that the year for which the rangers had enlisted was soon to expire, they were obliged to consume a great deal of time intended for exploring and seeking out Indians, in the killing and drying of buffalo meat before their return to Fort Gibson, which place they reached after an absence of fifty-four days. Thirty days of that time they lived on buffalo meat alone, without either bread or salt and for the last eight days before reaching Fort Gibson subsisted on buffalo meat boiled with tallow.

During the absence of the expedition there was almost incessant rain and an extraordinary rise in the streams of the country which was particularly disastrous in the vicinity of Fort Gibson. Distress on Arkansas River was said to be indescribable. That river, the Verdigris, and Grand, were reported higher than ever known before. At Fort Gibson several houses, fences, corn and other property belonging to the post were swept away. Colonel Arbuckle had a large farm about twenty miles below Fort Smith which was inundated with a loss to him of four thousand dollars. Other residents in that neighborhood lost much property. On the Verdigris, the trading houses of Colonel Chouteau and Colonel Hugh Love were swept away, together with most of their merchandise, Chouteau's loss being over ten thousand dollars. Two of the buildings at the Creek Agency on the Verdigris were washed down stream with a large amount of Government property, including rifles and traps intended for the Indians, of the value of twelve thousand dollars. It was reported also that the village of Van Buren was flooded.[140]

Experience had shown that the ranger organization was of little value. Undisciplined, they were organized as mounted free lances. The experiment had not long continued when Congress by the Act of March 2, 1833, provided for the establishment of a regiment of dragoons in place of the rangers with which most of of the latter were merged. The rangers were authorized during the Black Hawk War but were not recruited in time to be of service in that disturbance. Henry Dodge [141] of Wisconsin, was appointed to command them. He had earlier headed a company of mounted volunteers in the War of 1812 and had subsequently been a field officer in another organization. Upon the breaking out of the troubles with Black

---

[140] This, one of the greatest floods in the history of the country was noticed in a United States geological report (Hempstead, Fay. *A Pictorial History of Arkansas,* 245), and in many official letters concerning the removal of the Indians. This year was memorable with the Indians also for the great fall of meteors on November 13. The Kiowa noted it on their calendar as "Winter that the stars fell." – Bureau of American Ethnology, *Annual Report for 1895-1896* (Washington, 1898), Part ii, 260.

[141] Henry Dodge was born at Vincennes, Indiana, October 12, 1782. He commanded a company of volunteers in the War of 1812-15 and rose to rank of Lieutenant-colonel of Mounted Infantry. During the Black Hawk War he served as colonel of the Michigan Mounted Volunteers from April 15 to July 1, 1832, and on June 21 he became major of the newly organized Mounted Rangers. He was on March 4, 1833, made colonel of the Dragoon Regiment, with which he served at Fort Gibson. In 1836 he was appointed governor of Wisconsin and superintendent of Indian Affairs and served until 1841. He was delegate in Congress from that year until 1845 and United States Senator from Wisconsin from 1849 to 1857. He died in Burlington, Iowa, June 19, 1867.

Hawk, he had raised a company of volunteers and had several successful skirmishes with the Indians in Illinois.

When the rangers were merged with the dragoons, Major Henry Dodge was placed in command of this regiment. Major Stephen Watts Kearny, of the Third Infantry, was selected as Lieutenant-colonel. Captain Richard B. Mason of the First Infantry, was appointed major March 4, 1833. Jefferson Davis, only a few years out of West Point, became a first lieutenant in the regiment on the fourth of March, 1833, and adjutant during 1833 and 1834. Captains Boone, Ford, and Bean, and most of the other officers and the privates in the companies of rangers at Fort Gibson, took similar positions in the dragoon regiment.

Five companies of dragoons were soon recruited in eastern states and concentrated at Jefferson Barracks. The recruits had generally disposed of their clothing in anticipation of securing uniforms upon their arrival at that station. In this they were destined to be sadly disappointed. At the approach of winter, before any clothing or arms or many of their horses had been received, they were ordered to march to Fort Gibson. Encountering severe winter weather on the march and being inadequately clothed and organized, many men of these companies suffered severely before reaching Fort Gibson. The citizens of Saint Louis gave a farewell dinner to Colonel Dodge upon his departure to the western wilds and on the twentieth of November, the regiment left Jefferson Barracks for the frontier.

The cavalcade consisted of the regiment, baggage wagons, and retainers; eighteen prisoners sentenced for desertion and other offenses, wearing handcuffs and chains, marched under guard. Passing through south-

west Missouri and northwest Arkansas, through Fayetteville and across Illinois River, after a march of
five hundred miles they arrived at Fort Gibson on the
afternoon of December seventeenth; keeping on their
course for two miles below the post, they went through
the canebrake to a point on Grand River where they
were directed to camp.

The appearance of this canebrake where is now in-
tensively cultivated potato land,[142] was described by
a member of the Dragoons in a book he wrote about his
experiences.[143]   Stretching itself along the margin of
the river, it presented an apparently impenetrable
breastwork of dense green which extended beyond the
reach of the eye.   Its tall and slender stem reared itself
in the air to a height of thirty or forty feet.   From the
intersecting joints of the cane grew long and spiral
bunches of leaves, which retained their life and green-
ness throughout the winter.   And towering above their
heads were massive oaks, pecans, and walnut trees that
grew to an immense size on the rich bottom land.

They made their way with excessive toil through
the gigantic cane which was so close together that their
horses could not move forward without breaking
through by main force.   ·Floundering about, counter-
marching and retracing their steps, they could find no
place to camp and after waiting for an answer to an
inquiry sent to Colonel Arbuckle, they were directed
to camp on a sand bar projecting into Grand River.
There they pitched their tents and weary and half

---

[142] The value of this land for the growth of potatoes was discovered at
an early day. In the summer of 1828 the troops stationed at Cantonment
Gibson raised eighteen hundred bushels of potatoes from four and one
half acres of ground, some of which weighed one and one-half pounds.
– Arkansas *Gazette* (Little Rock), January 27, 1829, p. 3, col. 1.

[143] [Hildreth, J.] *Dragoon Campaigns to the Rocky Mountains*, 76 ff.

starved, having eaten scarcely anything for two days, they spent the first night at their new station.

The next day the dragoons laid out a camp for winter quarters in a little stretch of woods skirting the prairie and near a lake within one and one-quarter miles of the post and called it Camp Jackson. At first, provided only with tents, they suffered severely from the cold and they were obliged to resort to the woodsman's expedient of building a large fire in front of the open tent which by the reflection of the back tent-wall, in a manner retained the heat as long as the fire was burning. Provided with only one blanket and obliged to sleep on the low, wet ground their rest was far from comfortable. Later, large barrack rooms built of the timbers cut out of the woods and covered with oak clapboards, were erected at the edge of the woods upon higher ground. Each one of these structures housed a troop of about sixty men and they were but little more comfortable than the tents; for they leaked badly and during wet weather the man who owned a buffalo skin was extremely fortunate, for only when wrapped in this could he sleep without getting wet.

The flood of the previous summer had swept away the corn fields, as well as the surplus corn so that there was almost none in the country for the horses of the dragoon regiment, which were obliged to subsist on the cane. There were no stables and the life of the horses through that bitterly cold winter was more cheerless than that of the troopers. The winter clothing and rifles of the Dragoons were being forwarded on board the steamer Little Rock, which struck a rock and sunk just above the village of that name, and it was weeks before the salvaged property of the Dragoons, in a badly damaged condition reached Fort Gibson.

Soon after his arrival at Fort Gibson and establishment at Camp Jackson, Colonel Dodge addressed a letter [144] on Christmas day, 1833, to the Adjutant-general reporting that no arrangements had been made for quartering his troops or horses, but that Colonel Arbuckle had purchased eight thousand bushels of corn for him which would be delivered on the bank of Grand River. [145] However, on February second he wrote that the thermometer was twelve degrees below zero and the ice was six inches thick on the river so that it was impossible for the boats to ascend the rivers with the corn. The horses had been turned into the canebrake, but the extreme cold had frozen that food supply and the horses were suffering. Colonel Dodge expressed his disappointment at the quality of the arms issued to his men by the arsenal; but he found from the drills he had put them through that the men in his command knew nothing at all about the use of fire arms. However he took occasion to speak in high terms of Captain Nathan Boone, who had preceded him to Fort Gibson. He recommended that Boone and Ford be placed in command of two of the companies of dragoons. "Captain Boone is a first rate officer for the woods service. He commanded a company of U. S. Rangers under my command in 1812. He is a good woodsman and would be valuable on an expedition and has good knowledge of the southwestern frontier."

[144] Dodge's Military Order Book, 63. This is a manuscript document in the handwriting of Colonel Dodge, containing his military orders and correspondence from August, 1832, to March, 1836. This interesting and valuable document is in the possession of the Historical Department at Des Moines, Iowa. It contains a number of letters written at Fort Gibson pertaining to the preparations that were being made for the expedition in the summer of 1834 to the prairie Indians in the west.

[145] Anticipating the great demand for grain for the horses of the Dragoons about to arrive, speculators bought up all corn available and on

Determined not to be cast down by their hardships the Dragoons made the best of their surroundings; within the barn-like barracks they entertained themselves with musical efforts and on the ample space of floor, groups of Creeks, Osage, and Cherokee from their neighboring settlements, held powwows and dances in which they were frequently joined by the troopers. The Indian accompaniment, effected by patting the hands upon the knees with a gutteral sound from the lungs, was aided by two or three cracked fiddles. Around a tallow candle, in a corner of the building, were to be seen players engaged in thumbing over a deck of cards that were hardly distinguishable through the dirt that covered them; in some of the bunks could be seen others stretched and reading Robinson Crusoe or the Life of Colonel Gardner or General Marion, which with three or four other books formed the whole of the regimental library.

Spring finally came for the exiles in camp and the rigors of winter remained only as a memory; the parrakeets in large and happy flocks whistled as they sported through the trees; the prairie bedecked itself with azure larkspur, painted cup, American primrose, wild verbena, and wild indigo, and other habiliments of spring; the soft tints of the swelling buds of the forest trees turned green as the elm, sycamore, pecan, and walnut assumed the vernal garb that obscured the parasite mistletoe with which brown limbs were decked through the winter; the sassafras sent forth a delicious fragrance and the white of the dogwood, plum, and hawthorn blooms vied with the magenta of the redbud to decorate the landscape in brighest hues.

January 30, 1834, Colonel Arbuckle sent Lieutenant Collins to Louisville to purchase ten thousand bushels of that grain to be shipped by boat to Fort Gibson. (Adjutant-general, 47 A. 1834).

General orders [146] of February 12, 1834, directed
Brevet Brigadier-general Henry Leavenworth to
assume command of all the troops on the southwestern
frontier with headquarters at Fort Gibson. He arrived
there from Fort Towson on April 28, 1834, and assumed
command of the post which he did not relinquish until
June 12, when, the dragoons having departed for the
west he bestowed the command on Lieutenant-colonel
Many. On June 2, Leavenworth issued an order
creating three additional posts in advance of Fort
Gibson; one at the mouth of the Washita to be commanded by Captain Dean in charge of companies A
and C of the Third Infantry, then at Fort Towson.
Dean was directed to cut a road from Fort Towson
to the mouth of the Washita and there erect blockhouses and quarters for the troops of his command.
Brevet Major Birch was directed to proceed up the
road just being cut on the north side of the Arkansas
to the mouth of the Cimarron and there establish a
post to be occupied by two companies of the Seventh
Infantry from Fort Gibson. Captain Dawson who
was then engaged in constructing a road to connect
these posts was directed to take up his station with his
two companies at the mouth of Little River where the
road from the Arkansas would cross the Canadian.
Bridges were to be built, ferry boats constructed and
provisions made for moving troops over the road.[147]
The first post was called Camp Washita. The one on
the Canadian was sometimes called Camp Canadian
but was officially known as Fort Holmes. The third
at the mouth of the Cimarron was designated Camp

---

[146] [Hildreth, J.] *op. cit.*, 102.

[147] Leavenworth to Jones, Adjutant-general, April 29, 1834, Adjutant-general's office L. 1834, 101. Leavenworth's order 21, *Ibid.*, 137 M. 1834.

Arbuckle in compliment to General Arbuckle. The troops remained at these stations until fall, when after the death of General Leavenworth they were removed by order of Colonel Many.[148]

One of Leavenworth's first acts at Fort Gibson was to provide an escort of a company of dragoons for a body of traders going from Franklin, Missouri, to Santa Fe; Captain Wharton [149] was assigned to this duty by orders of Colonel Dodge May 9, 1834. He was directed to proceed north to White Hair's village of the Osage [150] and there await the arrival of the caravan of Santa Fe traders, whom he was to accompany and protect from attacks by the prairie Indians. He performed this duty, proceeding westward on Arkansas River to the limits of the United States, parted from the traders on June 27, and returned to Fort Gibson July 18.

General Leavenworth then gave orders for laying out a road from Fort Gibson to the mouth of the Washita. The remaining five companies of dragoons were enlisted during the winter and afterward organized at Jefferson Barracks; and in the spring and sum-

148 Camp Arbuckle was abandoned November 11, 1834, but not, however, before a blockhouse had been erected, ground cleared, and certain defensive works inaugurated. As these remained standing for many years, although unoccupied save by occasional trading parties enroute to and from Santa Fe, it became known in that section as old Fort Arbuckle (Reservation Division, Adjutant-general's office, Outline Index, Military Forts and Stations, A. page 376). On an undated map in the War Department made by Lieutenant Steen prior to 1841, on the west side of Arkansas River and on the north bank of the Cimarron is indicated "Camp Cedar".

149 Clifton Wharton was born in Pennsylvania and entered the army from the District of Columbia. As captain he was transferred to the Dragoons March 4, 1833, and saw many years of service at Fort Gibson and surrounding country. He was commissioned a major July 4, 1836, and Lieutenant-colonel June 30, 1846. He died on July 13, 1848.

150 White Hair's village was near Grand River in what is now southeastern Kansas.

mer they were marched to Fort Gibson. Company F, whose members were recruited mostly from Boston, arrived at Fort Gibson after a twenty-four days march from Saint Louis; Company G, enlisted largely in Indiana, came down two days later; and with the arrival of Companies H, I, and K, in a few days, the scene at the encampment became one of great animation in preparation for an extensive summer campaign. The blacksmiths' shops were in constant operation. Tailors and saddlers had all they could do, and no one had time to be idle.

Half of the regiment was daily detailed to watch the horses while grazing on the prairies, a trying employment for the troops exposed to the broiling sun, as the thermometer was registering daily over one hundred degrees. Besides these duties the officers were endeavoring to get the troopers into some kind of form; without discipline, experience, or training, these green soldiers were about to embark on a most arduous campaign that was to take an appalling toll of life.

The day the expedition of rangers and infantry left Fort Gibson under Colonel Many the previous summer, a report was received at the post that a party of Osage had returned to Clermont's village with a number of Pawnee scalps and prisoners. Pawnee was the elastic term by which they roughly classified prairie Indians in the southwest and denoted particularly Pawnee Picts or Pique, Tawehash or Wichita Indians. The story of the taking of these scalps and prisoners was a tragedy in the lives of these western tribes.

The Osage Massacre

In the Smithsonian Institution at Washington is a calendar made by the Kiowa Indians, covering a period of sixty years. Their calendars consisted of a series of crude drawings on buffalo hides. The summer of 1833 is indicated by a severed head with a knife by it, which translated reads, "Summer they cut off their heads." It is usually spoken of as the Osage Massacre. The next summer is indicated on the calendar by a crude figure of a girl, which reads, "Return of Gunpandama." [151]

When the treaty council with the Osage at Fort Gibson broke up in disagreement on April 2, 1833, three hundred Osage warriors under the leadership of Clermont departed for the west to attack the Kiowa. It was Clermont's boast that he never made war on the whites and never made peace with his Indian enemies. At the Salt Plains where the Indians obtained their salt, within what is now Woodward County, Oklahoma, they fell upon the trail of a large party of Kiowa warriors going northeast toward the Osage towns above Clermont's. The Osage immediately adapted their course to that pursued by their enemies following it back to what they knew would be the defenseless village of women, children, and old men left behind by the warriors.[152] The objects of their cruel vengeance

[151] U.S. Bureau of Ethnology, *Annual Report for 1895-96*, part i, Calendar History of the Kiowa Indians by James Mooney, 257 ff.

[152] *Journal of Rev. W. F. Vaill*, American Board for Foreign Missions, Congregational House Boston, Manuscript Library, vol. 73, no. 101.

were camped at the mouth of Rainy-Mountain Creek, a southern tributary of the Washita, within the present limits of the reservation at Fort Sill.

Warned of their danger by finding a buffalo with an Osage arrow sticking in it, part of the Kiowa fled and made their escape, but a considerable party stopped on a small tributary of Otter Creek just west of the mountain, where they were discovered by the Osage. In the morning at daylight, a youth went out to look for their ponies, and saw the Osage creeping up on foot. He ran back to the camp where all were sleeping and cried, "To the rocks, to the rocks!" The Kiowa sprang up and fled to the mountains, the mothers seizing the children, and the old men hurrying the best they could, with their bloodthirsty enemies close behind. One woman fled with a baby on her back and dragging another by the hand; a pursuing Osage caught the older girl and was drawing his knife across her throat, when the mother rushed to her aid and succeeded in beating him off with only a slight gash upon her head. A boy named Aya was saved by his father in the same way, and lived to tell his story in 1895 to James Mooney, who set it down in a Government report. His father seized and held him with his teeth, putting him down while shooting arrows to keep off the pursuers, and taking him up again to run.

The warriors being absent, the Kiowa made no attempt at a stand. It was simply a surprise and flight of panic-stricken women, children, and old men, in which every one caught was butchered on the spot. Two children were taken prisoners, a brother and sister, about ten and twelve years of age respectively. When the massacre was ended, the Osage cut the heads from all the dead bodies, and placed them in brass buckets,

one head in each bucket, all over the camp ground;
after which they set fire to the teepes and left the place.
The buckets had been obtained by the Kiowa from the
Pawnee, who procured them on the Missouri and
traded them to the southern tribes.

On their return to Clermont's village early in May
there was great rejoicing; feasting and dancing continued for several days and nights. They had brought
home with them over one hundred scalps including
many old ones taken by the Kiowa from their enemies.
Poles strung with scalps were raised over their houses.
Every grave in sight of the town was protected by a
scalp lifted on a pole. The Osage brought also over
four hundred horses and a number of Mexican dollars
the Kiowa or their neighbors, the Comanche, had taken
from Judge Carr's party the previous winter.[153]
Among the five prisoners they brought home were the
two terrified Kiowa children, whose mother they had
probably killed. The girl's name was Gunpandama,
and the little ten-year-old boy, Tunkahtohye. On another raid, they took home as captives two girls from
the Wichita Indians, who also lived in the vicinity of
where Fort Sill is located.

About the first of March, 1834, Colonel Hugh Love,
who had a trading establishment at the mouth of the
Verdigris, purchased from the Osage the two prisoners,
Gunpandama and Tunkahtohye, and took them home
with him. He paid seventy-five dollars for the boy
and one hundred forty dollars for the girl. It was
Love's intention to use these prisoners for his benefit,
expecting that by returning them to their people he
would be able to establish profitable trade relations
with them. On the arrival of Brigadier-general

[153] *Vaill's Journal*, Ibid.

Leavenworth at Fort Gibson, the commissioners suggested purchasing the prisoners from Love in order that the Government might have the benefit of whatever friendly impression could be created by returning them to their people. General Leavenworth was so impressed with the possibilities thus presented that he regarded the return of the girl to her home as the key to the success of the expedition planned for the summer of 1834. The commission had no money to pay for the prisoners, and General Leavenworth entered into a writing obligating himself to pay to Hugh Love the sum of two hundred dollars for the Kiowa girl, the boy, unfortunately, having been killed. Part of the sum represented board and clothing furnished her by Love. It developed that when the girl was delivered to General Leavenworth in June, Love had left his trading house for Philadelphia, and on his return in September he filed a complaint with Colonel Dodge of the Dragoons on the ground that he had not agreed to part with the prisoner for two hundred dollars, and that she had cost him much more than that sum.

The expedition from Fort Gibson in 1832 had accomplished little in the way of impressing the wild Indians in the southwest. The expedition of 1833 employed a much larger force, but had not achieved its object. It was now determined to send a formidable expedition to the Kiowa and Comanche country. The Secretary of War had directed that efforts be made to rescue Abbay, the ranger who was captured by the Indians while on the expedition in 1833. Gabriel M. Martin was a well-to-do planter who lived at Pecan Point on Red River now in Texas, but then claimed to be part of Miller County, Arkansas, in which county Martin held the office of judge. With his son and servants he was camped on Glass Creek, now called Glasses Creek, about fifteen miles above the mouth of the Washita and three miles west of that stream near where is now Medill, Marshall County, Oklahoma. About the fifteenth of the month Judge Martin sent two of his black men and a white man to hunt, and in their absence from camp the Kiowa Indians attacked and killed Martin and one of his black boys, scalped them both and took the son captive to their home in the Wichita mountains.[154] May 25, the day news of this outrage was received by General Leavenworth at Fort Gibson he addressed a communication, and at his request Governor Stokes's commission wrote another, to Colonel Almonte and Colonel Bean, Mexican officials in the military and Indian service respectively, at Nacogdoches, Texas; they were solicited to use their influence to induce the Texas Comanche Indians to meet Colonel Dodge's expedition at the mouth of the Washita and accompany it to the village of the Comanche on the north side of Red River in the hope that friendly relations and negotiations with the latter might be facilitated. General Leavenworth then entered into a written contract employing Benjamin Hawkins to carry these letters to the Mexican officials, and then to attend the Indian Council soon to be held on Trinity River and endeavor to induce some of the Indians in attendance to meet Leavenworth and Dodge at Camp Washita.[155] No Comanche were induced to attend but thirty-three Caddo Indians arrived at the mouth of the Washita July 22, and accompanied Captain Dean on the march to the western Indians after the departure

---

[154] Leavenworth to Jones, July 3, 1834, Adjutant-general's office, *Old Files,* 160 L. 1834.

[155] U.S. Quartermaster, Fort Myer Depot, *Book 14,* S 304, no. 151.

of Colonel Dodge. With the purpose of recovering Abbay and the Martin boy from the Indians, and, by exhibiting a large force of mounted troops, hoping to make an impression on them, and with the further object of inducing a number of representatives of these tribes to return to Fort Gibson with the Dragoons, the expedition to the southwest was ordered.

At Fort Gibson in June 1834, was George Catlin, the Indian painter. He was a Philadelphian who studied for the bar but became a painter and student of Indians among whom he lived for eight years, painting more than five hundred pictures that were shown and appreciated in London, where he published his absorbing two-volume account of his life with the Indians. The pictures were afterwards placed in the National Museum in Washington. Catlin was permitted to accompany the expedition, and he painted a large number of the western Indians, besides drawing a vivid word-picture of the expedition, the like of which had never before been seen in this country.

The Secretary of War had cast the Dragoons prominently in the theatre of western activity. It was intended, he represented to the President in 1833,[156] to order the whole regiment to proceed through the extensive Indian region between the western boundaries of Missouri and Arkansas, and the Rocky Mountains. It was deemed indispensable to the peace and security of the frontiers that a considerable force should be displayed in that quarter, and that the wandering and restless tribes who roamed through it should be impressed with the power of the United States by the exhibition of a corps so well qualified to excite their respect. "These Indians are beyond the reach of mere

---

156 U.S. Senate, *Executive Documents*, 23d congress, first session, no. i, 18.

infantry force. Without stationary residences, and possessing an abundant supply of horses, and with habits admirably adapted to their use, they can be held in check only by a similar force, and by its occasional display among them. Almost every year has witnessed some outrage committed by them upon our citizens, and as many of the Indian tribes from the country this side of the Mississippi have removed and are removing to that region, we may anticipate their exposure to these predatory incursions unless vigorous measures are adopted to repel them. We owe protection to the emigrants, and it has been solemnly promised to them."

While the rangers wore no uniforms, Congress went to the other extreme in the organization of the Dragoons, who must have created a sensation in all beholders, if one can visualize them in their splendor: A double-breasted dark blue cloth coat, with two rows of gilt buttons, ten to the row; cuffs and collar yellow, the latter framed with gold lace and the skirt ornamented with a star. Trousers of blue gray mixture, with two stripes of yellow cloth three-quarters of an inch wide up each outside seam. A cap like an infantryman's, ornamented with a silver eagle, gold cord, and with a gilt star to be worn in front with a drooping white horsehair pompon. Ankle boots and yellow spurs; sabre with steel scabbard and a half-basket hilt: sash of silk net, deep orange in color, to be tied on right hip and worn with full dress. Black patent leather belt, black silk stock, and white gloves. For undress uniform, the dark blue coat had only nine buttons on each breast, one on each side of the collar, four on the cuffs, four along the flaps, and two on the hips; an epaulette strap on each shoulder.

There was also a great coat of blue gray, made double-breasted and worn with a cape.[157]

Add the soldier's equipment of rifle and ammunition, and picture these helpless tender-feet from northern states starting in the middle of summer on an expedition of seven hundred miles, to impress the Indians with the splendor of their raiment and the menace of their arms and numbers; marching over the blazing prairies in heavy uniforms and through the suffocating thickets of underbrush and briars that entangled with the countless buttons and snatched off the towering cap with the white pompon.

The expedition was not in any sense fit or ready. Three of the companies had not arrived at Fort Gibson from their weary march from Jefferson Barracks until the twelfth, and the start was delayed for their arrival. Eight companies departed on June 15, leaving one to complete its preparation at Fort Gibson. Crossing the Arkansas near the mouth of the Grand, they proceeded eighteen miles southwest, where they stopped at what they called Camp Rendezvous until the twenty-first, when they took up their march for Washita River. The tenth company, that of Captain Wharton, was absent as an escort to the party of Santa Fe traders. They had not got under way when evidence of the unfitness of the organization for the undertaking ahead of them was disclosed by the fact that twenty-three men were sent back to Fort Gibson from Camp Rendezvous, having been pronounced by the surgeon unfit for service.

With the expedition were General Leavenworth, Colonel Dodge, Colonel S. W. Kearny,[158] and Major

---

[157] *Army and Navy Chronicle* (Washington), vol. i, 392.

[158] Stephen Watts Kearny, uncle of Philip Kearny was attending Col-

R. B. Mason. Jefferson Davis, first lieutenant, a few
years out of West Point, was in command of a company. Lieutenant T. B. Wheelock, a staff officer, was
the journalist of the expedition and wrote an account
to which we are indebted for interesting information
concerning the country and people visited by them.

A German botanist, Count Beyrick, a professor in
the University of Berlin, commissioned by his government to undertake scientific research in the United
States, was authorized by the War Department to
accompany the Dragoons. Traveling in a comfortable
dearborn wagon from Saint Louis to Fort Gibson, and
covering most of the route with the Dragoons, he had
made a valuable collection of plants and scientific
information; but soon after his return to Fort Gibson
he died from the disease that swept away so many of
the Dragoons.

There were also eleven Osage, eight Cherokee, six
Delaware and seven Seneca to serve as guides, hunters
and interpreters, and as representatives of their respective nations. The Cherokee were in charge of
Dutch,[159] remarkable for his personal beauty, daring

umbia University in New York when the War of 1812 broke out and he
left his studies to enter the army. As Lieutenant-colonel of the Dragoons
came to Fort Gibson where he saw many years of border service. In
1836 when Colonel Dodge was made governor of Wisconsin Territory,
Kearny succeeded him as colonel in command of the regiment; was in
command at Fort Gibson and in command of the Army of the West in the
War with Mexico; marched to California, conquering New Mexico on
the way. He established a provisional government at Santa Fe, pressed
on to California and was twice wounded in battle. In 1847, governor of
California; joined the army in Mexico; in March 1848, was governor, military and civil, of Vera Cruz and governor of the City of Mexico. In
August 1848, he was brevetted Major-general; he died in Saint Louis on
October 31, 1848.

[159] For an account and picture of Dutch see Smithsonian Institution,
Annual Report to July 1885, (Washington 1886), Part v. The George Catlin
Indian Gallery, 206. ff.

character and successful enterprise against the Osage. The Delaware party included Black Beaver,[160] who later became a well-known guide and interpreter, and had for a leader George Bullett, distinguished for his warlike qualities. Beattie, a Frenchman who had lived nearly all his life among the Osage and was a celebrated hunter, was in charge of that band. De-nath-de-a-go was in charge of the Seneca. There were also two Indian girls, one the Kiowa about fifteen years of age, captured by the Osage in 1833 with her brother, and the other a Wichita, eighteen years of age, taken by the Osage five or six years before.

The train of five hundred mounted troops, a large number of white-covered baggage wagons, and seventy head of beeves, with the necessary attendants, made a very imposing procession. Enthusiastic Catlin, riding to the top of a hill, described the view of the expedition as it started on the march: [161]

"Beneath us, and winding through the waving landscape were seen with peculiar effect, the 'bold dragoons', marching in beautiful order forming a train of a mile in length. Baggage wagons and Indians (*engages*) helped to lengthen the procession. From the point where we stood, the line was seen in minia-

[160] Black Beaver was born at the present site of Belleville, Illinois, in 1806, and died at Anadarko, Oklahoma, May 8, 1880. From 1834 until his death his services were in constant demand by the Government and were invaluable to military and scientific explorers of the plains and the Rocky Mountains. Black Beaver was chief of a band of five hundred Delaware Indians living on Canadian River in the early fifties in the vicinity of Old Camp Arbuckle northeast of where Pauls Valley now is. He served in the Mexican War at the head of a company of mounted volunteer Shawnee and Delaware Indians. As the Federal troops of forts Washita, Cobb, and Arbuckle fled before the Confederate forces in April 1861, Black Beaver acted as guide for the fugitives and piloted them toward Fort Leavenworth.

[161] Catlin, George. *Letters and Notes on the Manners, Customs, and Condition of the North American Indians*, vol. ii, 466 ff.

ture; and the undulating hills over which it was bending its way, gave it the appearance of a huge black snake, gracefully gliding over a rich carpet of green."

But there was a touch of sadness for Catlin at the beginning of the journey. "Wun-pan-to-mee (the white weazel) a girl, and Tunk-aht-oh-ye (the thunderer) a boy, who are brother and sister, are two Kioways who were purchased from the Osages, to be taken to their tribe by the dragoons. The girl was taken the whole distance with us on horseback, to the Pawnee village, and there delivered to her friends, as I have before mentioned; and the fine little boy was killed at the fur trader's house on the banks of the Verdigris, near Fort Gibson, the day after I painted his portrait, and only a few days before he was to have started with us on the march. He was a beautiful boy of nine or ten years of age, and was killed by a ram, which struck him in the abdomen, and knocking him against a fence, killed him instantly." [162] The picture of the little boy and his sister with her arm affectionately about him is one of the Catlin collection hung in the National Museum at Washington.

They marched over the new road recently laid out by orders of General Leavenworth, to the mouth of the Washita; leaving Camp Rendezvous at eight o'clock in the morning, they went over waving prairies. The lush grass varied with gorgeous patches of coreopsis, golden rudbeckia, and pink phlox in bloom, and the more modest centaurea and a riot of other prairie flowers; they made twenty miles through beautiful

---

[162] Smithsonian Institution, *Annual Report of the Board of Regents to July, 1885,* part v, 52. Here in Catlin's Gallery the Kiowa girl's name is spelled Wun-pan-to-mee. In Mooney's account of the Kiowa Massacre, [U.S. Bureau of Ethnology, *Seventeenth Annual Report 1895-1896*, part i, 261], she is Gunpandama.

undulating prairie and patches of timber, reaching the north fork of the Canadian that evening; there they had great difficulty in getting their wagons across, thirty or forty men being required to pull and push one up the bank. The next day a company was compelled to drop behind to care for wagons that had broken down, and Wheelock [163] records [164] that they early discovered baggage wagons to be a great handicap to such an expedition.

General Leavenworth had preceded the command, and was overtaken at the Canadian on the twenty-fifth by Colonel Dodge and his staff, the regiment coming on a few hours later. They crossed the Canadian just below the mouth of Little River, which is near the present town of Holdenville. Lieutenant T. H. Holmes [165] with one company of the Seventh Infantry, was then constructing a fort and quarters for two companies at the junction of Little River and the Canadian, which was afterward known as Camp Canadian and

---

[163] Thompson B. Wheelock was born in Massachusetts and on September 24, 1818, entered West Point Military Academy; graduated July 1, 1822. June 30, 1829, he resigned from the army and served until 1833 as president of Woodward College at Cincinnati, Ohio. September 19, 1833, he re-entered the army as first-lieutenant of the First Dragoons. Ordered to Florida in the Seminole War where he died on June 15, 1836, at the age of thirty-six.

[164] Wheelock kept a daily journal of the expedition which presents a fascinating narrative of that adventure. It was submitted by Wheelock to his commanding officer Colonel Dodge on August 27, 1834, and is to be found in *American State Papers*, "Military Affairs" vol. v, pp. 373-382. The journal was published with the President's Message of December 2, 1834. [U.S. Senate, *Executive Documents*, 23d congress, second session, no. 1, pp. 73-93.]

[165] Theophilus Hunter Holmes was born in North Carolina and from that state entered West Point Military Academy on September 1, 1825, graduating July 1, 1829. With the Seventh Infantry at Fort Gibson from 1832 to 1838. Served in the Mexican War. Resigned from the army April 22, 1861, and joined the Confederate Army with which he served in Indian Territory and later became a Lieutenant-general. He died June 20, 1880.

Fort Holmes.[166]   Before leaving here, General Leavenworth sent orders back to Fort Gibson for Lieutenant
Chandler to proceed to Fort Holmes with several cannon then at Fort Gibson.

After crossing the Canadian, they found the dragoon
camp on the south side of the river.   Beginning their
daily march at eight or nine in the morning and camping at four, the men had been pushed through the
hottest part of the day, and by the time they reached
Camp Canadian or Fort Holmes, twenty-seven more
men were past going, and they were left at that place
with Assistant-surgeon Hailes and a command under
Lieutenant Edwards.   Here Lieutenant Cooke [167] was
left sick, but he lived to return to Fort Gibson and to
write his scorching indictment of the Administration
for its folly in sending these inexperienced men from
the north on this disastrous expedition.

On the twenty-sixth, about ten miles below the Canadian, in the vicinity of where the town of Allen now
is, they came across a band of between five hundred

166 This fort was afterward called Old Fort Holmes when Major
Mason established the fort higher up Canadian River near the site of the
town of Purcell, Oklahoma, which was also called Fort Holmes.

167 Philip St. George Cooke was born near Leesburg, Virginia, June 13,
1809.   He was graduated from West Point July 1, 1827; participated in the
Black Hawk War in 1832, and served at Fort Gibson in 1834.

In 1846 in charge of a battalion of Mormons recruited from a company
of emigrants from Missouri.   During the following winter he made the
first wagon road from the water shed of the Atlantic to that of the
Pacific ocean.   In 1847, as major of the Second Dragoons served in California.   In 1848 he was in command of a regiment at the City of Mexico.

Colonel Cooke served in numerous Indian campaigns in the west and
prepared a system of cavalry tactics which was adopted for the service
in 1861.   As Brigadier-general he was in command of the cavalry in the
army of the Potomac and took part in the defense of Washington and in
many other engagements in the Civil War.   Brevetted Major-general March
13, 1865, he was retired in 1873 and died in Detroit, Michigan March 20,
1895.

and six hundred Osage under their chief Black Dog,[168] engaged in curing buffalo meat; and soon after they began to see large numbers of buffaloes. Catlin describes how General Leavenworth, Colonel Dodge, and other officers yielded to the temptation to chase these great beasts, a folly which they had repented as a cruel waste of the energy and strength of their horses, soon to be put to a severe test. General Leavenworth then sternly announced that there should be no more chasing of buffalo. This resolution was joined in by his companions, the while they were traveling through a section in which no buffalo were to be seen. They had hardly finished discussing the subject when General Leavenworth who was in the lead sighted some buffalo grazing just over the knoll ahead. With an inconsistency any true hunter will excuse him for, General Leavenworth gave a few hasty orders to Dodge, Catlin and Wheelock calculated to compass the destruction of the buffalo, and dashed into what was to be his last ride after that animal. Catlin details at length the exciting chase which ended in General Leavenworth being thrown when his horse plunged into a hole. The General got up and declared he was not hurt, and immediately fainted. Catlin says he was hurt, and that he began to fail from that hour until the time in camp near the Washita, when Catlin describes him under a raging fever:[169] "The General lies pallid and emaciated before me, on his couch, with a dragoon fanning him, while he breathes forty or fifty breaths a minute, and writhes under a burning fever, although he is yet unwilling even to admit that he is sick."

[168] Colonel Chouteau had recommended (Dodge's Military Order Book 92) that Black Dog be employed to head a body of Osage Indians to accompany the expedition and furnish buffalo meat to the men of the command who did not know how to kill the animals.

[169] Catlin, George, *op. cit.,* vol. ii, 473, ff.

Colonel Dodge Reaches Villages of Western Indians

Trailing through broad and verdant valleys, they went, their progress often arrested by hundreds of acres of plum trees bending to the ground with tempting fruit; crossing oak ridges where the ground was covered with loaded grapevines, through suffocating creek-bottom thickets, undergrowth of vines and briars, laboring up rocky hillsides and laboring down again, the horses picking their way through impeding rocks and boulders, until on the twenty-ninth of the month, two hundred miles from Fort Gibson, General Leavenworth and his staff reached Captain Dean's camp, a mile or two from the Washita, where there were quartered two companies of the Third Infantry from Fort Towson. Reports of sickness among the men were alarming. They were dying daily, and failure of the expedition was threatened. General Leavenworth, who had intended to send the command on from the Washita in charge of Colonel Dodge, announced that he himself would proceed in charge to the Wichita country. It was not until the first day of July that the regiment came dragging into camp with forty-five men and three officers ill from exposure, the surgeon said, brought on by marching through the heat of the day. A contributing cause was the strange diet to which these untrained, undisciplined men gave themselves, and the sudden and intemperate indulgence of their appetite in abundant buffalo meat. On arrival at the Washita, seventy-five horses and mules were also disabled past proceeding.

Several days were consumed here in disposing of and caring for the sick, and reforming the badly disorganized regiment. Whole companies were incapaciated by sickness, and as the hardest part of the campaign was ahead of them, the prospect was discouraging, but General Leavenworth did not falter.

The third and fourth of July were employed in crossing the Washita River, with the loss of five horses and a mule by drowning. Where they crossed was a narrow, deep stream with miry shores and steep banks, requiring nearly a company of men to pull a wagon out. A ferry was arranged by building a platform on two canoes, and all of the third was consumed in crossing the left wing of the expedition. The right wing was put over on the fourth, but it was after night before the last wagon was safely across. To add to the difficulties caused by sickness and the terrific heat, many of the horses and mules had worn out their shoes and were traveling on tender, sore feet. There was bitter disappointment in the regiment on arrival at the Washita, when it was found that horseshoe nails that were expected from Fort Towson had not arrived, and the blacksmith was at once sent to that post to make the nails.

By the fourth of July, General Leavenworth realized that he was too sick to travel, and reluctantly gave over his plan to accompany the expedition. He accordingly ordered Colonel Dodge to head the reorganized command of two hundred fifty able-bodied men, half the number that had left Fort Gibson less than three weeks before. Eighty-six sick men, including General Leavenworth and Lieutenant McClure, were left behind at Camp Leavenworth, about twelve miles west of the Washita, with one hundred nine men fit for duty under Captain Trenor [170] to hold the post and care for the sick.

The new command was composed of six depleted companies, with Colonel Dodge, Colonel Kearny, Major Mason, Lieutenants Wheelock and Hamilton as field officers. The captains at the head of the companies included Nathan Boone, Sumner, Hunter, and others. Jefferson Davis [171] was transferred to Company E, under Captain Perkins. Lieutenant Izard was in command of a company. The command was furnished with ten days rations and eighty rounds of cartridges to a man, and baggage was reduced to the lowest possible quantity; and thus they started upon the hardest part of their journey, with two hundred miles between them and their objective. All seemed gay and buoy-

---

[170] Eustace Trenor born in New York; attended at West Point from October 1, 1817, to July 1, 1821. Served at Fort Gibson in 1833 as captain of of the First Dragoons. He became major of the First Dragoons June 30, 1846, and on February 16, 1847, died in New York City at the age of forty-four.

[171] Jefferson Davis was born in Christian County, Kentucky, June 3, 1808. Appointed from Mississippi to West Point, he was graduated July 1, 1828. As second-lieutenant of infantry he served at Fort Crawford and Fort Winnebago, Wisconsin, Yellow River, Dubuque, Iowa, Rock Island, Illinois, and Jefferson Barracks; as first-lieutenant and adjutant of the First Regiment of Dragoons he began his service at Fort Gibson early in 1834. After his return that summer from the expedition to the prairie Indians he was absent on leave until 1835 when he resigned from the army June 30, 1835. Served in the war with Mexico as colonel of the First Regiment of Mississippi and was severely wounded in the battle of Buena Vista. He was disbanded on July 12, 1847, and reappointed in the United States Army with the rank of Brigadier-general on May 17, 1847, but declined the appointment. Subsequently served as presidential elector, congressman, senator, secretary of war, and President of the Southern Confederacy.

ant at the fresh start which they hoped was to release
them from the fatal miasma hanging over the Washita.

The country west of the Washita was frequented by
the western tribes as their hunting grounds, and as the
dragoons were then crossing hostile territory, they were
keyed up to the possibility of combat, though with less
assurance of their own prowess since their force was so
much reduced. Their situation and the state of mind
of the green recruits of this organization were illustrated by an incident of the first night after they got
away. For safety they formed a camp on four lines,
forming a square fifteen to twenty rods across. Upon
these lines their saddles and packs were all laid at a
distance of five feet from each other; and each man,
after grazing his horse, had it fastened with a rope or
lasso to a stake driven in the ground at a little distance
from his feet; thus enclosing the horses all within a
square for security in case of an alarm or attack. On
the night mentioned, a poor horse that had strayed
away the night before and had faithfully followed the
trail of the dragoons, in the darkness of the night was
picking his way through a thicket of bushes into camp
to join its comrades, when a stupid sentinel mistook the
horse for an Indian and fired, and killed him. The
report of the gun and the groaning of the horse alarmed
the camp and set off in a stampede the rest of the
horses; and the whole command was kept in camp the
next day while the troopers combed the country for
the lost horses, all but ten of which were brought in.

It was not long before they began to see roving bands
of Comanche hunters on horseback, who warily
avoided the dragoons, for the officers tried by every
means to come up with them for a talk. Finally, on
the fourteenth, by dint of much patience and tact, they

were able to make a favorable impression on a small band after the interesting process described by Wheelock:

"The command had advanced today about half a mile, when on a hill to our right, we discovered a party of horsemen. Our spy glasses soon determined them to be Indians; Colonel Dodge halted the columns; ordered a white flag; and with it and his staff, moved in the direction of the Indians. After some delay, one of the party advanced upon full gallop, bearing a white flag on his lance; he proved to be a Spaniard, who, early in life, had been taken by the Camanches. Colonel Dodge received him kindly; and through our interpreter, who spoke a little Spanish, made known to him our pacific disposition; gradually the whole band, about thirty Indians, came to us and shook hands. They proved to be Camanches; discovered a good deal of alarm and eagerness to convince us of their disposition to be friendly; they rode good horses; they were all armed with bows and arrows and lances; and carried shields of buffalo hide."

They told Colonel Dodge that they were a very numerous people, whereupon the Colonel, not to be outdone in assurance, answered that the whites were a very numerous people, and that more troops were coming behind with large guns.[172] After the dragoons camped for the night, the Comanche came to buy tobacco and to talk with Colonel Dodge. The Colonel told them

---

[172] After Dodge's departure General Leavenworth took up the march again with sixty men and a six-pounder cannon to support Colonel Dodge, but proceeded only about twenty-five miles west of the Washita where they encamped at a place they called Camp Smith. Unable to travel farther General Leavenworth remained here where he died July twenty-first. He had appointed Kearny in charge of Camp Smith and Camp Washita. (Dodge to Jones, Adjutant-general, August 24, 1834, Adjutant-general's office, 114 D. 1834).

that the President, the Great American Captain, had sent him to shake hands with them, and that he wished to establish peace between them and the red brothers, to send traders among them, and be forever friends. The Indians shook hands with the Osage, Cherokee, and Delaware, and with the Dragoons, and offered to accompany them to the Tawehash village. Wheelock says:

"The Camanche is a fine looking Indian, in general naked; some of them wear blankets. The squaws are dressed in deer skins, and are good looking women. Among them were several Spanish women; evidently long used to Camanche habits. Appearance of a Camanche fully equipped, on horseback, with his lance, bow and quiver, and shield by his side – beautifully classic. This has been an interesting day for us; our goal seems in sight; uncertainty of reaching the Pawnees much lessened."

Colonel Dodge learned that the Kiowa, Comanche, and the tribe called by them Pawnee Picts, but correctly termed Tawehash or Wichita, were allies; but as the Comanche were the largest band, the proudest and boldest, he decided to visit this band first. As they proceeded they were joined by more Comanche, among whom the Wichita girl recognized a friend, and through her Colonel Dodge was able to converse more freely by way of the Osage tongue, which she had acquired during her stay with that tribe. Arriving near the Comanche town in the vicinity of the Wichita Mountains, they were greeted by a hundred mounted warriors who had come out to meet them.[173]

Sickness continued to take toll of the men and horses,

---

[173] "The Comanches are represented as wild, savage-looking fellows, armed with bows, well filled quivers, spears, knives and shields, well mounted, and appeared to be accomplished and daring horsemen. Their

and some of the former were carried in litters, seriously retarding the movement of the troops. When they reached the camp at the Comanche village, there were thirty-nine sick, and six of them, including Mr. Catlin, were in litters. The Kiowa girl even was very ill. Colonel Dodge decided the success of the expedition could not be jeopardized by the care and delay occasioned by the sick, and ordered breastworks to be constructed, within which the fever-stricken men were to be left protected. Twenty-six able men under Lieutenant Izard [174] were detailed to protect the sick, and the command, reduced to one hundred eighty-three men, proceeded to the Wichita village. Game had been scarce for several days and Colonel Dodge, anxious to complete the undertaking that now seemed so near achievement, pushed on as rapidly as possible, so there was little time to hunt. After four days of marching west, they arrived at the Wichita village on the north side of the North Fork of Red River, about four miles below the junction of Elm Fork. Their provisions consumed, the country destitute of game, and no wholesome water to drink, men continued to fall sick, and there was the added misery of the suffering horses laboring, bare-footed and sore, over the granite rocks.

camp consisted of about two hundred lodges, made of skins, and having a conical form; and the number of Indians occupying them appeared to be about four hundred. It appears scarcely credible, but the officers unite in saying that the number of horses possessed by this small hunting party, and were grazing in the vicinity of the camp, exceeded three thousand." From account by S. C. Stambaugh in *Niles Register,* vol. xlvii, p. 74 ff.

[174] James Farley Izard was the son of Major-general George Izard, who served in the War of 1812-15 and was governor of Arkansas Territory from 1825 to 1828. Born in Pennsylvania he was graduated from West Point in 1828 in class with Jefferson Davis; in 1829 he accompanied Major Bennet Riley on an expedition for the protection of Santa Fe traders, and served at Fort Gibson until 1835 when he was ordered to Florida to engage in the war with the Seminole Indians. He died there March 5, 1836.

On the twenty-first of the month the expedition entered upon the last day of their westward march, which is full of interesting details graphically set down by Lieutenant Wheelock:

"The command marched at 8 o'clock for the Toyash village – proceeded a mile or two, when we met about sixty Indians who had come out to meet us, and shook hands with them and moved on in company with each other. They stated that the principal chief was absent on a visit to the Pawnee Mohaws' country; passed their corn fields on our way to their town; these fields are well cultivated, neatly enclosed and very extensive, reaching in some instances several miles. We saw also here melons of different kinds, squashes, &c. The Indians discovered a good deal of alarm as we approached their village – frequently halted and begged Col. Dodge not to fire on them; Col. Dodge promised them safety. These Indians are chiefly naked, and are armed with bows and arrows. They have few horses and seem altogether an unwarlike people. Before we started this morning, the uncle of the Pawnee girl rode up to our camp – he embraced his relation and shed tears of joy on meeting her. We soon reached the village, which was situated immediately under mountains of granite, some six hundred feet in height – in front of the village runs the river; we counted near two hundred grass lodges. These are made of poles, fixed firmly in the earth, fastened together at the top, and thatched substantially with prairie grass and stalks from their corn fields; many of these lodges are thirty feet high and forty feet in diameter; in the center of the floor a shallow excavation serves as a fireplace; around the sides are comfortable berths, large enough to accommodate two persons each. We encamped on a fine position about one mile from the village. Toyash men are less fine looking than the Camanches; their women are prettier than the Camanche squaws; indeed some of their girls are very pretty – naked save a broad garment of dressed deerskin, or red cloth worn about the middle; some of the men wear coats of red cloth, obtained from the Spaniards of Mexico; most of our officers visited them on the day of our arrival, and were hospitably entertained; our own provisions were almost entirely exhausted; we had met with little or no game for several days, and found most excellent fare in the dishes of corn and beans, which they dress with buffalo fat; they served us thus liberally, and for desert gave us watermelons and wild plums. Our men purchased green corn, dried horse meat and buffalo meat; we depended, during our stay with them, on their dried meat and corn; which, with vermillion and articles of clothing, knives, &c., we were able to purchase of them. The Camanches now began to arrive."

Colonel Dodge then told the Indians that he wished to make a treaty of friendship with them; that he desired information concerning the ranger Abbay, who was taken prisoner the summer before; and the boy, Matthew Martin, who was made captive in May when his father was killed near the mouth of the Washita. He told them further that they had brought from Fort Gibson a Pawnee girl, who would be restored to them if the white persons were given up, and that they would all then be friends. The Indians replied that they had nothing to do with the taking of Abbay, but said that a roving band of Indians living near San Antonio in Mexico had captured him, and that when they reached the vicinity of Red River they killed him. They produced little Matthew Martin, a boy of about eight or nine years, who was entirely naked. He was delivered to Colonel Dodge, who expressed to the Indians his pleasure at the exchange of prisoners and told them he was going to restore the little boy to his mother; that her heart would be glad, and she would think better of the Pawnee. The exchange of prisoners had established the friendliest feelings between the Indians and whites, where before had existed distrust and resentment.

Colonel Dodge then passed to the question of the selection of members of the tribe to accompany him to Fort Gibson. After extended discussion, and with much reluctance, the next day it was agreed that one of the Waco chiefs would go.

Here the following interesting ceremony took place: "The boy whom we recovered yesterday is the son of the late Judge Martin of Arkansas, who was killed by a party of Indians, some weeks since. The son was with the father on a hunting excursion, and being parted from him (his death, however, he did not witness, and is now in ignorance of it), the boy relates that, after being parted from his father, the Indians who had taken him were disposed, save one, to kill him; this one shielded him and took care of him in sickness. Colonel Dodge, as a reward for this noble kindness, gave him a rifle, and at the same time caused the little boy to present him, with his own hand, a pistol. Colonel Dodge now assured the chiefs that they should have further presents if they would go with him to his country."

The chiefs responded in satisfactory manner, and speeches were made by the Indians who came with the dragoons. Colonel Dodge assured the western Indians that if they would come to Fort Gibson and enter into treaties of peace, the Government would cause trading posts to be established among them, of which they were much in need; they would no longer have to rely on the Spaniards for their commerce, and the Americans could furnish them articles of trade much better and much cheaper. Before the conference was over, a band of thirty Kiowa, in a very threatening manner, rushed into camp on horseback and almost into the door of Colonel Dodge's tent. The indignation of these Kiowa

". . . against the Osages had kindled to a great pitch, and could scarcely be kept in respectful bounds in their relation to us. The Osages, not many months previously, had murdered a large number of the women and children of the Kiowas, whilst the men were absent hunting. We held in possession, of which they were informed, a Kiowa girl, who was taken on the occasion of the massacre alluded to. The Kiowas, who had just arrived, were not aware of the intention on our part to restore the girl, and consequently presented themselves in warlike shape, that caused many a man in the camp to stand by his arms. Colonel Dodge, however, immediately addressed them with the assurance of our friendly disposition, and gradually led them into gentleness. They are bold, warlike-looking Indians; some of their horses are very fine; they ride well, and were admirably equipped, today, for fight or flight; their bows strung and quivers filled with arrows; they kept their saddles chiefly. A relation of the Kiowa girl's embraced her and shed tears of joy at the intimation that she should be restored to her father and friends. She proved to be a relation of one of the chiefs."

Success of the Expedition and the Cost

The ice having been broken by councils with portions of the Comanche, Wichita, and Kiowa Indians, it was arranged that a grand council should be held between the white officers and the chiefs of the tribes present. At ten o'clock the next day the chiefs began to assemble at the place appointed for the meeting, which was in a wood two hundred yards from the Dragoons' camp. The Indians came from every direction until there were more than two thousand mounted and armed Indians around the council, against whom the pitiful little handful of sick, weary, and emaciated Dragoons would have had small chance; and that the Indians were restrained from violence against the whites who by their association were in the position of espousing the Osage, was due to the tact of Colonel Dodge, and to the good feeling made possible by bringing and delivering to their friends the prisoners taken by the Osage.

"The father of the Kiowa girl, having learned that she was to be restored, in a speech addressed to the Kiowas whose numbers every moment increased, gave vent to his joy and praise of his white friends. . . Great excitement prevailed among the Indians; but especially with the Kiowas, who embraced Col. Dodge and shed tears of gratitude for the restoration of their relative. An uncle of Wa-ha-sep-ah, a man of about 40 years of age, was touchingly eager in his demonstrations, frequently throwing his arms around Col. Dodge, and weeping over his shoulder, thus invoking blessings upon him, in a manner the most graceful and ardent. The women came in succession and embraced the girl, who was seated among the chiefs. The council being now in order, and the pipes having made their rounds, Col. Dodge addressed the Camanche chief, who sat at his right, and who interpreted his words to the Kiowas, whilst a Toyash Indian, who speaks the Caddo tongue, communicated with the Toyash men from Chiam, and one of our Cherokee friends, who speaks English and Caddo."

During Colonel Dodge's speech, another band of Kiowa, about sixty in number, rode up led by a chief, handsomely dressed.

". . . He wore a Spanish red cloth mantle, prodigious feathers, and leggings that followed his heels like an ancient train. Another of the chiefs of the new band was very showily arrayed: He wore a perfectly white, dressed deer-skin hunting shirt, trimmed profusely with fringe of the same material, and beautifully bound with blue beads, over which was thrown a cloth mantle of blue and crimson, with leggings and moccasins entirely of beads. Our new friends shook hands all around, and seated themselves with a dignity and grace that would well become senators of a more civilized conclave."

The Indian prisoners having been restored to their friends, the naked little Matthew Martin delivered to Colonel Dodge, and the delicate negotiations having achieved the ultimate purpose of the expedition – the promise of representatives of western tribes to accompany Colonel Dodge to Fort Gibson, that officer at once set his face toward the east. With his command were fifteen Kiowa, including Titche-totche-cha, who were the first mounted and equipped ready to march. The Comanche chief, cautious and suspicious, deferred until late, when four Comanche and squaws and their early acquaintance the Spaniard, joined the command. Wa-ter-ra-shah-ro, a Waco chief, speaking the language of the Wichita, and two warriors of the latter tribe, also rode into camp prepared for the adventure.

Wheelock does not give the numbers, but many of the men, including the officers, were sick from eating the green corn, dried horse and buffalo meat furnished by the Indians, and there was no doctor with them. Their provisions were so far reduced that they were obliged to subsist on parched corn and dried buffalo meat obtained from the Kiowa. On their arrival at the sick camp at the Comanche village, they found lieutenants Izard and Moore both down with fever, and Mr. Catlin was still very ill, among the total of twenty-nine sick. The next day they broke up the camp, and all started on the march to Fort Gibson. From there they pursued a course farther to the north than their western route. That day the heat was overpowering, and before night there were forty-three ill, seven of whom were past sitting on their horses and had to be carried on litters suspended between those animals. They were almost famished for nourishing food and that with raging fevers, the waste of physical strength and a scourging sun had filled their cup of misery. It was nearly noon of the third day, Wheelock records, that "the cry of buffalo was heard and never was the cheering sound of 'land' better welcomed by wearied mariners, than this by our hungry columns. The command was halted, and soon went together the report of Beatte's rifle and the fall of a fat cow. Halted at 4 o'clock; killed two more Buffaloes, passed today more plaister of paris; rode today over open rolling prairies, between two forks of the Washita. Met a small party of Toyash Indians; our red friends suffered exceedingly from the heat of the sun; we covered them this morning with shirts."

The next day they crossed the Washita River, and the next found them still in the buffalo country. Wheelock notes "men in fine spirits; abundance of buffalo meat; course northeast; distance 10 miles; encamped on a branch of the Canadian; three buffaloes killed this morning; no news yet from express; anxiously looked for . . . One of the Kiowas killed three buffaloes with *three arrows*."

On the first day of August they crossed to the north side of Canadian River fifteen or twenty miles south of where is now Oklahoma City. There they rested for two days, moved camp a mile on the third; on the fourth followed the course of the river south eight miles where they again camped near the site of the future Oklahoma State University. They remained until the sixth. During these five days they were engaged in killing buffaloes and curing the meat for the anticipated march to Fort Leavenworth, four hundred miles away, to which post they were under orders to report; fortunately for these pitifully emaciated dragoons these orders were later changed so they went to Fort Gibson first.

In these camps Wheelock says they saw "large herds of buffaloes; the Kiowas dashed in amongst them and killed with their bows a vast many of them. Grass very much dried. . . The prairie took fire today near our camp and was with difficulty extinguished." Though very sick Catlin was able to enjoy the prairies

upon which Norman, Oklahoma, is built; he said: [175]
"We are snugly encamped on a beautiful plain, and in
the midst of countless numbers of buffaloes; and halting
a few days to recruit our horses and men, and dry meat
to last us the remainder of the journey.

"The plains around this, for many miles, seem actually speckled in distance, and in every direction, with
herds of grazing buffaloes." The officers and men who
were well enough to sit on their horses were engaged in
killing buffaloes much in excess of any possible
demand for their meat; Catlin deplored the riot of
killing: ". . . the men have dispersed in little squads
in all directions, and are dealing death to these poor
creatures to a most cruel and wanton extent, merely for
the pleasure of *destroying*, generally without stopping
to cut out the meat. During yesterday and this day,
several hundreds have undoubtedly been killed, and
not so much as the flesh of half a dozen used. Such
immense swarms of them are spread over this tract of
country; and so divided and terrified have they become,
finding their enemies in all directions where they run,
that the poor beasts seem completely bewildered – running here and there, and as often as otherwise, come
singly advancing to the horsemen, as if to join them
for their company, and are easily shot down. In the
turmoil and confusion, when their assailants have been
pushing them forward, they have galloped through
our encampment, jumping over our fires, upsetting pots
and kettles, driving horses from their fastenings, and
throwing the whole encampment into the greatest
instant consternation and alarm."

On the fifth an express brought word of the death of

---

[175] Catlin, *op. cit.*, vol. ii, 511, 512.

General Leavenworth west of the Washita, July 21, of bilious fever. Colonel Dodge then sent orders to Colonel Kearny at Camp Smith near the Washita, to move his command with the sick to Fort Gibson. The stop on the Canadian was intended as a rest for the sick as well as to secure meat, and while encamped there nearly all the tents belonging to the officers had been converted into hospitals for the patients; and Catlin who was one of them records that:

". . . sighs and groaning are heard in all directions. . . From day to day we have dragged along, exposed to the hot and burning rays of sun, without a cloud to relieve its intensity or a bush to shade us, or anything to cast a shadow except the bodies of our horses. The grass, for a great part of the way, was very much dried up, scarcely affording a bite for our horses; and sometimes for the distance of many miles, the only water we could find, was in stagnant pools, lying on the highest ground, in which the buffaloes have been lying and wallowing, like hogs in a mud-puddle. We frequently came to these dirty lavers, from which we drove the herds of buffaloes, and into which our poor and almost dying horses, irresistably ran and plunged their noses, sucking up the dirty and poisonous draft, until, in some instances, they fell dead in their tracks – the men also (and oftentimes amongst the number, the writer of these lines) sprang from their horses, and ladled up and drank to almost fatal excess, the disgusting and tepid draft, and with it filled their canteens, which were slung to their sides, and from which they were sucking the bilious contents during the day.

"This poisonous and indigestible water, with the intense rays of the sun in the hottest part of the summer, is the cause of the unexampled sickness of the horses and men. Both appear to be suffering and dying with the same disease, a slow and distressing bilious fever, which seems to terminate in a most frightful and fatal affection of the liver."

Having received the news of General Leavenworth's death, after a rest of five days, Colonel Dodge's command took up their march southeast for the mouth of Little River. At once they entered the Cross Timbers where the black jack saplings were so close together they were frequently compelled to cut an opening with axes before the horses could pass. Five extremely sick men were then being carried on litters swung between the horses and the condition of these men was wretched in the extreme as their horses fought through the thickets that clawed and buffeted the improvised litters carrying the miserable burdens.

While they had acquired buffalo meat in plenty, they had no other wholesome food; and the man who had saved a little of his allowance of corn was envied by the others. The scarcity of water added to the suffering of man and beast, both sick and well. After hours of weary travel under a broiling sun, a fringe of low lying timber indicated the bed of a stream and shade, and seemed to invite them to refreshing water. Winding down the steep bank through cottonwoods and willows, to the dry crossing at the bottom, the patient horses looked longingly up and then, turning, gazed down the parched surface for the pools that instinct told them should be there. And the men gazed in vain at the cottonwoods and willows which marked only where water had been.

And so they continued to Camp Holmes, at the mouth of Little River, where they found a large number of sick to add to their list of thirty, but here at least Dodge's men were rejoiced by pork and flour. They received word from Colonel Kearny that there were one hundred forty-one sick and seventy-nine men fit for duty on the Washita. At the Creek settlements on North Fork, the horses were made happy by the first feed of corn, and Colonel Dodge learned that the frantic mother of little Matthew Martin had offered two thousand dollars for his return, little knowing that she was so soon to be made happy by his restoration, without price. Against a hot wind that burned the face, alternately walking and leading and riding the enfeebled horses, they marched on to Fort Gibson, where they arrived on the fifteenth, a handful of sorry looking figures, half-naked and emaciated, with nothing to identify them as the splendid, vigorous troopers who left that place two months before.

Colonel Dodge and staff and the Indians crossed to the Post, while the dragoons camped on the west side of the Arkansas. It was the twenty-fourth of the month before part of Colonel Kearny's command arrived from the Washita with his pitiful caravan of sick men and worn-out horses; those too sick to travel with the first contingent followed in wagons and litters. The scenes at Fort Gibson after the return of the dragoons are well described by Catlin.[176]

"Fort Gibson, Arkansas. The last Letter was written from my tent, and out upon the wild prairies, when I was shaken and *terrified* by a burning fever, with home and my dear wife and little one, two thousand miles ahead of me, whom I was despairing of ever embracing again. . . I am yet sick and very feeble, having been for several weeks upon my back since I was brought in from the prairies. I am slowly recov-

---

[176] Catlin, *op. cit.*, vol. ii, 517.

ering, and for the first time since I wrote from the Canadian, able to use my pen or my brush.

"We drew off from that slaughtering ground a few days after my last Letter was written, with a great number sick, carried upon litters – with horses giving out and dying by the way, which much impeded our progress over the long and tedious route that lay between us and Fort Gibson. Fifteen days, however, of constant toil and fatigue brought us here, but in a most crippled condition. Many of the sick were left by the way with attendants to take care of them, others were buried from their litters on which they breathed their last while travelling, and many others were brought in to this place, merely to die and get the privilege of a decent burial.

"Since the very day of our start into that country, the men have been continually falling sick, and on their return, of those who are alive there are not well ones enough to take care of the sick. Many are yet left out upon the prairies, and of those that have been brought in and quartered in the hospital, with the soldiers of the infantry regiment stationed here, four or five are buried daily; and as an equal number from the 9th [Seventh] Regiment are falling by the same disease, I have the mournful sound of 'Roslin Castle,' with muffled drums, passing six or eight times a-day under my window, to the burying ground, which is but a little distance in front of my room, where I can lay in my bed and see every poor fellow lowered down into his silent and peaceful habitation. During the day before yesterday, no less than eight solemn processions visited that insatiable ground.

". . . After leaving the headwaters of the Canadian, my illness continually increased, and losing strength every day, I soon got so reduced that I was necessarily lifted on to and off from my horse; and at last, so that I could not ride at all. I was then put into a baggage wagon which was going back empty, except with several soldiers sick, and in this condition rode eight days, most of the time in a delirious state, lying on the hard planks of the wagon, and made still harder by the jarring and jolting, until the skin from my elbows and knees was literally worn through, and I almost '*worn out*'; when we at length reached this post, and I was taken to a bed, in comfortable quarters, where I have had the skillful attendance of my friend and old schoolmate, Dr. Wright under whose hands, thank God, I have been restored, and am now daily recovering my flesh and usual strength."

The expedition was rated as successful,[177] inasmuch as it resulted in actual contact with the wild western prairie Indians, and subsequent treaties with them, though at an appalling cost. The Administration was subject to scathing criticism for the management of the expedition which left Fort Gibson six weeks too late, exposing to the perils of the climate recruits unprepared for the risk by training or experience; three troops of the dragoons having but three days to rest between their arrival from Jefferson Barracks and their departure for the Southwest.

Soon after the return of Colonel Dodge to Fort Gibson runners were sent to the chiefs of the Osage, Cherokee, Creek, Choctaw and other tribes, for the purpose of assembling them in council with the western Indians who accompanied the expedition to the post. On September 2, the council met at noon. Major F.

---

[177] See sixth Annual Message of President Andrew Jackson, December 1, 1834. Richardson, James D., *A Compilation of the Messages and Papers of the Presidents,* vol. iii, 112, 113.

W. Armstrong, who had been commissioned to wind up the affairs of the late commissioners stationed at Fort Gibson, had just arrived from Washington in time to take part in the conference. Governor Stokes, whose commission of office had expired, had remained at Fort Gibson while the expedition was in the west; at the request of Colonel Dodge and Major Armstrong to give them the benefit of his information gained as commissioner, he took an unofficial part in the council.

There were present at the council, Colonel Dodge, Major Francis W. Armstrong, Superintendent of Indian Affairs for the Western Territory; Civil John and To-to-lis, chiefs of the Seneca; Moosh-o-la-tu-bee for the Choctaw; Chisholm and Rogers for the Cherokee; McIntosh and Perryman for the Creeks; Clermont for the Osage; Titche-totche-cha of the Kiowa; We-ter-ra-shah-ro for the Pawnee Picts and We-ta-ra-yah for the Waco. Besides these, braves of all the other tribes represented brought the number to about one hundred fifty. Lieutenant T. B. Wheelock was the secretary and recorded the proceedings of the council.[178]

With mingled feelings of curiosity and suspicion, uncertainty and caution, these half-naked and wild-looking representatives of the western tribes, warily entered the rudely constructed council house at the post, and tentatively yielded to the novel experience of a council with the white men and with tribes they had

[178] Indian Office, Retired Classified Files, *1834 Western Superintendency,* Journal of Lieutenant T. B. Wheelock. This journal consists of twenty-five pages of manuscript in Wheelock's handwriting, and is signed by Colonel Dodge and Wheelock. It is entitled, "Proceedings of a Council held at Fort Gibson, Ark. in September 1834 between Col. Dodge, U.S. Dragoons, and Col. Armstrong Supt. Ind. Affairs, I. Territory U. States, on the part of the U. States, and the Chiefs of the following tribes of Indians – viz. The Seneca, Choctaw, Cherokee, Creek, Osage, Kiawa, Pawnee Pict (or Toyash) and Waycoah. The three last named being the tribes known by the name of Pawnee."

never before met. The conference lasted three days and at its conclusion Colonel Dodge presented to the western Indians medals and flags given by Governor Stokes, and explained that they were symbolic of the friendship of the Great Father at Washington. Dodge and Armstrong, having no authority to enter into a treaty of peace with the western Indians, the latter requested that a promise be made to them that in the buffalo country "when the grass next grows after the snows, which are soon to fall, shall have melted away", another conference would be held at which formal treaties would be entered into, entailing of course more substantial presents. Armstrong and Dodge assured them that they would recommend it to the President. Then the meeting adjourned.

Thus ended what was probably the most important Indian conference ever held in the Southwest; for it paved the way for agreements and treaties essential to the occupation of a vast country by one hundred thousand members of the Five Civilized Tribes emigrating from east of the Mississippi; to the security of settlers and travelers in a new country; to development of our Southwest to the limits of the United States and beyond and contributed to the subsequent acquisition of the country to the coast, made known to us by the pioneers to Santa Fe and California traveling through the region occupied by the wild Indians who, at Fort Gibson, gave assurances of their friendship. It is true, these assurances were not always regarded, and many outrages were afterwards committed on the whites, but the Fort Gibson conference was the beginning and basis upon which ultimately these things were accomplished.

After the conference, Colonel Dodge reported [179]
that he had presented to the chiefs of the western
Indians thirteen guns and two hundred fifty dollars'
worth of merchandise and tobacco as presents; and
recommended that commissioners be sent to the buffalo
country the next spring to make treaties with the tribes
in that country.   He said that on September fifth the
western Indians started home, and he had sent a small
detachment of dragoons to escort them out of the settlement and a small body of Cherokee to accompany
them through the Cross Timbers.[180]   Major Mason's
company, he said, was stationed twenty miles up the
Arkansas, convenient to building-timber for the erection of huts and stables for the winter, and forage for
the horses.

On the eighth the Osage Chiefs, Black Dog and
Tal-lai, with one hundred members of the tribe, came
to Fort Gibson and said they had just heard of the conference and desired to know what was done.   They
then demanded two hundred dollars for the woman
prisoner who had been turned over to General Leavenworth by Hugh Love, and threatened that if the amount
were not forthcoming they would overtake the western
Indians who were returning home, and recapture the
girl or take another in her place.   Fearful that they
might carry their threat into effect and destroy all that
had been accomplished at an appalling cost, Colonel

---

[179] Dodge's Military Order Book, 90.

[180] "There is already in this place [Fort Gibson] a company of eighty
men fitted out, who are to start tomorrow, to overtake these Indians a few
miles from this place, and to accompany them home, with a large stock
of goods, with traps for catching beavers, etc., calculating to build a trading-
house amongst them, where they will amass at once an immense fortune,
being the first traders and trappers that have ever been in that part of the
country." – Catlin, *op. cit.,* vol. ii, 523.

Dodge paid them the money on his own responsibility. He also had the great satisfaction of reporting that on the twelfth the officer had returned after restoring to his mother in Miller County, Arkansas, the little prisoner, Matthew Wright Martin.

Western Garrison Life

Holland Coffee was a trader operating at Fort Smith with Robert M. French and others, under the name of Coffee, Calville and Company. When Colonel Dodge's expedition to the Comanche country was being arranged, this firm of traders saw in the plans an opportunity for profitable enterprise, and organized a trading expedition to the western country. Soon after the dragoons took up their march from Fort Gibson, Coffee's company, forty strong, left Fort Smith on the first of August. Proceeding as far as the Canadian River, they halted and went into camp to await the result of Colonel Dodge's conference with the western tribes. When it was known that the meeting of the dragoon officers and eastern Indians with the Indians of the prairies was friendly and conciliatory, so that it was safe to proceed, Coffee's company resumed their march to the west, and upon arrival set up a trading establishment on Red River at what was called the old Pawnee village, about twenty miles above the Cross Timbers and seventy-five miles in a direct line above the mouth of the Washita River.[181] The trading

---

[181] Armstrong to the Commissioner of Indian Affairs March 6, 1835 (Indian Office, 1835, *Southwestern Territory*). Captain Stuart writing from Fort Coffee says, "The trading post is at the extreme west edge of the Cross Timbers on Red River." (Stuart to Lieutenant W. Seawell, March 28, 1835, *Ibid.,* 1835 *Western Superintendency*). The trading post was first established in 1834 within what is now the southwest part of Tillman County, Oklahoma.

Col. A. P. Chouteau (Chouteau to Armstrong May 22, 1837, Indian Office, *1837 Western Superintendency* A-183) locates Coffee's trading house at that

house was on the north bank of Red River, and surrounded by a picket fortification about one hundred
feet square.

Isaac Pennington was another trader who had been
associated with Colonel Chouteau and Colonel Hugh
Glenn on the Verdigris. He also went out among the
western Indians directly after the conference at Fort
Gibson in September. In March 1835, Coffee, Calville, and Pennington came east to the Choctaw
Agency, a few miles west of Fort Smith, and called
upon Major F. W. Armstrong, Acting Superintendent
of Indian Affairs for the Western Territory, and then
visited Captain Stuart in command at Fort Coffee near
by. They informed these officials that the conference
of the preceding fall had made a favorable impression
on the western tribes who were friendly and peaceable,
and inclined to continue so as long as their confidence
in the white officers lasted. But these Indians were
becoming restless for further assurances of the conference and treaty which Colonel Dodge had allowed
them to believe would be held with them in their
western country, and which they desired to be near
Coffee's trading establishment. There was some question of Dodge's authority to give this assurance, but
having given it, the western officials realized the im-
importance of keeping faith with the Indians. Within
a short time after the visit of these two traders, two
Wichita and a Waco Indian came to Fort Gibson,
commissioned by their tribes to inquire when the council would be held. On the arrival of these Indians,

time on Walnut Bayou, which empties into Red River within what is now
Love County, Oklahoma. At approximately this location there was subsequently a trading post known as Warren's, which was abandoned in 1848
and located at the mouth of Cache Creek.

General Arbuckle[182] had much difficulty in ascertaining their business. As there was no interpreter at the post, General Arbuckle sent to the Osage village for a woman living among them, who was known to be able to speak the language of these Indians; she was away from home in the woods, as the messenger expressed it, and it was some weeks before it was possible to converse with the western Indians.

In the meantime a commission was received from the Secretary of War appointing Governor Stokes, General Arbuckle[183] and Major F. W. Armstrong,[184] commissioners to hold a conference with the Comanche, Kiowa, and other western tribes at Fort Gibson. The object of the treaty and conference, as recited in the letter of instructions, was to establish amicable relations between the Comanche and other predatory tribes roaming along the western border, and the United States; and between these and other Indian tribes.

The board of commissioners organized early in May and having secured an interpreter, discussed with the western emissaries the matter of holding a conference at Fort Gibson. After two days of discussion, the commissioners learned that it would be impossible to secure even an interview with the Comanche and other chiefs

---

[182] General Arbuckle had been returned to the command of Fort Gibson after the death of General Leavenworth.

[183] Secretary of War Cass, to Stokes, Arbuckle, and Armstrong, March 23, 1835; Indian Office, *Letter Book* no. 15, p. 195.

[184] Francis W. Armstrong born in Virginia; appointed to the army from Tennessee; captain of the Seventh Infantry with brevet of major from June 26, 1813. He resigned April 30, 1817; served as United States Marshal for the District of Alabama. March 1831, Major Armstrong was appointed agent for the Choctaw in Arkansas Territory and later became Acting Superintendent of Indian Affairs for the Western Territory, which office he held until his death.

until late in July. They were informed that a war party had gone over the line into Texas, and the remaining bands were hunting on the great prairies; and that neither party would return until the green corn raised by the Wichita was ripe enough for eating. Wandering and hunting bands annually visited the Wichita, the farming Indians described by Wheelock in his journal, and procured corn from them. Because of the promise made these Indians by Colonel Dodge, that the council would be held in their country, they would not consider any other arrangement. The commissioners deemed it imprudent to vary from the plans which the western Indians had understood were to be followed, and decided to conform to their views unless they could yet be brought to Fort Gibson by inducements which would not shake their confidence in the white officers.

The commissioners therefore decided to send Major Mason,[185] with a party of dragoons, from Fort Gibson to the headwaters of Little River to establish a camp at a suitable place for holding the conference with the western Indians, if their chiefs could not be prevailed upon to come to Fort Gibson. Accordingly, on May 18, Major Mason left Fort Gibson with a detachment of dragoons, and marched about one hundred fifty miles southwest to a point where he would be in touch with Coffee's trading post on Red River, about seventy miles south. A report had reached Fort Gibson that the Mexicans planned an attack upon the Comanche, and had warned Coffee to abandon his post. Mason's

---

[185] Richard Barnes Mason was born in Virginia; major of the Dragoon Regiment March 4, 1833, and for several years saw much service at Fort Gibson. He was made Lieutenant-colonel July 4, 1836, colonel June 30, 1846; brevet-major July 31, 1829, for ten years faithful service in one grade, and Brigadier-general May 30, 1848, for meritorious conduct. In 1848 Colonel Mason was in command of the Tenth Military Department, with headquarters at Monterey, California. He died July 25, 1850.

post, which he located at the edge of the Cross Timbers and called Camp Holmes, was described as a beautiful location, with a border of timber to the east, ten miles of prairie to the west, encircled with sparse woods and having a fine running creek and a number of springs.[186]

On June 16, Lieutenant Seaton of the infantry was dispatched from Fort Gibson with a force of thirty men, to cut a wagon road through to Major Mason's position, and to convey provisions for the troops stationed there, and he returned to Fort Gibson on July 19. Excessive rains prevailed during Seaton's absence from Fort Gibson, and for eleven days he and his men were camped on a ridge surrounded by water near Little River. For nearly a month the men in his command were without dry clothing, and Seaton [187] contracted an illness from which he died at Fort Gibson in the fall.

Near the first of July, the Comanche and other tribes began arriving at Mason's fort in great numbers, and refused to yield their determination to have the conference in the west. They established themselves in camp eight or ten miles from Camp Holmes in such numbers that one report said there were seven thousand

---

[186] "In 1835, shortly after the treaty with the Comanche at Camp Holmes, Colonel Auguste Chouteau built on the same site a small stockade fort, where a considerable trade was carried on with the Comanche, Kiowa, Wichita, and associated tribes until his death three years later, when the place was abandoned. The exact location of Camp Holmes and Chouteau's fort, was at a spring on a small creek, both still bearing the name of Chouteau, on the east or north side of South (main) Canadian River, about 5 miles northeast of where now is the town of Purcell, Indian Territory. It was a favorite Indian camping ground and was the site of a Kichai village about 1850." _ U.S. Bureau of Ethnology, *Seventeenth Annual Report*, 1895-1896, part i, 171.

[187] Augustine Fortunatus Seaton was born in the District of Columbia, from which place he was appointed to West Point, graduated July 1, 1833, and he served with the Seventh Infantry at Fort Coffee and Fort Gibson until his death November 18, 1835, at Fort Gibson at the age of twenty-five years.

present. Their number was so large and their attitude so menacing, upon viewing the handful of men under Major Mason, that on the third day of July this officer dispatched messengers to General Arbuckle and requested reinforcements. General Arbuckle returned an answer at once by the Osage Indians who brought the message, assuring Major Mason that he should have reinforcements, and directly dispatched to his assistance companies T and H of the Seventh Infantry, numbering one hundred men under Captain Lee, together with a piece of ordnance.

While the commissioners were making their plans to go to Camp Holmes for the conference, Major Armstrong was taken seriously ill, and on the sixth of August he died at his home at the Choctaw Agency.[188] On the same day, General Arbuckle and Governor Stokes departed from Fort Gibson for Camp Holmes, with an escort of companies A and D of the Seventh Infantry, under Major Birch.[189] Accompanying them were delegations from the Creek, Osage, Seneca, and Quapaw; the Cherokee, Choctaw, and Delaware were to follow immediately. On their arrival at Camp Holmes, the force of soldiers amounted to two hundred fifty; this number the commissioners decided necessary to enable them to maintain their position and secure the respect of the Indians, and as a warning to the western tribes that if they refused to enter into the treaty desired by the United States, the latter were able to, and would if they chose, occupy the position permanently.

[188] The Choctaw Agency was fourteen miles southwest of Fort Smith and five miles south of Fort Coffee and the Arkansas River. The payments were made here to the Choctaw whose name for money is "Iskuli-fehna" whence the place became known as Skullyville.

[189] George Birch was born in England and December 12, 1808, was appointed to the army from Pennsylvania; made brevet-major, August 31, 1826, for ten years faithful service in one grade; died September 26, 1837.

The commissioners left Fort Gibson at a much later period in the summer than that in which the Dragoons left the year before. The distance traveled was not so great, and it was probably not so hot; for no great number of deaths resulted. Governor Stokes was not well when they left Fort Gibson, and a report came back to the post that he was dying at a camp along the road; but this resolute seventy-five-year-old campaigner not only took part in the conference with the wild prairie Indians, and performed all the labors required by his commission, but intrepidly covered the three hundred miles entailed by the journey through July and August, and returned to Fort Gibson in good health.

After the usual preliminaries and speech making, and with the assurance of presents to be made after the signing, the treaty was finally entered into on August 24,[190] between the Wichita, their associated bands or tribes, and the United States; and between these western Indians and the Cherokee, Creek, Choctaw, Osage, Seneca, and Quapaw. The Kiowa did not remain to participate in the treaty, and in fact left before the commissioners arrived. It was reported that they became impatient with the delay, and departed for their homes; it was also said by officers present that they left through fear of the Osage, instigated by Clermont. The treaty contained assurances of peace and friendship between the contracting parties, and a grant of free passage through the western Indian country for citizens of the United States to Santa Fe and to Mexico; and provided that the eastern Indians might hunt and trap throughout the country west of the Cross Timbers as far as the limits of the United States. Camp

---

[190] Kappler, *op. cit.*, vol. ii, 322.

Holmes was located within the country granted by treaty to the Creek Indians, whose right to occupy this country had not, up to the time of the treaty, been recognized by the western tribes. After the conference the infantry left Camp Holmes for Fort Gibson, but the dragoons arrived there first, on the fifth of September. Governor Stokes and General Arbuckle reached Fort Gibson on the twelfth.

Thus was enacted the first treaty with the wild western prairie tribes so essential to the plans of the Government for the location of the eastern Indians west of the Mississippi, and necessary to the peace and security of the West and to the traders and pioneers in all that great expanse of country. And thus was consummated what for years the Government was trying to accomplish, with Fort Gibson as the basis of operations, and for which many lives had been sacrificed.

But the object of the Government was not yet fully gained, and it now became a matter of importance to induce the Kiowa Indians to go to Fort Gibson; an enterprise these Indians were reluctant to engage in, because it would entail one hundred miles of travel between the Cross Timbers and Fort Gibson, nearly destitute of buffalo, and they were not yet well enough assured of the candor of the white men to trust a few of their number among them so far from their friends.

"The celebrated *Cross Timbers,* of which frequent mention has been made, extend from the Brazos, or perhaps from the Colorado of Texas, across the sources of Trinity, traversing Red River above the False Washita, and thence west of north to the Red Fork of Arkansas, if not further. It is a rough hilly range of country, and, though not mountainous, may perhaps be considered a prolongation of that chain of low mountains which pass to the northward of Bexar and Austin City in Texas.

"The Cross Timbers vary in width from five to thirty miles, and entirely cut off the communication betwixt the interior prairies and those of the great plains. They may be considered as the 'fringe' of the great prairies, being a continuous brushy strip, composed of various kinds of undergrowth; such as black-jacks, post-oaks, and in some places hickory, elm, etc., intermixed with a very diminutive dwarf oak, called by the hunters 'shin-oak'. Most of the timber appears to be kept small by the continual inroads of the 'burning prairies'; for, being killed almost annually, it is constantly replaced by scions of undergrowth; so that it becomes more and more dense every reproduction. In some places, however, the oaks are of considerable size, and able to withstand the conflagrations. The underwood is so matted in many places with grape-vines, green-briars, etc., as to form almost impenetrable 'roughs', which serve as hiding-places for wild beasts, as well as wild Indians; and would, in savage warfare, prove almost as formidable as the hammocks of Florida."[191]

In early days, traders and trappers employed the Cross Timbers as a datum line for location, and measured distances of places from this well-known landmark, as in populated parts of the world reference is made to the Meridian of Greenwich.

On some of the old maps [192] the Cross Timbers is shown extending up the ninety-eighth meridian, be-

[191] Thwaites, *op. cit.*, vol. xx, 254 ff.

[192] Notably, a "Map of Texas and the countries adjacent, compiled in the bureau of the Corps of Topographical engineers from the best authorities for the State Department under the direction of Colonel J. J. Abert, Chief of the Corps, by W. H. Emory, First-lieutenant Topographical Engineers War Department 1844."

tween Red and Canadian rivers which gives it a north
and south course through the country embracing Chick-
asha and El Reno, Oklahoma.   On a Government map
of 1834 [193] a legend is printed up and down this line
"Western Boundary of Habitable Land."   In the
adjustment of the affairs of the Choctaw and Chickasaw Indians in 1866, this line was taken as the western
boundary of the possessions of those tribes and all west
of it was ceded to the United States for the use of the
prairie tribes of Indians, who at all times claimed that
the rights of the emigrant Indians did not extend west
of the Cross Timbers.   This line so established became
part of the dividing line between Indian Territory and
Oklahoma Territory.

After three years of patient labor it was late in 1827
before the fort and other defenses at Cantonment Gibson were completed; the quarters were spacious and
comfortable and ample to garrison a regiment.   The
troops, after three or four years of fatigue duty, began
a strict course of drill and discipline.   The fort itself
was a square three hundred feet on a side, surrounded
by a log barricade with blockhouses at the northwest
and southeast corners, and contained barracks, store
houses, and officers' quarters.   A hospital and several
log houses used for quarters were some distance east of
the fort and toward the rising ground.   One building
was erected for an Indian council house.   It was called
the Theatre and here the soldiers entertained themselves
by getting up plays and presenting them.   A cemetery,
sawmill, stables, and hay-barn were southwest of the
fort; two sutlers' stores were on the bank of the river
northeast of the fort.   From a ferry across the river a

---

[193] U.S. House. *Reports*, 23d congress, first session, no. 474.   Report of
Committee on Indian Affairs.

road lay northwest to Creek Agency and the traders' stores at the falls of the Verdigris. Three miles out on this road Houston established his store.

Cantonment Gibson soon began to assume a place of great importance in the Southwest and was the center of all the civilized life and interest for hundreds of miles around. A lively celebration of the Fourth of July, 1826, serves to illustrate the isolation of the post and its importance as a center of southwestern activity. At the dinner given on this occasion, thirteen toasts were drunk; the formula – "The President of the United States" one gun and three cheers; the number of guns and cheers measured by the subject of the toast. The twelfth toast was "The Festive Board", four cheers. The thirteenth, "The Fair Sex", seven cheers. There is something touching in the picture of these men exiled to the wilderness hundreds of miles from friends and relatives, trying to be gay and patriotic. Speeches were made by Captain Pierce M. Butler, Colonel John Nicks,[194] Captain Nathaniel Pryor, John Dillard, Colonel A. P. Chouteau, and others. They were probably well sustained in their efforts at gaiety; fortified by six thousand gallons of good proof whiskey

---

[194] John Nicks was born in North Carolina and on July 1, 1808, was appointed captain in the Third Infantry; October 9, 1813, major in the Seventh Infantry and honorably discharged on June 15, 1815. Reinstated December 2, 1815, as captain in the Eighth Infantry with brevet of major from October 9, 1813; major in the Seventh Infantry June 1, 1816, and Lieutenant-colonel June 1, 1819; June 1, 1821, shortly before his regiment removed to Fort Smith, Colonel Nicks was honorably discharged. He was sutler at Fort Gibson from the time of its establishment and was appointed postmaster at the post February 21, 1827, and was therefore the first postmaster within what is now Oklahoma. He was sutler and postmaster there at the time of his death December 31, 1831. In partnership with John Rogers, under the name of Nicks and Rogers, he maintained a trading establishment at Fort Gibson and one at Fort Smith. Upon the death of Major William Bradford, Brigadier-general of Militia of Arkansas territory, Colonel Nicks was by the President appointed to that post in 1827.

the post should have been well prepared for the demands of any Fourth of July. This consignment of whiskey was one of the established items purchased annually by the War Department for Cantonments Gibson, Towson, and other western posts. Some of the other items for annual consumption at the post were four hundred barrels of pork; eight hundred barrels of flour; three hundred sixty bushels of beans; sixty-six hundred pounds of hard soap; thirty-five hundred pounds of hard tallow candles with wicks; fifteen hundred bushels of salt, and fourteen hundred gallons of vinegar.

Fort Gibson occupied the central position of the five out-posts marking our western frontier; from north to south, Forts Snelling, Leavenworth, Gibson, Towson, and Jesup. The position of Fort Gibson in the center was reckoned the most responsible and important, and in 1832 it had ten companies of infantry and three of rangers, nearly as many as the combined forces of the other four posts.

While Fort Gibson was linking up the Southwest with the United States – for they were spoken of separately – other news was emanating from that out-post. Fort Gibson of that day was not located on the fine elevation where it was rebuilt during the Civil War and where the village of the same name is now to be seen. For some unknown reason it was located below the hill on the lowland along Grand River, surrounded by a canebrake where the water remained stagnant after rains and bred mosquitoes and deadly malarial germs. The dragoon expedition of 1834 had occasioned wide interest and the press of the country contained frequent accounts of that unprecedented adventure and subsequent conditions and events at the post. The most impressive item of news was that concerned with the fearful death rate of the members of the command. Nearly every issue of the weekly papers and frequent numbers of the dailies, reproduced accounts of Fort Gibson and there was no lack of willing correspondents crying out to the country against conditions under which they were forced to live. One account [195] said: "I think Fort Gibson the worst, and without doubt the hottest and most unhealthy in the U. States. Besides, our quarters are truly rotting over our heads, and not sufficient by one-fourth to accommodate the third of the officers of the regiment, if present, and *none to be built*; but patch, patch, patch the old ones up, here and there, to stop a leak.

"This, however, is not the greatest of our troubles or vexations, for almost every day, surely every week, an armed command leaves here either for the prairies, or to seek and destroy whiskey in the Cherokee Nation. Our garrison, as to troops, are reduced to the smallest number from these causes and sickness. Captain L., from necessity, had to command a detachment of two companies that left here last week for the headwaters of the False Washita, and neither was his own. Lieutenant Seaton has another detachment of thirty men escorting provisions to Major Mason, who is encamped on the headwaters of Little River. Major B. commands two companies encamped out on the hills, to scatter the troops on account of the sickness in the garrison, and Lieutenant G. has another detachment of ten men taking villianous white people out of the Indian country, and Lieutenant P. another detachment hunting for whiskey. Such is our constant occupation and duties, harassing to officers and soldiers. . .

[195] Army and Navy Chronicle (Washington), vol. i, 279.

God grant that by your influence united you could get the regiment removed; it would meet the approbation of every one in it, except three." Another wrote in the fall of 1835: [196] "Sickness still prevails at this most infernal of all military posts, . . . if you were to visit Fort Gibson you would pronounce it the most perfect caricature of a military establishment that was ever seen in any service; it is situated, it may be said with a good deal of truth, in the bottom of a sink hole. . . These bottoms are low and subject to inundation, and contain several large sloughs and lakes of stagnant water." Another wrote: "Two hundred dragoons now await the sound of the 'last bugle' in its graveyard, a majority of them laid there in less than nine weeks (September and October 1834) besides many of the 7th Infantry and some strangers. . . On this date (17 October, 1835) out of six officers in the dragoon garrison, four, including the assistant surgeon, are on the sick report and nearly half of the men."

Official reports showed that during the two years preceding December 8, 1835, two hundred ninety-two soldiers and six officers had died at the post; from the establishment of the post in 1824 five hundred sixty-one soldiers and nine officers had died. And during the third quarter of the year 1835 there were six hundred and one distinct cases of disease at the post in the infantry alone. It is not surprising that there were a large number of resignations, and that a movement was inaugurated for the removal of the post, which assumed such proportions that in February, 1836, Major-general Macomb recommended the removal of the garrison to Fort Coffee ten or twelve miles above Fort Smith.

[196] Army and Navy Chronicle (Washington), vol. i, 357, 397.

Among those who resigned was Lieutenant Jefferson Davis, whose resignation took effect on June 30, 1835. He went from Fort Gibson to Kentucky, to meet Miss Sarah Knox Taylor, daughter of General Zachary Taylor, to whom he was engaged, and they were married directly afterward. An error has persisted that Davis courted his wife at Fort Gibson while her father was in command there. General Taylor's daughter never saw Fort Gibson and it was long after her death when General Taylor served at the post.

General Taylor was in command at Fort Crawford, Prairie du Chien, on the upper Mississippi in 1832, and serving under him was young Lieutenant Davis. It was there that Davis and Miss Taylor fell in love and became engaged. Her father was unalterably opposed to the match and said he would never give his consent. After the two young people became engaged, Davis was transferred to the Dragoons with which organization he served at Fort Gibson in 1834; but after two years had passed and her father refused to relent, Miss Taylor, who had inherited some of his determination, took matters into her own hands. A steamboat having arrived at the post she induced her brother-in-law to secure a stateroom for the return passage to Saint Louis. Before the boat started Miss Taylor went again to her father and told him she was determined to marry Davis and was leaving home for that purpose but that she hoped he would consent. He again refused and she sorrowfully gave up hope of winning his approval. Departing from Fort Crawford, Miss Taylor went by boat to Saint Louis and from there to the home of her aunt in Kentucky. In refuting the story of an elopement, Davis once said: [197] "In

197 Davis, Varina Jefferson, Jefferson Davis, *A Memoir by his wife*. 162.

1835 I resigned from the army, and Miss Taylor being then in Kentucky with her aunt – the oldest sister of General Taylor – I went thither and we were married in the home of her aunt, in the presence of General Taylor's two sisters, of his oldest brother, his son-in-law, and many others of the Taylor family."

The estrangement between Lieutenant Davis and General Taylor was not healed during the lifetime of Mrs. Davis. After their marriage they went to live on a tract of land given to him by his brother in Mississippi, called Brierfield; Davis set to work to clear it up, and he and his wife were both taken sick of malarial fever, from which she died on September 15, 1835.

As soon as they were able to travel after the disastrous dragoon expedition of 1834, several of the companies of dragoons were sent to Fort Leavenworth and Fort Des Moines. Lieutenants T. B. Wheelock and James F. Izard, who had figured so prominently in the dragoon expedition were ordered to Florida in the service against the Seminole Indians, where they were both killed. On February 28, 1836, in a skirmish with the Indians on the Withlacoochee, Izard was wounded, and died on March 5, at Camp Izard. His death was deplored by the members of the dragoon regiment who in their remote stations adopted resolutions setting forth the high regard in which he was held. On the tenth of June, 1836, Lieutenant Wheelock, at the head of a detachment under orders from his chief, Major Heileman, had creditably carried out a sortie against the Indians at Micanopy. His service had been so arduous that he was seized with a fatal aberration in which, five days later, he killed himself with his rifle.

Much of the life of the frontier post of those days

is reflected in the order books and letter books of Fort Gibson.[198]   Daily routine orders for the conduct of the post are recorded; when the commanding officer leaves the post an order is made delegating the command to another.   Detachments are ordered out of the post in the discharge of the numerous duties required of them. On January 1, 1839, Captain Bonneville is ordered to take his company and start on the long march to Tampa, Florida.   John Howard Payne is entertained at the post in October 1840 by Captain George A. McCall. Payne spent that winter at Park Hill as the guest of Chief John Ross.

One of the soldiers is reported a deserter and a small party under a non-commissioned officer is detailed to scour the woods or descend Arkansas River in search of him as he is probably headed for the settlements. Desertions are of frequent occurrence, and the most familiar entries on the books are those ordering a court-martial, and the subsequent proceedings of the court. Punishments were brutal and apparently not deterrent. Sanford Lacy stole a pair of trousers and decamped but he was captured after a week of desertion.   He was convicted and sentenced to receive fifty lashes on the bare back with a raw hide well laid on at intervals of forty-eight hours; to be confined at hard labor for six months with a ball and chain and to reimburse the United States for the expense of apprehending him. Private James Laden on sentry duty at post number three on the night of August 14, 1838, was found asleep. The court-martial adjudged him guilty and sentenced him to four months confinement in the post, sixty days in the cells on bread and water, and the remainder at

---

[198] Adjutant General's Office, Old Records Division, *Fort Gibson Letter Books 15, 17; Order Book 10.*

hard labor with ball and chain. Another for habitual drunkenness was sentenced to forfeit his pay, have half his head shaved and be drummed out of the post and service. Drunkenness was common and soldiers frequented disorderly houses kept by Cherokee individuals on the tribal land just outside the reservation where they were beyond the control of the garrison. Drinking and fighting, bloodshed and frequent killings occurred at these places. Some years later, in 1846 authority was given for the sutler to sell liquor to the soldiers under the regulations of the commanding officer, with the result, Colonel Mason reported, that disorderly houses were abandoned and drunkenness was much reduced.

Extended reports are required in connection with the killing by Lieutenant Charles Wickliff,[199] a West Point graduate, of Robert Wilkins who lived near Fort Gibson. Wickliff had an affair with Wilkins's wife, a half-breed Cherokee and on January 9, 1842, the former shot Wilkins in the back with a double barrelled shot gun. Wickliff was arrested but broke arrest and became a deserter. Another lieutenant was court-martialed for being heard to express approval of what Wickliff did. Complaints are recorded by Chief John Ross and other Cherokee that their negro slaves in considerable numbers have fled toward Texas. A number of them settled in the west in a community that became the town of Wewoka. Frequent complaints are received concerning Josiah Hardridge, and Osiah Harjo, Creek Indians, who are engaged in kidnapping free colored people, running them off and

---

[199] Wickliff was dropped from the army rolls April 12, 1842, but was reinstated as captain March 5, 1847; he was honorably discharged July 22, 1848; served with the Confederate army as colonel of the Seventh Infantry; died April 24, 1862 of wounds received at the Battle of Shiloh.

selling them into slavery. Several hundred Seminole negroes who surrendered in Florida to General Jesup under promise of emancipation from the slavery by which they were held by the Seminole, are settled around Fort Gibson and are clamoring for the officers of the post to secure them in their freedom.

A feud existed between Colonel Mason in command and Governor Butler, Cherokee agent and the former had an order made requiring the agent to remove from the reservation as his Indian visitors were obnoxious to the officers. An order was made also that the sutlers at the post should not sell to or traffic with the Indians, but it was afterwards relaxed. In July 1844, the Fort Gibson Jockey Club was organized with Governor Butler as president, and races were held near the post on September 24, and through the week, on an old race course laid out many years before by the Seventh Infantry. This was objected to by Colonel Mason. The Cherokee caught some of the colored servants of the officers and horse-whipped them. Two of Captain Boone's men were murdered on March 12, 1845, at a disorderly house three-fourths of a mile south of the dragoon barracks, kept by Polly Spaniard, a part Cherokee. The next night the soldiers burned her house and one or two others. An anonomous proclamation was then circulated saying that the Cherokee would meet at Tahlequah to consider measures for protecting themselves against the military. Mason charged that this was prepared by Butler.

Colonel Loomis reports December 18, 1843, that the post was in bad police when he took charge and the command has been engaged for some time in white-washing and policing the garrison. Deaths of officers are reported from time to time. July 22, 1844, Captain

Boone is reported ill to the point of death, but he recovered and in the fall, reports tell of his expedition to the Indians on the Brazos, his return, and report.

Colonel Mason becomes ill and the wordy controversy as to which of two captains has succeeded to the command, and the records of attempted arrest of each by the other become amusing and consume many pages before Mason leaves his sick bed again to assume command and end the quarrel. Mason reports the building of a house twenty-two by forty feet for a church and school room. The church had formerly been held in the post library room which was too small for a congregation. Numerous reports are received concerning disturbances in the Cherokee Nation where several murders were committed during the election in the fall of 1845. A large number of Cherokee collected at the home of Lewis Ross at Grand Saline and Captain Boone was sent out with his company to maintain order; he remained in camp several months near Evansville, Arkansas.

Entries are made of the movements of troops on numerous missions to the prairies, to Fort Smith, Fort Towson and elsewhere; officers leaving the post and officers returning; reports of visiting Indians of different tribes and traders from near and far who bring accounts of many things – movements of the Indians, of white prisoners among them, of difficulties among the Indians, rumors, small talk. Captain Boone has seen a young Kickapoo chief who is on his way with a small party to see their principal chief on the Missouri River to request him to send a mission to the Pawnee on the Platte to induce the latter to cease their depredations on the Kickapoo living along the Canadian. Measures for removing the Seminole settled around

Fort Gibson consume much space. As the Mexican War draws the seasoned troops from Fort Gibson, they are replaced by numerous detachments of volunteers from Arkansas and Kentucky. Soon after their arrival measles broke out among them and many died. Work on the new buildings at Fort Gibson was stopped in 1846 for lack of funds.

Governor Houston at His Trading Post on the Verdigris

In February, 1828, the vanguard of Creek immigrants arrived at the Creek Agency on the Verdigris, in charge of Colonel Brearley, and they and the following members of the McIntosh party were located on a section of land that the Government promised in the treaty of 1826 to purchase for them. By the treaty of May 6, 1828, the Government assigned the Cherokee a great tract of land, to which they at once began to remove from their homes in Arkansas. The movement had been under way for some months when there appeared among the Indians the remarkable figure of Samuel Houston. The biographers of Houston have told the world next to nothing of his sojourn of three or four years in the Indian country, an interesting period when he was changing the entire course of his life and preparing for the part he was to play in the drama of Texas.

When Houston was a first-lieutenant in the First Regiment of the United States Infantry in 1817, General Andrew Jackson appointed him Cherokee sub-agent under Colonel Return J. Meigs. Houston conducted from Knoxville to Washington City a delegation of Arkansas Cherokee chiefs who were favorable to the views of the Government, for the purpose of making a treaty which would locate the Cherokee west of the Mississippi. In 1819, Jackson, who was Houston's warm friend, offered him the position of agent for the Cherokee in Arkansas – the place held by William J. Lovely up to the time of his death – but Houston declined the appointment. Houston resigned from the army March 1, 1818, and went to Nashville as he himself stated, "without education more than ordinary – without friends – without cash – almost without acquaintances – consequently without much credit, and here, among talents and distinction, I have made my stand." [200] He studied law and was selected as Attorney-general for that section of the state; elected to Congress in 1823, and again in 1825; on June 5, 1826, he was appointed chairman of the Board of Visitors to West Point; in 1821 he had been made Major-general of the militia of his section of the state. During part of the time he was in Congress, his warm friend, Andrew Jackson, was senator from Tennessee. In 1827,[201] Houston was elected governor of Tennessee, and his campaign for reelection began at Nashville, in April, 1829. His rise had been remarkable, and he seemed to want only one thing to fill his cup of success. In January, 1829, he married Miss Eliza H. Allen, daughter of a rich family of Sumner County, Tennessee. It was the sensation of the whole country and the mortification of his friends and admirers, when he left his wife a few weeks after the wedding, and shortly after the beginning of his campaign for reelection as governor.

The public sought to throw the mantle of oblivion over the family troubles that blasted his reputation and career, and various speculations as to the cause of his separation from his wife were offered. The friends

[200] Houston to Governor Joseph McMinn, February 15, 1823, Indian Office, Retired Classified Files, *1823 Cherokee Nashville.*

[201] At the same time David Crockett and James K. Polk were elected to represent Tennessee in Congress.

of Mrs. Houston's family in Sumner County felt it was due to her to call a meeting of the citizens of the county at the courthouse, to give expression to the opinion entertained by them as to her character. The committee appointed for the purpose prepared a report in which they charged that Houston rendered his wife unhappy by his unfounded jealousies and his repeated suspicions of her coldness and want of attachment, and that she was constrained by a sense of duty to herself and her family to separate from her infatuated husband and return to her parents. Houston was chivalrous enough to address a letter to Mrs. Houston's father, in which he acquitted her of any blame in the matter, and this letter the committee made public. Houston refused to discuss the matter with any one, and his version of the difficulty never became known.[202]

Such was Houston's bitterness, that he abandoned not only his wife but all his friends and the civilized country that had honored him; and he turned to the Cherokee Indians whose society he had learned to enjoy in his youth, while he was sub-agent among them and whose language he spoke fluently. The next month, Houston passed two days at Little Rock on his way up Arkansas River to join the Cherokee. At the mouth of the Illinois River he stopped with John Jolly, a chief of the Cherokee, who had adopted him as his son and whom Houston called his Indian father. Houston made his home with the Cherokee, adopted their dress, drank to excess, and in every way emphasized the renunciation of the former life and friends from whom he had turned.

The Cherokee Agency was then located on the north

---

[202] Guild, Joe C. *Old Times in Tennessee, with Historical, Personal, and Political Scraps and Sketches*, 269 ff.

side of Arkansas River, above Fort Smith and not far from where Fort Coffee was located in 1834. Houston was there during the payment of the annuity in October, 1829, and on the twenty-first of that month he was adopted as a member of the Cherokee Tribe of Indians, and a certificate was given him in the following language: [203]

"Whereas, an order has been published by the agent, of the Cherokee Nation, requesting all white men who reside in the Nation without the consent of the chiefs of the said nation, to comply with certain rules, and regulations set forth in said order: Now, Be it known by these presents: That General Samuel Houston, late of the State of Tennefsee, has been residing in the Nation for sometime past and has manifested a disposition to remain with us: In consideration of his former acquaintance with, and services rendered to the Indians, and his present disposition to improve their condition and benefit their circumstances and our confidence in his integrity, and talents, if he should remain among us; We do, as a committee, appointed by order of the principal chief John Jolly, solemnly, firmly, and irrevocably, grant to him forever, all the rights, privileges, and immunities, of a citizen of the Cherokee Nation, and do as fully empower him with all the rights, and the liberties, as though he was a native Cherokee, while at the same time the said Houston, will be required to yield obedience to all laws, and regulations made for the government, of the native citizens of the Cherokee Nation.

---

[203] Arbuckle to Secretary of War July 23, 1830, enclosing Houston's papers; Indian Office, Retired Classified Files, *1830 Cherokee West.* Houston was at Fort Gibson in June 1829, and on the 24th of that month at the post wrote a letter to the Secretary of War recommending Colonel A. P. Chouteau to undertake to make treaties between the Osage and Pawnee, and volunteering to accompany him on the mission.

"In witness whereof we have this day set our hands this 21st day of October, 1829.

"Cherokee Nation, Illinois. Walter Webber, his mark, President Commt. Aaron Price, his Mark, Vice President. APPROVED. John Jolly, his mark, Principal Chief."

After the payment of the Cherokee annuity at the agency, Houston went up the river to Cantonment Gibson, and from October to December he seems to have employed his time in and around the Creek Agency and Cantonment Gibson, where he either built or purchased a house nearby, which he called The Wigwam, in which he engaged in trading with the Indians. There he listened to the tales of the wrongs which the Creek Indians claimed to have suffered at the hands of their agent, Colonel Brearley, and with Houston's help they prepared a memorial to President Jackson which Houston, because of his close relation to the President, was able to bring promptly to his notice. It contained a number of charges, some of them indicating faults of the governmental method of dealing with the Indians, and others charging turpitude at the hands of their agent; that for personal gain he had speculated on their contracts for subsistence, had retained the cash provided for their annuities, and had given them due bills instead. Houston became a bitter critic, not only of Brearley and Crowell, their agent in the east whom they blamed for the killing of their chief, General McIntosh, but of Colonel Thomas McKinney, head of the Indian Department at Washington. He charged that McKinney's department had failed to give the Indians, who were very needy indeed, the blankets, guns, ammunition, beaver traps, and kettles promised them in the treaty; and that later, when Mc-

Kinney selected Luther Blake to succeed Brearley, he was appointing a relative of Crowell, who was interested with him in speculating on the necessities of the Indians, and charged that McKinney was to blame for many of their wrongs.

In December, 1829, Houston, clad in the turban, leggins, flap or breech-clout and blanket of the Indian went to Washington in company with Walter Webber and John Brown, both prominent Cherokee Indians. They arrived in Washington January 13, 1830. Webber was engaged in trading with the Indians, and was hostile to the Cherokee Agent, E. W. duVal. Carnes and duVal were traders at Fort Smith, and their goods to the value of ten thousand dollars, shipped into the Indian country, had been seized by Colonel Arbuckle because a barrel of whiskey was found among them. Later, on September 24, 1829, the War Department ordered the release of the goods, and rendered the naïve opinion that the act was not a violation of the law, because a barrel of whiskey was not suited to Indian consumption and did not fit the description of whiskey "which they can purchase in quantities to produce the inconvenience which it was the object and policy of the law (Act of May 6, 1822) to provide against."

Houston spent some time in Washington, and, for good measure, included the name of the Osage Agent, Hamtramck,[204] among those condemned by him as fit

---

[204] John F. Hamtramck was born in Indiana and graduated from West Point July 1, 1819; at the age of sixteen he was a sergeant in Major Zachary Taylor's expedition up the Mississippi River in 1814, and received his appointment as cadet for his good conduct in action, opposite the mouth of Rock River, Illinois, July 19, 1814, against seven hundred Sauk and Fox Indians, supported by British batteries. He was the son of Captain John F. Hamtramck, distinguished in the battle of Miami in 1794. Resigned March 1, 1822, and became a planter near Saint Louis. In May 1826, appointed United States Indian Agent for the Osage tribe and served until

subjects for removal; and the list of those removed included the names of Colonel Brearley, Major E. W. duVal, Hamtramck, and Colonel McKinney himself. Following Brearley's removal, his assistant, Anthony, served for a short time, until General John Campbell of Tennessee was appointed to the post at the Creek Agency on the Verdigris. In March, 1830, Campbell was reported as passing Little Rock, up-bound in a keel boat with his family, destined for the Creek Agency. During that month, however, a question arose resulting in recalling Campbell's appointment and directing Luther Blake to repair to the agency and assume the duties of agent. This was only temporary, and in a short time Campbell began his duties as Creek agent. Upon the removal of duVal as agent for the western Cherokees, Captain George Vashon, formerly of the Seventh Infantry, was appointed to the place on March 12, 1830. P. L. Chouteau, a brother of Colonel A. P. Chouteau, and who had been acting as Osage sub-agent, was on April 30, 1830, confirmed by the Senate as Osage Agent to replace Hamtramck.

Houston had other business in Washington beside securing the dismissal of Indian agents. He went to President Jackson and proposed that the Government make a contract with him, authorizing him to supply rations to the Indians who, in the future, would be removed to the Indian country. He claimed that the Government had been paying contractors too much, and that the Indians had been defrauded by them, and represented that if the contract were given to him he would furnish the rations at much less than had been paid. Jackson referred Houston to General J. H.

1830; served in the Mexican War as colonel of Virginia volunteers; and was governor of Saltillo from March 8, to July 20, 1848; died April 21, 1858.

Eaton, Secretary of War, and upon Houston's explaining his proposition to him, the Secretary disapproved the suggestion, and wrote a letter to the President [205] February 16, 1830, saying that the Government could not make a private contract with Houston without being censured for it, and that no contract could be made without advertising for proposals. To this Houston assented, and he and the Secretary prepared notices to be published in the papers. These were given to McKinney at the head of the Indian Service, for his signature and delivery to the newspapers; they were dated February 18, and called for bids to be submitted by the twentieth of March, 1830.

Houston went to New York where he interested John Van Fossen, a man of means, in joining with him and his friend Benjamin Hawkins in an effort to secure the contract. Van Fossen made a bid of thirteen cents per ration, and twelve other bids were submitted ranging from eight to seventeen cents per ration. A ration was to consist of one pound and a quarter of fresh beef, or one pound of fresh pork, with two quarts of salt to every hundred rations; or, if salted meat were used, one pound of beef and three-quarters of a pound of pork, with a quart of corn or corn meal to each ration of meat, whether fresh or salt, or eighteen ounces of flour.

After the notice had been duly advertised and the bids all received, and the matter had been under consideration for some weeks, the Secretary refused to let the contract to the lowest bidder for the reason, it was charged, he was trying to favor Houston, whose bid put in by Van Fossen was not the lowest. It was then

205 U.S. House. *Reports,* 22d congress, first session, no. 502. Report of Investigating Committee, p. 66.

discovered that thirty days was not enough time to permit responsible bidders from Illinois, Missouri or Arkansas to submit proposals, and charges of misconduct promising a scandal were frequent. However, the Secretary refused to let the contract to any one, and it was finally announced that as no treaties had been ratified by the Senate providing for the removal of any more Indians, there was no occasion for the letting of any contract. These facts and others were discussed in a congressional inquiry two years later.

On April 4, before his return to Fort Gibson, Houston wrote to Van Fossen from Baltimore: [206]

"I have just seen Mr. Rose on the subject of the contract for Indian rations, and find that he is anxious to engage in the business. When I advised you to put in your *bid,* I did expect to be equally concerned with you in the business. What number of *bids* were actually put in, I do not know: Blake told me that he would withdraw his bid. If these things have been done, ascertain if these are not less than twelve or thirteen cents. If all others are withdrawn under twelve cents and you can get the contract at twelve, it will be *safe* business. It may be that you can not get it at thirteen! if so, take it at twelve. I do not know what the conversation was between you and Mr. Blake, or that you had any on the subject. To Mr. Prentiss, I presume there was nothing said, as Blake told me that he got P. to put in for him; so, if he withdrew one, I suppose both were withdrawn.

"To act in good faith with all parties and to get just as much from Government as will indemnify us for the use of the capital employed and the labor bestowed, is what I wish; and further, to do ample justice to the

---

[206] *Ibid.,* p. 36.

Indians in giving to them the full ration, and of good quality, should we get the contract, must be regarded as a 'sine qua non' with us.

"If Mr. Rose and you can obtain the contract upon the foregoing premises, I will be very happy to unite with you jointly, and will furnish the capital necessary for the next six or nine months. So if you get it, it will be necessary for one of you to be out before *fall!* The other may take his station about Cincinnati and watch the fall market. All this in the event that emigration goes on with the Indians. If needful, you are hereby authorized to sign my name to the bond, and bind me, equally with yourself and Mr. Rose, for the performance of the contract."[207]

After his return to the Verdigris, Houston wrote again to Van Fossen on August 22, about the contract, advising the latter to be in Washington to attend to the matter, and intimating that he and the Secretary of War were not friendly. "I am just about to make a grand purchase of Salt Springs,[208] and trust in God that I will be in a way to 'do well'. *My fortune must not wane,* it must *full,* if I live and meet with my deserts (in my humble opinion)." He told Van Fossen also to watch the papers for articles written by him over the signature of "Tah-lon-tusky", the name of the old Cherokee Chief, attacking certain officials in the Indian Service and defending himself.

After leaving Washington, Houston started on his return to Fort Gibson, stopping at Nashville and Little

---

[207] Houston had written over the signature of Tah-lan-tuskee: "Cherokee Nation, Wigwam, Neosho, 23d December, 1830. . . Under the *notice issued* I made *no* offer, nor did I put in a bid. To say that Gen. Van Fossen did make a bid, I believe is true, but *I was not* in partnership with him in this bid." *The Advocate* (Little Rock), Feb. 16, 1831, p. iii, cols. 1, 2.

[208] The Osage reserve on Grand River which Houston purchased from Colonel Chouteau, near the present site of Salina, Oklahoma.

Rock on the way. At some place in the east he had purchased a supply of goods for his trading house, for at the latter place, he wrote the following letter to Colonel Arbuckle:[209]

"Wigwam, 21st July, 1830.

Colonel Arbuckle. Sir: I have the honor to inform you of the arrival of my Boat at the Verdigris in the Cherokee Nation on yesterday, with an afsortment of goods which I will proceed to open and make sale of so soon as convenient.

"I have thought proper to report to you for the reason that I do not wish to be molested by either misapprehension or design. You are the only public officer in this country to whom I will or could report. There is no agent of the Cherokees in the Nation at this time (Capt. Vashon [210] not having arrived) or I would with great pleasure report to him and if necefsary obtain from him a license to trade and as there is no one else authorized to grant a license, I now report to you and will await the arrival of Capt. Vashon.

"My situation is peculiar and for that reason I will take pains to obviate any difficulty arising from a supposed violation of the intercourse laws. I am a

---

[209] Arbuckle to Secretary of War, July 23, 1830, enclosing Houston's letter. Indian Office, Retired Classified Files, *1830 Cherokees West.*

[210] George Vashon was born in Maryland 1786, and entered the army from Virginia. He was transferred to the Seventh Infantry May 17, 1815, and resigned from the army on December 31, 1819. April 15, 1829, Captain Vashon was appointed by the Secretary of War, Indian Agent for the Delaware, Shawnee, and other small tribes in Missouri. Upon the removal of Major E. W. du Val as Cherokee Agent, Captain Vashon was, on March 12, 1830, appointed to that office and afterward took up his residence at Fort Gibson. He held this agency until it was abolished and then was appointed sub-agent for the Cherokee and Seneca Indians, which post he held until his death, which occurred at the Seneca Agency on January 2, 1836. His remains were brought to Fort Gibson and buried with military honors. He was succeeded in office by Governor Stokes.

citizen of the Cherokee Nation and as such I do contend that the intercourse laws have no other bearing upon me or my circumstances than they would have upon any native born Cherokee; as I exercise all the rights which anyone is enabled to do.

"The certificate of my adoption and the evidence of my citizenship I have the honor of enclosing to you.

"I ordered to this point for my own use and the convenience of my establishment, five barrels of whiskey (four of Monongahela and one of corn), one barrel of cognac brandy, one of gin, one of rum and one of wine intended for stores and for the accommodation of the officers of the Government and such persons as are duly authorized to purchase the same. The whiskey excepting one barrel will be stored with the sutler Gen'l Jno. Nicks, subject to your orders or the orders of the Government and not to be used or broached without your knowledge and consent – nor shall one drop of whiskey be sold at my establishment to either soldier or Indian without the orders of the commanding officer or the agents of the respective tribes.

"In making this rule I have a threefold motive; first I entertain too much respect for the wishes of the Government – second – too much friendship for the Indians and third too much respect for myself to make a traffic of the baneful curse.

"Should you require bonds for the performance of the pledges given I am prepared to execute them with security as solvent as any in this country.

"So soon as my establishment is opened I will request of you that you will (if you please) direct an officer or officers to examine and see that there is a perfect agreement between my report and the stores on hand.

I have not my invoices at hand at the moment but believe my report is correct. Should it not be so it shall be corrected the moment I can detect any error which it may contain. I have the honor to be your obed*t*. serv*t*,

Saml. Houston,

To Colonel M. Arbuckle, Comdg. Cant. Gibson, Neosho."

Colonel Arbuckle submitted General Houston's novel proposition to the Secretary of War, who asked for an opinion of Attorney-general Berrien who, as might have been expected, held that General Houston could not thus evade the operation of the intercourse laws enacted for the regulation of trade among the Indians.

Governor Houston's Life Among the Indians

The year following his failure to secure the contract, Houston spent writing letters defending his acts and denouncing the officials who had been discharged. In addition to the Indian officials, he poured his wrath and denunciation on Colonel Hugh Love, a trader on the Verdigris whom Houston accused of being in league with the Indian Agent to rob the Creeks; Love replied [211] to Houston with some spirited charges against the latter. Stung by the contents of an article appearing in a Nashville paper, in a burst of passion Houston gave to the press of Nashville a most intemperate letter, July 13, 1831, beginning: "A proclamation! That all scoundrels whomsoever that they are authorized to accuse, defame, calumniate, traduce, slander, vilify, and libel me to any extent in personal or private abuse, and that I will in no wise hold them responsible, in law or honor," and much more to the same effect.[212]

Writing letters, offensive and defensive, through the years 1830 and 1831, did not interfere with Houston's further activity as the Nemesis of Indian officials who came under his disapproval, and he even attacked General Clark. On June 2, 1831, a complaint concerning their agent was forwarded to the Secretary of War

[211] Arkansas *Gazette* (Little Rock), Oct. 30, 1830, p. 3, col. 1.
[212] Arkansas *Gazette* (Little Rock), Aug. 3, 1831, p. 3, col. 2.

by John Jolly and a number of other Cherokee. It was witnessed and probably prepared by Houston. December 1, 1831, Jolly addressed President Jackson on the subject of a delegation he had appointed to visit Washington to present certain grievances and other matters of concern to the western Cherokee. The subjects they were authorized to discuss included their shares of the annuities of the whole tribe, and reparation for property destroyed by white people in Arkansas on their removal. One of the matters submitted has particular interest in connection with General Houston: "Fourth. The delegation are directed to solicit a literal fulfillment of the treaty of 1828; and one point in said treaty is for the Cherokee Nation to be possessed of all lands and improvements within their marked limits (Cantonment Gibson, only, excepted). By treaty with the Osages in 1825, seven reservations were made to certain half-blood Osages and laid off for them on the east side of Neosho River. These lie within the limits of the Cherokee Nation, and so long as they remain the property of individuals it will subject the Cherokees to many troubles and may lead to unhappiness."

Jolly's letter was by Jolly and Houston submitted to Captain George Vashon, Cherokee Agent, for transmission to the President. Vashon forwarded it to the Secretary of War with a letter [213] in which he said: "The instructions of the Chief to the delegation are in the handwriting of General Samuel Houston who purchased two of the Osage reserves from Colonel A. P. Chouteau. . ." Vashon had written the Presi-

---

[213] Vashon to Secretary of War, Jan. 4, 1832. Indian Office, Retired Classified Files; *1832 Cherokee West.*

dent from Fort Gibson:[214] "I am informed from a source entitled to confidence, that Col. Augs^t P. Chouteau a trader, & brother to the present Agent for the Osages, has purchased up the Reserves on the Neosho, granted by treaty 2 June 1825, to half breed Osage Children & others and that two of said reserves containing a valuable saline has just been sold by said Chouteau to Genl S. Houston & a Mr. Drenen a Merch^t of Nashville, who appears to be connected in trade with Genl H. in the Cherokee country & within 3 miles of this post, and I have good reason to believe they have purchased these reserves from Col. Chouteau with the view & expectation of prevailing on the Govern^t. to purchase them out at an exorbitant price by availing themselves of an undue influence over the Cherokees to induce them to demand of the Govern^t. the removal of persons unacceptable to them, under the 3 Article of the treaty of 6 May 1828" – Vashon added that he believed Houston planned also to have a request made for the removal of Union Mission which he deprecated for "I consider Union Mission most judiciously located as affording the superior advantage of conferring moral instruction to the children of the Cherokees, Creeks and Osages."

In his letter forwarding to the Secretary of War Houston's proposition that he be permitted to trade with the Indians as a member of the tribe without conforming to the intercourse laws, Colonel Arbuckle said [215] that Houston was impatient of restraint and had made exceptional remarks concerning what he pro-

214 Vashon to President Jackson, Sept. 12, 1830. Indian Office, Retired Classified Files; *1830, Cherokee West, Agency.*

215 Arbuckle to Secretary of War, July 23, 1830, Indian Office, Retired Classified Files; *1830 Cherokee West.*

posed to do if the Government did not gratify his wishes, which Arbuckle attributed to momentary excitement connected with the newspaper controversy in which Houston was then engaged.

While Houston was undoubtedly a man of passion and intolerant prejudices, that he was also capable of the warmest sympathy and indignation where injustice was done was shown by him during his stay at Fort Gibson, in other ways than with the Indians. Two letters written in behalf of Nathaniel Pryor sufficiently illustrate that fact.

It is incomprehensible that the Administration should have persistently ignored the ability of Pryor as an employe in the Indian Service. Nothing but sheer incompetence and indifference can account for passing him by and appointing the many poorly equipped men who were sent to the West; for no other man probably up to that time had such convincing endorsements as to character and ability by men who knew him and were acquainted with the country and the Indians, and work for which his experience and temperament had peculiarly fitted him. However, on May 7, 1830, Pryor was, by the Secretary of War, appointed sub-agent to the Osage,[216] under P. L. Chouteau, at the munificent salary of five hundred dollars annually. At the time of his appointment he was a sick man trying to perform the duties of sub-agent under a temporary appointment by Governor Clark. Within a month of his appointment, Pryor died at his home at the Osage sub-agency, southeast of where Pryor, Oklahoma, is located and near the creek bearing his name.

Washington was not yet through with Houston and

---

[216] Indian Office, *Letter Book* 9, p. 5.

his contract. On March 31, 1832 William Stanbery, a representative in Congress from Ohio was speaking in the House on the subject of discharging the judiciary committee to which had been referred the matter of the removal of a collector in the service of the Government, at Wiscasset. Criticising the attitude of the Administration for not recognizing the turpitude of the collector and removing him, Stanbery said: "Was the late Secretary of War [General Eaton] removed because of his attempt fraudulently to give Governor Houston the contract for Indian rations?"

On April 4, Houston, who was in Washington, addressed a letter to Stanbery demanding to know whether he meant to impute fraud to him. At the request of Houston, Cave Johnson another member of the House, conveyed the letter to Stanbery, who answered that he did not recognize the right of Houston to question him concerning the matter. This made Houston furious, according to witnesses, and arming himself with a heavy hickory walking-stick, he waited his opportunity to obtain satisfaction. Stanbery fearing trouble armed himself with a pistol. On the night of April 14, Houston met Stanbery on the street, knocked him down with his cudgel and beat him severely, giving Stanbery no opportunity to use his pistol. The next day Stanbery, who was confined to his bed by his injuries, sent a note to the Speaker of the House reporting the assault "for words spoken in my place in the House of Representatives."

The House was then obliged to determine what, if any, action should be taken to maintain its dignity and the rights of the members. After a debate, by a vote of one hundred forty-five to one hundred twenty-five, the House decided to issue a warrant for Houston's arrest, and on April 16 he was brought before the Bar of the House. There then ensued another debate concerning the procedure for the unprecedented situation. That being settled, the trial started on April 19, and lasted nearly a month. Houston was defended by Francis Scott Key.[217] In mitigation of the fierceness of the assault by a man of Houston's great stature, it was testified that since the year 1815 Houston had suffered from an injury to his right arm received in battle. Affairs on the Verdigris and Houston's attempt to secure the Indian rations contract figured prominently in the trial, and on May 11, the House found Houston guilty; and as a penalty, by a vote of one hundred eighty-six to eighty-nine, adjudged him guilty of a contempt and violation of the privileges of the House.

But affairs at the Mouth of the Verdigris were to receive further notice in Congress. The day the House voted on Houston's guilt, a resolution was adopted calling for an investigation as to whether the Secretary of War, John H. Eaton, had fraudulently attempted to give to Samuel Houston or to any other person or persons concerned with him, a contract to furnish rations to the Indians emigrating to the Indian country; whether Houston had made a fraudulent attempt to secure such a contract, whether President Jackson had knowledge of such attempted fraud, and whether he had approved or disapproved of it.

The investigating committee began its labors on May

---

[217] Francis Scott Key who was born in Frederick County, Maryland, August 9, 1780, was a lawyer and poet and in 1814 wrote the Star Spangled Banner. In 1833 he was in the Indian service engaged under the Secretary of War in investigating the oppression of the Creek Indians in Alabama and made a number of reports on the conditions he found there. [U.S. Senate. *Documents,* 23d congress, first session, no. 512, vol. iv, 655 ff.]

18, and made its report July 5, by a divided vote acquitting the Secretary and Houston of the charge, but without mentioning the President.[218] The testimony was conflicting. It developed from Houston's letters that were introduced, and he admitted, that he was endeavoring to obtain the contract for subsisting the Indians, which he had previously denied. His principal accuser was Luther Blake, agent at the Creek Agency on the Verdigris, and himself the low bidder for the contract. He testified that Houston had solicited him to withdraw his bid and join Houston and his friends on a higher bid, so they could all make money out of the contract. In his defense, Houston offered Colonel A. P. Chouteau and others as witnesses, to prove that near the Creek Agency on the Verdigris at the time under Blake's charge, cattle were killed in a dirty pen on the bank of the river, without allowing the carcasses to bleed, and the meat was issued to the Indians in a dirty and unwholesome condition; and other evidence was offered attacking Blake, only slightly relevent to the inquiry.

Though having no official connection with the Government, and declaring that he would accept no appointment, Houston was most persistent in offering suggestions in connection with the Indian Service. While he was in Washington in 1830, in connection with the contract for subsisting Indians, he made a written proposition that he, Colonel Arbuckle and Colonel Chouteau be commissioned to go among the Pawnee and undertake to make peace between them, the Osage and Comanche, so that peace would rest on the prairies and the Santa Fe caravans could travel in safety. Houston stipulated, however, that he did not expect

---

[218] U.S. House, *Documents*, 22d congress, first session, no. 502.

any pay for his services. Two years later, when he was in Washington, attending the Congressional investigation of the attempted letting of the contract for subsisting emigrant Indians, Houston informed the Secretary of War of his intention to go west among the Pawnee and Comanche Indians, and offered to secure for the Government information concerning those tribes. July 16, 1832, the Secretary of War wrote Houston,[219] expressing his confidence in the ability of the latter to secure information along certain lines which the Secretary at some length detailed, and concerning which he requested Houston to report; he also informed Houston that he would be allowed a reasonable compensation for the services he should perform, to be determined upon his return.

On the sixth day of August, a passport was issued to Houston, reading as follows:[220]

"I, the undersigned, Acting Secretary of War, do hereby request all the Tribes of Indians, whether in amity with the United States, or as yet not allied to them by Treaties, to permit safely and freely to paſs through their respective territories, General Samuel Houston, a Citizen of the United States, Thirty-eight years of age, Six feet, two inches in stature, brown hair, and light complexion; and in case of need, to give him all lawful aid and protection. Given under my hand and the impreſsion of the Seal of the Department of War, at the City of Washington, this 6th day of August, in the year of our Lord, one thousand, eight hundred & thirty two, & of the Independence of the United States the fifty seventh.

John Robb, Act^g. Sec^y. of War."

---

[219] Indian Office, *Letter Book* 9, p. 54.
[220] Indian Office, *Letter Book* 9, p. 122.

On December 1, Houston reported from Fort Towson to Mr. Ellsworth at Fort Gibson; again February 13, 1833, he sent from Natchitoches, Texas, another report to Mr. Ellsworth, and at the same time he wrote a letter to President Jackson. To the latter he gave his reasons [221] for believing the time to be ripe for the United States to acquire Texas, which he strongly favored. He also told the President that he expected to make Texas his home.

To the Commissioners at Fort Gibson Houston reported that he had met some of the Comanche near San Antonio de Bexar, [222] and had secured their promise to visit Fort Gibson in May for the purpose of entering into a treaty of peace; they would not be able to travel sooner than that for lack of pasture for their horses. However, nothing seems to have come of this engagement; the Comanche were said to have been influenced by the Mexicans not to go to Fort Gibson.

Houston wrote to the Secretary of War [223] of the difficulties he had encountered due to the extraordinary floods; he submitted an account of thirty-five hundred fifty-two dollars for services and expenses for the period from July 25, 1832, to May 28, 1833. On October 4, the Assistant Secretary of War replied, [224] denying the implication that Houston had been appointed to any office in the Government, and calling his attention to the fact that he had planned to make the trip to the western country on his personal business, and had consented to give only part of his time to securing information desired by the Government. The letter said

[221] Yoakum, H. *History of Texas*, vol. i, 465.

[222] Yoakum, H., *op. cit.*, vol. i, 467.

[223] Houston to Cass, July 31, 1833, Indian Office, Retired Classified Files; *1834 Creeks West.*

[224] Indian Office, *Letter Book* no. 11, p. 219.

Houston's services had been of little value, as he had made no reports other than a letter to Mr. Ellsworth on December 1, 1832, containing information he had received from others, for which he said he was unable to vouch. The Secretary offered to pay him only twelve hundred dollars unless he was able to submit information showing that he was entitled to more.

From this time on, Fort Gibson saw little of Samuel Houston. Correspondence with him at Nacogdoches within the next two or three years indicated the removal of his activities to the vicinity of Texas, whose cause he later espoused and with which he became identified.

The possibilities of Houston's expedition among the western Indians were matters of great concern to the Government, for the establishment of peace with them was earnestly desired. After Houston had departed, the Government was favored in the spring of 1833, by a letter from Albert Pike,[225] who had traveled extensively among the Indians, and offered to give the Government the benefit of his information. He said the Comanche numbered eight or ten thousand; that they were divided into two bands, one living near San Antonio, who were staunch friends of the Americans; and the other, by the machinations of the Wichita, were our enemies. "Governor Houston of Tennessee," he says, "will effect nothing with the Comanches, He goes to treat with the southern portion of them who are already friendly – he will never meet one of the northern portion from whom is our only danger, and even should he do so he would be immediately scalped. You can never make war upon them. Possessed of

[225] Pike to Cass, Secretary of War, March 16, 1833, Indian Office, Retired Classified Files; *1833 Western Superintendency.*

numberless horses and having a prairie to flee to as barren as the Sahara, they defy pursuit. The Llano Estacado where they dwell is a byword and a curse to the Spaniard."

Albert Pike, who was one of the most remarkable and interesting characters in the annals of the Southwest, was born in Boston, December 29, 1809. At the age of sixteen he entered Harvard College, and shortly afterward became a teacher. In the spring of 1831 he went west on an expedition to Mexico, but got no farther than Santa Fe. There, in the summer of 1832, he joined a party of trappers and hunters that included the picturesque Bill Williams, Aaron B. Lewis, and about thirty other Americans and twice as many Mexicans and Indians. Lewis had left Fort Towson the year before by way of the Washita, the Canadian and Taos, on a trapping expedition to Santa Fe, and his account of the incredible hardships he experienced was preserved by Pike in 1835 under the title of "Narrative of a Journey in the Prairie", as a serial in the columns of his paper, the Arkansas *Advocate*.[226]

In September, 1832, Pike left Santa Fe with forty-five men and traveled through the Comanche villages on his return to Van Buren and Fort Smith. In his letter he stated that he had just heard that Judge Carr of Saint Louis, who had left Santa Fe in December, 1832, with twelve men, had been attacked on the Canadian by the Comanche; that one man was killed and another wounded, and the survivors were at Fort Gibson. He concluded his letter by suggesting that if the Government proposed to send a treaty party among the Comanche, he and Lewis would go along as guides; and if the "government cannot obtain an interpreter,

---

[226] The Arkansas Historical Association. *Publications* vol. iv, 66-139.

my knowledge of Spanish which many of the Comanche speak, will enable me to act as such."

Houston had been charged with designs on Texas soon after his arrival at Fort Gibson in 1829; and President Jackson had been impelled to write him, June 21 of that year: "It has been communicated to me that you had the *illegal* enterprise in view of conquering Texas; that you declared that you would, in less than two years, be emperor of that country, by conquest. I must have really thought you deranged to have believed you had such a wild scheme in contemplation; and particularly, when it was communicated that the physical force to be employed was the Cherokee Indians." [227]

Houston evidently counted on his friendship with the Indians in his plans and schemes of conquest in Texas. With the Cherokee he was on terms of warmest friendship which he improved on his arrival at the mouth of the Illinois in 1829 by seeking and accepting membership in their tribe, and by interesting himself in their affairs. He immediately began sedulously to cultivate the Creeks near Fort Gibson, the little store which he maintained near the post lending itself well to this undertaking. The poorly organized Indian service in the west and instances of dereliction of duty on the part of some of the officials, gave great opportunity for Houston to demonstrate his fervent devotion to the Indians; counselling with them on the subject of their wrongs, writing complaints for them, and in his own name making wholesale charges against officials, several of whom were removed, he stood before the Indians as their great friend to whom they were bound by ties of profound obligation.

---

[227] Yoakum, H. *op cit.*, vol. ii, 307.

While the watchful eye of the Government kept the Creeks and Cherokee from participating in the affairs of Texas on anything like an extensive scale, there was frequent evidence that Houston sought in a guarded way to interest them in the state south of Red River.

"It was during the year 1834 that an attempt was made by the Creek Indians to obtain a settlement in Texas.[228] Through some influence, the chiefs, Apoth-tayoha and Ben Hawkins came to Nacogdoches, and entered into an agreement to procure the lands lying north of that town, which were then under the control of a New York company. A part of the purchase-money was advanced by the Indians, and further steps were taken to complete the title. In the meantime, the report of this project having gone abroad, and been made public by the newspapers, aroused the American settlers, and also the Cherokees. Colonel Bean, the Indian Agent, was consulted; and in a short time the public mind became so exasperated, that the matter was abandoned. Hawkins was killed by the Cherokees." [229]

Benjamin Hawkins was a Creek living in the Cherokee Nation with his wife, a half-breed member of the latter tribe. He was engaged in trading, and in 1832 landed sixty barrels of whiskey on the east side of the Verdigris; he was a friend and business associate of Houston. January 4, 1834, Hawkins executed to Houston a power of attorney to collect from the Government money owing him for the loss of his improvements east of the Mississippi. The collection of this

---

[228] Yoakum, H. *op. cit.,* vol. ii, 328.

[229] "September 15, 1835: F. Thorn, president; T. J. Rush, Secretary. *Resolved,* that General Houston be appointed to take such steps as he may deem necessary in attempting to arrest the progress of one Benjamin Hawkins, who, we have every reason to believe, is attempting to introduce a large body of Indians from the United States into Texas. *Proceedings of* Vigilance Committee, Nacogdoches." – H.Y.

claim was the subject of some correspondence between Houston and the Secretary of War, as late as 1835, after Houston had taken up his residence in Texas. The other Creek chief, "Apothtayoha" mentioned by Yoakum is easily recognized as the venerable Opoethleyahola, to whom Houston was writing in 1837 when one of his letters [230] was intercepted by Government officials, disclosing plans for locating the Creek Indians in Texas. So that the influence spoken of by Yoakum that brought these Indians to Texas was obviously that of Houston.

---

[230] Indian Office, *Western Superintendency* 1837, File A 174.

The Stokes Treaty Commission

The Osage who left their old home and removed to the Verdigris, were known as the Arkansas Osage. They had no agent until 1822 when Nathaniel Philbrook was appointed sub-agent for them. He was drowned at the mouth of Grand River the latter part of March, 1824 as related by Colonel Chouteau. David Barbour was then appointed in his place at a salary of five hundred dollars yearly. Governor Alexander McNair[231] of Missouri had been appointed agent for the Great and Little Osage on the Missouri and Upper Grand rivers. The difficulties caused by the Arkansas Osage were so frequent and continuous, and interposed such obstacles to the policy of the Government of locating the eastern Indians peaceably in the western country, that it was determined to remove them to a region farther north, where they would be less in the way. Clermont and his people, however, would not consent to leave, and it required many years to bring about their removal. The conferences to provide compensation for losses occasioned by the Osage

---

[231] Alexander McNair was born in Derry, Pa., in 1774; served in the Whiskey Insurrection as a lieutenant in 1794; appointed a lieutenant in the regular army April 23, 1799; removed to Missouri in 1804 where he was appointed United States Commissioner, and in 1812 Adjutant and Inspector-general. He was the first governor of Missouri, serving from 1820 to 1824. On May 18, Congress passed an act providing for an agent (in the place of sub-agent) for the Osage living west of Missouri and Arkansas territory, and Governor McNair was appointed to that post, at a salary of fifteen hundred dollars per year. While in that service he died on May 9, 1826, and he was succeeded by Captain Hamtramck, sub-agent for the Arkansas Osage.

and for the adjustment of ever-recurring difficulties became almost annual affairs.

In 1831 it became necessary to have another conference and treaty between the Osage, Creek, and Cherokee. By the efforts of Colonel Arbuckle, Captain Pryor, Captain Vashon, Cherokee Agent, Mr. McNair, and Major P. L. Chouteau, representatives of the three tribes met at Fort Gibson to adjust claims of Creeks and Cherokee for depredations committed by the Osage. The conference lasted two weeks, and resulted in two treaties: [232] one between the Osage and Creeks, dated the tenth of May, and the other between the Osage and Cherokee, dated May 18.

A large part of the work of securing the attendance of the Osage devolved upon Captain Pryor, who devoted himself industriously to the task; though his efforts were delayed by serious illness that confined him for several weeks in Fort Gibson during January and February, and prevented his return home until the latter part of February, where he remained a convalescent for some time before he could resume his duties. June 10, within a month after the adjournment of the conference at Fort Gibson, Pryor died at his post seven miles from Union Mission. It is a singular fact that a few days before occurred the deaths of two other men who had taken part in the conference; D. D. McNair, Osage Sub-agent, and his horse were killed June 2 by lightning on the prairie near Union Mission, as he was riding home from Fort Gibson; and May 27, Louis P. Chouteau, [233] Sub-agent for the Creeks, died at the western Creek Agency on the Verdigris.

---

[232] U. S. Senate. *Documents*, 23d congress, first session, no. 512, vol. ii, 499.

[233] Louis Pharamond Chouteau, half-brother of Colonel A. P. Chouteau, born August 18, 1806, and died May 27, 1831.

Governor Stokes gives us a picture of the MacNairs in a letter he wrote to the Secretary of War, July 20, 1833:[234]

"The late Governor McNair was a reputable man who had frequently been employed by the United States. He died leaving a reputable family in moderate circumstances. His son (Dunning D. McNair) was employed as a sub-agent with the Osages, and set apart a portion of his Salary for the support of his mother and sisters now residing at St. Louis. This son was killed by lightning in the Prairie above Fort Gibson, and his younger brother [Alexander] was appointed sub-agent in his place. He also dedicates a part of his small salary to the support of his mother and sisters. When we held the conference with the Osages at Fort Gibson in March last, the Osages to the number of eight or nine hundred were encamped on the Neosho River opposite to the Fort. It was the wish of Paul L. Chouteau, the Osage Agent, that the Indians should be prevented from croſsing the river of nights, and mixing with the soldiers of the Garrison, and he ordered young McNair his sub-agent, to encamp with the Osages for that purpose. – By means (*which* no *Gentleman* would be guilty of using) it was discovered that young McNair had slept some nights in his tent with an Osage squaw. For this offense I am told he has been reported to your Department for removal. I cannot believe, Sir, that you will be influenced by the charges of these Hypocritical informers. However meritorious some of the Miſsionaries may be, it is a fact that others will never be satisfied unleſs they get the management of the Indian affairs West, into their own hands."

234 Stokes to Secretary of War, July 20, 1833, Indian Office, Retired Classified Files; *1833 Western Superintendency, Missionaries.*

Immediately on the arrival of Governor Stokes at Fort Gibson early in February, 1833 the commission organized, and with the Governor as chairman set itself to one of the most important tasks responsible for its creation – the adjustment of the boundary line between the Creeks and Cherokee.

The blunder of the officials at Washington in giving the Cherokee tribe in the treaty of 1828, land on the Verdigris and Arkansas rivers occupied and claimed by the Creek Indians had occasioned contention and bitter feeling between the tribes, for the Creeks were then enjoying some of the richest river bottom land, had built their homes and farms, and were profitably engaged in raising corn, cotton, and other crops and they were selling their surplus of corn to the Government for use at the garrison.

Through tactful negotiations the commissioners and the tribes reached an agreement, and the boundary line between the tribes was established, starting twenty-five miles north from where the old territorial line of 1824 crossed the Verdigris, thence south on that line to the Verdigris, thence down the Verdigris and Arkansas to the mouth of Grand River, and thence southwest to the mouth of the North Fork of the Canadian; this latter line lies just east of the corporate limits of the city of Muskogee. Two separate treaties [235] were enacted between the United States and the Cherokee, and between the United States and the Creeks, both bearing date of the fourteenth of February, 1833. Captain Nathan Boone was stationed at Fort Gibson, where he had recently arrived in command of his company of rangers, and he was employed by the commissioners to survey the line agreed upon between the

---

[235] Kappler, *op. cit.*, vol. ii, 283, 285.

two tribes; he performed the work over a period of twenty-five days in March and April.

The commission then met the representatives of the Seminole Tribe and made a treaty with them; by authority of the treaty just completed with the Creek Indians, the Commissioners assigned to the Seminole for their future residence the tract of Creek country lying between the Canadian River and the North Fork and extending west to the forks of Little River. This treaty was signed March 28, 1833.[236]

The commissioners next took up the perennial task of negotiating with the Osage, who were in a destitute condition. In February 1833, members of this tribe had made a raid on some white people in Miller County, Arkansas, in the vicinity of Red River, and returned to the Verdigris loaded with clothing, bed quilts, spoons, knives, and merchandise; in addition to these thefts they had killed much live-stock. Notice was given that the conference would be held February 25, at the home of Colonel Chouteau on Grand River; but as the weather was more than usually inclement, the Osage did not appear, and an adjournment was taken to Fort Gibson for March 11. On this occasion eight hundred Osage came to Fort Gibson accompanied by their chiefs.

A contract was made with Colonel A. P. Chouteau to furnish the rations for the Indians attending the conference. His cousin, Augustus Aristide Chouteau, son of Auguste Chouteau, was selected to interpret from English to French; and the United States interpreter, Baptiste, rendered the French into the Osage language.

The meetings continued from day to day over a period of nearly three weeks, and the efforts of the

---

[236] Kappler, *op. cit.*, vol. ii, 290.

commissioners would probably have been successful but for the stubborn opposition of Clermont to the Government's purpose to remove them. As if to show their contempt for the efforts of the Government to control their actions Clermont's warriors immediately set out to renew their warfare against their enemies in the West.

In their report to the Secretary of War dated April 2, 1833,[237] the Commission said: "In conformity with our instructions, we consulted Col. A. P. Chouteau (as well as his brother the Agent) as to the course to be pursued to obtain the object of the Government, and requested Col. Chouteau to aid the Commissioners in effecting a treaty. Col. Chouteau has long been the great friend and counsellor of the Osage Nation, and the unlimited influence the Chouteaus seem to possess over the nation together with the assurance of a belief that a treaty could be made, induced the Commissioners to intrust the management of the nation principally to them. Indeed, such is their influence that it would be difficult if not impracticable to make a treaty against their opinion." The commission reported that the large attendance of Osage at Fort Gibson was due to the fact that they were nearly naked, destitute and hungry, and came to the meeting for the food that would be given them. In fact, all of the six thousand members of the Osage Tribe were suffering for food except the members of Requa's band who had been taught by the missionaries to raise food from the soil.

---

[237] U. S. Senate. *Documents,* 23d congress, first session, no. 512, vol. iv, p. 228.

Governor Stokes's Views and Difficulties

After the commissioners adjusted the boundary dispute between the Creeks and Cherokee they executed treaties with the Seminole, Seneca, and Shawnee and adjusted difficulties of the Quapaw. In April, Mr. Ellsworth left his post for a visit with his family in Connecticut intending to return in September. The next month Schermerhorn and the secretary, Stambaugh, started for the East. Cholera was raging in the South and there were many deaths from this disease at Fort Gibson.[238] Whether this occasioned the departure of the other members of the commission or not, the venerable Governor Stokes remained at his post to perform the duties of the Commission, of which he was chairman.

The Secretary of War had directed the commissioners to consult freely with Colonel A. P. Chouteau, upon whose integrity, intelligence, and information the Government placed great reliance. Two of the commissioners, Schermerhorn and Ellsworth, chose not to follow that part of their instructions, and displayed a violent prejudice against Chouteau, because, with Governor Stokes, he opposed their plan to remove the Osage to a worthless tract of land, a move justified by

[238] A party of five hundred fifty Cherokee emigrants who embarked at Waterloo on the Tennessee River about the first of March, 1833, were attacked by cholera and compelled to encamp near Little Rock; by the last of April sixty of them had died besides Dr. J. C. Roberts, one of the two physicians who accompanied them.

the two commissioners as a good bargain for the Government.

Governor Stokes who was ill, and Colonel A. P. Chouteau were both in Saint Louis in July writing to the Secretary of War. Governor Stokes was joined there by Mr. Ellsworth who was returning from the east; they had business to attend to at that place with representatives of the Shawnee and Kickapoo tribes. Ellsworth desired to proceed to Fort Leavenworth and then to the Pawnee villages for the purpose of making treaties with those Indians.

After securing Governor Stokes's promise to follow as soon as he should be able to travel, Mr. Ellsworth departed with a little party of eight for Fort Leavenworth; there he waited several weeks for Governor Stokes and in the meantime endeavored to secure a military escort sufficient to overawe the Pawnee Indians. The state of the garrison enfeebled by sickness made this impossible however, and he was obliged to content himself with an escort of seven soldiers with which his little party left Fort Leavenworth after giving up Governor Stokes. The latter made an effort to join Mr. Ellsworth however and had proceeded as far as the Shawnee,[239] the Delaware and Kansa Agencies when he learned that his associate had left Fort Leavenworth two weeks before; Governor Stokes then proceeded to Fort Gibson.

With some of them mounted on horses and others in two dearborn wagons and accompanied by two wagons, each drawn by six oxen, loaded with baggage and presents for the Indians, Mr. Ellsworth's little party left Fort Leavenworth and visited all the villages of the Pawnee Republic. They then returned to the

[239] Where Kansas City, Missouri, now is.

Grand Pawnee village where on October 9, a treaty [240] was made with the chiefs of these four confederated bands of Pawnee. Delegations from these four bands and from the Oto then joined Mr. Ellsworth's party on their return to Fort Leavenworth. Here in November a conference was held by representatives of fourteen tribes who were induced to enter into a mutual treaty of peace to put an end to the warfare that had raged among them. These included the Pawnee, Kansa, Oto, and Osage and the emigrant tribes, the Delaware, Peoria, Piankashaw, Potawatomi, Kickapoo, and Shawnee. The Osage delegation included Clermont and Tal-lai.

An amusing difficulty threatened the success of the conference. The Delaware cherished a tradition that they were the source from which sprang the numerous and powerful tribes throughout the whole of North America. They called themselves the great-grandfathers of the whole Indian race, including those most unfilial of all great-grandchildren, the rebellious Pawnee. The latter looked upon the little handful of Delaware warriors with contempt and indignantly denied that they had ever sprung from the "Delaware dogs" or that a drop of Delaware blood was mingled with that which coursed through their veins. They concluded their expressions of ill will by refusing to commence the council if they were to be looked upon as the descendants of that race. The Delaware, on the other hand were equally obstinate. They insisted on being acknowledged by the refractory Pawnee as their great-grandparents.

For a short time Commissioner Ellsworth was perplexed. But at length, privately assembling the Paw-

---

[240] Kappler, *op. cit.*, vol. ii, 308.

nee chiefs he begged that, for the sake of peace the Delaware should be humored; telling them that no person would for a moment believe so brave and powerful a people as the Pawnee should have sprung from so paltry a stock as the Delaware. The chiefs smiled grimly as they received the pleasing unction of flattery and at length consented, though with wry faces, to submit to the degrading appellation, until the conference should be ended; reserving the right, however, privately to consign the Delaware to purgatory.[241]

In order to make the peace between the tribes complete, at the request of Mr. Ellsworth, one hundred Pawnee who had walked all the way to Fort Leavenworth, continued their journey to Fort Gibson to meet the Creeks, Cherokee, Choctaw, and Osage at their homes, entailing a journey on foot of over a thousand miles before they again reached their villages. They arrived at Fort Gibson in December and were rewarded by securing from the Osage a Pawnee prisoner captured from that tribe.

Ellsworth's party on the Pawnee expedition included his son Edward and John T. Irving,[242] the nephew of Washington Irving, who sought to emulate his distinguished uncle by writing a graphic and entertaining account of the expedition and of the Indians visited by them. Mr. Ellsworth's chance meeting with Irving and his invitation to the latter to visit Fort Gibson in 1832 seem to have been followed by a pronounced attachment between the two families. Ellsworth's son accompanied his father to Fort Gibson in 1832; there is no evidence that Irving's nephew was in the party,

---

[241] Irving, John T. *Indian Sketches,* vol. ii, 277.

[242] Son of Judge John Treat Irving of New York City, a brother of Washington Irving.

but that he later came to Fort Gibson appears from the fact that in 1834 the young men, Irving and Ellsworth were engaged in the business of freighting in that country; and one of their bills for transporting to Fort Gibson supplies ordered by the Commission, provoked criticism by the secretary, Stambaugh, in the charges he made against Ellsworth and Schermerhorn.

By the following winter the commissioners were together again at Fort Gibson, but their relations were not pleasant. In February, 1834, the Commission made a long and interesting report [243] of their work and of conditions among the Indians of the southwest. This report contained a recommendation that the garrison at Fort Gibson be removed to Fort Smith, the "head of navigation on the Arkansas River." [244] To this Governor Stokes filed a dissenting report [245] with the Secretary of War. He wrote: "It is my firm belief that hostilities will take place between the Osages and one or more of the surrounding tribes, if this Garrison is removed. In addition to this, the removal would be a serious injury, and cause great diſsatisfaction among the Indians. This place is their market and their only home market for the sale of their produce. The contracts for corn and Beef for supplying the Troops have been taken by Indians and furnished from Indian families. There is not a day in the year that they do not bring in and sell, neceſsary articles for house consumption, such as Beef, pork, venison, fowls,

[243] U.S. House. *Reports,* 23d congress, first session, no. 474, pp. 78-103. Early in that year the Committee on Military Affairs of the House reported favorably on a bill for removing the garrison from Fort Gibson to Fort Smith, but it was not carried into effect. The buildings had become so dilapidated that it was decided to rebuild the post there or elsewhere.

[244] U.S. House. *Reports,* 23d congress, first session, no. 474, p. 104.

[245] Stokes to Herring, March 27, 1834, Indian Office, Retired Classified Files; *1834 Western Superintendency.*

eggs, butter, and vegetables of all kinds. They also bring many articles of domestic manufacture, such as Wampum, socks, gloves, fans, ornamented slippers, Belts and shot pouches, drefsed deer skins and drefsed Bear skins and Buffalo robes. The ready sale of these articles greatly encourages them in habits of Industry. I do not pretend to say that the Garrison ought to be kept here, merely as a market for Indian traffic, but I do say that this is the proper place for the location of a Military Post intended for the protection of the Indians connected with the Government. It is at the head of Steam Boat navigation, where Boats can come at all times that they can reach the Boundary line. There were seventeen arrivals of Steam Boats at this place last year. It appears to be an object with the Government to protect and satisfy the emigrating Indians in their new and permanent homes; and there is no place West of the Mifsifsippi better adapted for this purpose than Fort Gibson, at the junction of the Rivers Arkansas, Verdigris and Neosho."

Early in the year 1834 the commissioners addressed a communication [246] to the Secretary of War in response to his request that they do something about the recovery of the ranger Abbay. They recommended that they be provided a small steamboat with which to ascend the Arkansas during the high water in summer, to a point where they could meet with the Pawnee Indians, and follow up the friendly overtures made by the delegation of one hundred who had visited Fort Gibson the winter preceding. It was planned to take troops, supplies, and presents for the Indians and hold a con-

---

[246] Stambaugh to Cass, Secretary of War, Feb. 2, 1834. *Ibid.* 1834 *Western Superintendency.*

ference with those western tribes. The dragoon expedition was provided instead, and with this the commissioners had nothing to do. However, the suggestion seems to have been considered. In June, the William Parsons, a small steamboat of one hundred sixteen tons, with a cargo of provisions ascended the Arkansas, the first steamboat to proceed higher than the mouth of the Verdigris. It was intended to proceed to Camp Arbuckle, at the mouth of Cimarron River, a post garrisoned by two companies under Major Birch who had already proceeded with his command to the place and was erecting quarters for his men and the year's supply of provisions on board the William Parsons. The boat had not reached its destination however, when a fall in the river compelled the captain to return down stream.

In May, Stambaugh had written that the Creek, Benjamin Hawkins, a close friend of Samuel Houston, had told him a meeting had been planned on Brazos or Trinity River for the twentieth of June; it was to be attended by the Comanche of Texas, Shawnee, Delaware, Creeks, Kichai, and Cherokee. Sam Houston was the moving spirit in this effort to establish peace between the tribes which he sought to accomplish through the medium of his friends, the Cherokee. Hawkins extended an invitation to the government officials at Fort Gibson to attend. Stambaugh stated that the commissioners had been for over a year considering plans for meeting the western Indians but had not been able to agree. General Leavenworth told him in May that the Secretary of War had entrusted the matter to him. When Hawkins went to the meeting in Texas he carried messages from Leavenworth.

General Leavenworth relieved Colonel Arbuckle of his command in May 1834, and on the thirtieth of that month a dinner and ball were given at Dillard's Hotel in honor of General Leavenworth. Colonel Arbuckle had left for a visit to his farm below Fort Smith and among the toasts was one by Governor Stokes: "Our absent friend Colonel Arbuckle, an honest man and an efficient and faithful public servant. May his journey through life be prosperous and happy."

After Colonel Arbuckle returned on June seventh, a farewell dinner was given him by the officers of the post upon his leaving,[247] "On furlough, in consequence of ill health. It was the largest party ever convened at Fort Gibson upon any occasion. There were numerous talks by Colonel Many who presided, Lieutenant-colonel Burbank, Lieutenant Seawell, Governor Stokes, Colonel Stambaugh, Colonel Nowland, Colonel Henry Dodge, Lieutenant-colonel Kearny, Lieutenant Hamilton, and Captain Perkins. Colonel Arbuckle returned thanks and said 'as my impaired health obliges me to seek for its restoration in a different climate, and as I may never return, it is a source of no inconsiderable gratification to leave this frontier in a state of perfect peace as relates to Indian tribes with which the United States has intercourse.' " [248]

Directly afterward Colonel Arbuckle, who had been sick during the preceding winter and spring, left for his home at White Sulphur Springs, which he reached a month or two later; but he had not been there long when on September ninth, he was assigned to the command vacated by the death of General Leavenworth.

[247] *Army and Navy Chronicle* (Washington), vol. iii, 474.
[248] *Niles Register* (Baltimore), vol. xlvi, 379.

His new command embraced all troops on the south-west frontier over a territory bounded on the east by the Mississippi, on the north by the southern line of Missouri and the Santa Fe Trail to the Mexican terri-tory; on the west by the boundary of the United States, and on the south by Red River; with headquarters at Fort Gibson, where he at once established himself.

Indian Warfare Between Texas and Mexico

The Kiowa having left the treaty grounds at Camp Holmes before the arrival of the commissioners, they were not parties to the treaty of 1835, signed by the Comanche and other western tribes. Different reasons were given for their leaving; one was that the commissioners delayed too long leaving Fort Gibson; Governor Stokes said the Indians became alarmed at the display of military force sent by Colonel Arbuckle. At any rate the commissioners immediately took steps to make the Kiowa acquainted with the contents of the treaty made with the other tribes, and extended to them an invitation to attend a conference at Fort Gibson and become parties to its terms. In response to this invitation, in the early part of December, 1835, a Kiowa warrior, accompanied by a Wichita chief, came to Fort Gibson to ascertain how his tribesmen would be received if they should come. He explained that the Kiowa were willing to treat, but said that as their horses were poor and they themselves constantly engaged in hunting to support their families, they would not be able to come before spring.

Governor Stokes and Colonel Arbuckle immediately commissioned Major P. L. Chouteau to proceed to the Kiowa country and seek an interview with those Indians to induce them to come to Fort Gibson as soon as possible. In December, Major Chouteau went to Coffee's trading house on Red River and finding no news of the Kiowa there, proceeded sixty-five miles farther up the river to Cache Creek [249] to question the Indians in that neighborhood about them. He found none there; but in two days farther travel he came up with some bands of Tawakoni and Waco who were returning to occupy the country from which they had been driven by the Osage some years before, and which in view of the treaty just signed, they felt safe in reoccupying. They were agriculturists, and told Chouteau they were preparing to plant corn in the spring.

From there Major Chouteau went on to the village of the Wichita, who informed him that the Kiowa would be found south of Red River on the headwaters of the Colorado. For twenty-two days he ranged the country between those rivers, and was about to start on his return to Cache Creek, being compelled to do so by the weakness of his horses, when he found himself surrounded by innumerable camp fires of the Comanche, Kiowa, and Kiowa Apache; [250] these Indians had just commenced their annual migration to the buffalo grounds to the north. Traveling north with them to Cache Creek, he halted and invited the Indians to his camp for an interview. They were suspicious and circumspect, and for a number of days sent minor members of the tribe to Major Chouteau to learn his business and reflect on the matter before the chief finally appeared. At last however, he discussed the object of his visit with some of the head men of the tribe, who agreed to send a deputation to Fort Gibson in the early part of the succeeding May. These Indians reported that they had been at war, though with

[249] Sixty-five miles below Cache Creek would locate Coffee's trading post in Love County, Oklahoma.

[250] Major Chouteau estimated that in 1836 there were forty-five hundred Comanche and fifteen hundred Kiowa warriors in these two tribes, indicating a population of thirty-six thousand individuals.

whom Major Chouteau does not state; and their horses and mules, probably stolen from the Mexicans or Texans, were not in fit condition for traveling to Fort Gibson before the spring grass would sustain them.

The expedition had taken Major Chouteau all winter, and was a most arduous undertaking. He returned to Fort Gibson in April and made his report [251] to Governor Stokes and Colonel Arbuckle. He concludes with the following interesting paragraph: "I should feel myself wanting in gratitude to the Comanches, Kioways, Catakahs and the various bands of Pawnees whom I met with, were I, in this communication to omit to bear testimony to their uniformly kind attention and respectful bearing towards me throughout the whole of my intercourse with them, seeming never for a moment to forget the courtesy due to an agent of the Government." The great influence of the Chouteau family with the Indians may be accounted for by the sense of justice to them reflected in this sentiment.

The Kiowa did not come to Fort Gibson in 1836, as they promised, but instead ominous reports of war among the prairie Indians complicated with the Mexican and Texan situation found their way to that post. In the following winter, Major Chouteau, accompanied by his son Edward and Doctor Richie, went to Camp Holmes where A. P. Chouteau had built a trading post after the treaty made there in 1835 with the Comanche and other tribes, and where he was trading with those Indians. Major Chouteau sent his son with four other men to visit the Comanche and Kiowa Indians in their winter camp south of Red

---

[251] Chouteau to Stokes and Arbuckle, April 19, 1836, and April 25, 1836, Indian Office, *Choctaw Agency, Western Superintendency, 1836,* S 275.

River; he returned in January and reported to his father. On February first, 1837, Major Chouteau wrote [252] that his son had reported the Comanche Chief, She-co-ney, who had signed the treaty of 1835, was angry with the white people, and threatened to destroy Camp Holmes with its inhabitants. Information had also come from Coffee's trading post on Red River that the Comanche had burned their copy of the treaty because they were just beginning to realize that it admitted the Osage, Creeks, Cherokee, Choctaw, and other eastern tribes into the country they had been accustomed to regard as their exclusive hunting ground. And from indications Chouteau predicted that the Comanche would soon engage in a war with the Osage, Delaware, and other tribes who were then hunting in the country claimed by the former.

Camp Holmes and Chouteau's trading house were within the country given the Creeks, but members of that tribe had not ventured so far west except on hunting excursions. To avoid conflicts, Major Chouteau was directed to warn the Delaware, Creeks, Choctaw, and Shawnee not to trespass on the country not belonging to them. At that time a number of white people had been made prisoners by the Comanche in Texas and brought across the border into the United States. Chouteau was directed to secure information concerning these prisoners, supposed to number forty or fifty. He learned of two women prisoners in the village of She-co-ney, one of them a Mrs. Martin, whose youngest children were killed by the Indians because they were unable to walk with the party who made them captives. The Kiowa and Wichita also had a number of prison-

---

[252] P. L. Chouteau to Armstrong, Feb. 1, 1837, Indian Office, *Western Superintendency, 1837,* A 131.

ers, including persons named Richards, Parker, and Forest; but the Comanche had the largest number. In May, 1837, a war party of Comanche, brought to Major Chouteau at Camp Holmes three white women and children prisoners. Jack Ivey,[253] a half-breed mulatto, reported to Chouteau that at a Waco village he had purchased a white woman and a two-year-old girl; the woman had a daughter and a brother still prisoners, the former with the Wichita and the brother with the Waco. They were all taken prisoners in Texas. Because they had no horses to ride, Ivey was obliged to leave the woman and child at Coffee's trading house until his return.

Among the white captives of the Comanche were Cynthia Ann Parker, twelve years of age, and her brother who were taken by the Comanche on a raid in the summer of 1835, from the home of their father on Navasota River in Texas. The girl later became the wife of No-co-ne and the mother of the famous chief, Quanah Parker, who was born about 1845.

Captain Marcy stated [254] that Cynthia, having an Indian husband and children, could not be persuaded to leave them. The brother, who had been ransomed at Fort Gibson and brought home, told Captain Marcy that he was sent by his mother to try to induce his sister to return home. When he interviewed her, she refused to listen to his suggestion, saying that her husband,

---

[253] Jack Ivey is frequently mentioned by early trappers and explorers and was a well known figure among the Indians. John Ivey accompanied James to the west in 1821, and again in 1823 to the Comanche country [James, *op. cit.*, 98, 197, 198], where he was well received by the Indians, and was probably among those who remained in that country when James returned home.

[254] U.S. Senate. *Executive Documents*, 32d congress, second session, no. 54, Explorations of the Red River of Louisiana in the year 1852, by Randolph B. Marcy, p. 103.

children and all that she held most dear were with the Indians, and there she should remain.

In 1860 a company of Texas Rangers and United States Cavalry attacked a body of Comanche Indians on Pease River in north Texas. The Indians who were not killed fled; one of those captured proved to be Cynthia Ann Parker. She was carried with her little daughter, Prairie Flower, back to the home of her childhood. After her twenty-four years of captivity, she was compelled to re-learn the English language; but she pined for her Indian associates and freedom of the plains, and in 1870 died in civilized surroundings to which, it was said, she never became reconciled.

In 1837 the authorities in the Southwest reported the situation as critical.[255] From the large number of Indians of different tribes ranging the prairies as a common hunting ground, conflicts seemed inevitable, and Indian warfare on a large scale was expected. Reports continued to reach Fort Gibson of the activities of agents of Mexico among the western Indians who were inciting the Comanche and Wichita to make war on the whites. The Government was beset in several quarters, and much of its little army was engaged in the Seminole War in Florida. Part of it had just returned from the expedition from Fort Gibson to the Mexican border.

---

[255] The following winter Major-general McComb, commander-in-chief of the army, submitted to Congress a new and comprehensive plan for the defense of the western frontier [U.S. House. *Documents,* 25th congress, second sesson, no. 311]. He proposed the building of a number of new army posts and a system of railroads to facilitate the removal of troops to meet emergencies. One road proposed by the plan was to run directly from Saint Louis to Fort Gibson; another from Memphis to Little Rock and thence to Fort Gibson, extending up the Arkansas River to a new post to be located on the upper part of that stream at the western boundary of the United States; the site of this proposed new post is approximately that of the subsequently located Fort Dodge, Kansas.

In January, Captain Bonneville at Fort Gibson wrote [256] the Adjutant-general offering to head an expedition to the western Indians to reach an understanding with the Kiowa and other prairie tribes. This offer was not accepted, but as the situation became more alarming, on April 7, 1837, Colonel A. P. Chouteau was commissioned by the Secretary of War to go among the prairie Indians and endeavor to execute further treaties among the tribes, and between them and the United States. Colonel Chouteau was described by Governor Stokes in a letter to the Secretary of War [257] as "better acquainted with the situation of Indian tribes, and of Indian manners, habits and dispositions, than any man west of the Mississippi River." With his previous long experience among the Indians, and from the operation of his trading house at Camp Holmes, he had a wide knowledge of, and acquaintance with them, and held their confidence, giving him advantages in such negotiations no other man of his time possessed. And the Government confidently turned to him and his brother, Major P. L. Chouteau, for service of the greatest importance in the critical situation.

It seems incredible, but the Government had no money to pay for the important service required of Chouteau; his commission concluded as follows: [258] "There is no appropriation out of which any part of your expenses can be paid. I wish, therefore, that all your pecuniary engagements should rest upon your

---

[256] Bonneville to Jones, Adjutant-general, January 24, 1837, Indian Office, *Western Superintendency, 1837,* A. 120.

[257] Stokes to Poinsett, Secretary of War, May 30, 1837, Indian Office 1837, *Fort Gibson, Western Superintendency,* S. 385.

[258] U.S. House. *Executive Documents,* 25th congress, second session, no. 3, Report of Secretary of War, p. 598, Report from the Office of Indian Affairs, December 1, 1837.

individual responsibility, and that you should rely upon Congress for idemnification of your expenses. The Department is aware that the duties of the mission cannot be successfully executed without presents to the Indians, and you are therefore authorized, under the restrictions just stated, to provide the necessary supplies for this purpose, to an amount not exceeding five thousand dollars." [259]

The situation was described by an observer: "Choctaw Agency, April 21, 1837. The Indian country on the southwest frontier is filled with Mexican emissaries. Some five or six have been seen among the wild Indians, and have induced them to take up arms against Texas. They have, regardless of the treaty, crossed over our line, to meet the wild Indians, and have made a general invitation to our emigrant tribes to join in the contest, offering horses, arms, ammunition, and all the plunder they can take –besides a peaceable possession of Texas if they can succeed in driving off the inhabitants. These invitations, I assure you, have created no little sensation among our Indians, many of whom are poor, and are ready for adventure – spiced a little with feelings of *an ardent love* for the Texans – they being a branch of the American family; and if we have not a war immediately on this frontier, it will be owing to the prompt gathering of a military force at some point on Red River, which I do not see any sign of. Parties of friendly Indians come in daily, complaining of depredations being committed on them by the wild Indians. Several travelling parties (American),

[259] After his death, his estate was paid by the Government $3049.25 for his services as Commissioner to the western Indians, and five thousand dollars was paid for presents made by him and his brother, P. L. Chouteau, to the Indians.

have been plundered and driven from the prairies by Camanches, who have been urged to these acts by their Mexican allies. This state of things ought not to last long." [260]

In May, 1837, Major P. L. Chouteau returned to Fort Gibson from Camp Holmes with a delegation of twenty-four of the principal chiefs and head men of the Kiowa, seven Kataka or Kiowa Apache, and two Wichita for the purpose of meeting the commissioners and entering into the long-deferred treaty of peace and friendship. They arrived at Fort Gibson on the eighteenth, and two days later they were followed by the principal chief of the Tawakoni and eleven of his people, for the same purpose as the Kiowa.[261] After a conference and the usual preliminaries, on the twenty-sixth, a treaty [262] was entered into at Fort Gibson and signed by Governor Stokes and Colonel Chouteau for the United States, General Arbuckle having left on a journey to the east; and by the chiefs and representatives of the Kiowa, Kiowa Apache, and Tawakoni tribes of Indians. The treaty embraced much the same subjects as those in the treaty of 1835 – assurances of peace and friendship, consent for all to hunt on the great prairies west of the Cross Timbers, promises of indemnity for property of traders taken or destroyed, and guarantee of safety of Santa Fe traders en route. With this accomplished, the Government had concluded treaties with nearly all the bands of prairie Indians in the Southwest with whom there was intercourse or possibility of collision within the United States; and

---

[260] *Army and Navy Chronicle* (Washington), vol. iv, 318.

[261] Stokes to Poinsett, Sept. 8, 1837, Indian Office, *Western Superintendency*, S 576.

[262] Kappler, *op. cit.*, vol. ii, 363.

if faithfully observed, was believed to insure the safety of traders going to Santa Fe as well as all licensed traders on the southwestern frontier.

The making of this treaty was a consummation much desired by the officials of the Government. Conditions in the Southwest more and more justified and required the presence of Fort Gibson and its influence over the untamed expanse between the post and the limits of the United States. The efforts of Texas and Mexico to embroil the southwestern Indians in their quarrel,[263] aggravated on our side of the line the differences already existing among the Indians and between them and the traders, trappers, and travelers engaged in legitimate enterprise, whom we were unable to protect by force.

When the Comanche visited Fort Gibson, the only white settlement in the United States they had ever seen, they believed that the few hundred soldiers and civilians at that little post represented the great strength of the United States, of which Colonel Dodge in their villages had boasted, in his well-meant efforts to impress them, but they refused to be impressed; feeling that the whites were few in comparison with them – the hundreds of the white soldiers' horses insignificant com-

[263] Even Samuel Houston himself, now president of the Republic of Texas, was using his friendship with the Creeks and Cherokee to enlist them on the side of Texas in her contest against Mexico. Superintendent Armstrong sent to Washington a copy of Houston's letter intercepted in the hands of a Creek chief, with a report [William Armstrong to C. A. Harris, Commissioner of Indian Affairs, May 10, 1837, Indian Office, *Choctaw Agency*, 1837 A 174] in which he said: "The Creeks as well as Cherokees have a great disposition to engage in the contest between the Texans and Mexicans, and there is those amongst them, more especially with the Cherokees who are secretly encouraging such a design. It is calculated to operate injuriously upon the Indians, to have anything to do with this contest, thereby withdrawing them from their proper pursuits, and calculated to alienate their confidence from the Government of the United States."

pared to their thousands. This impression coming to the knowledge of the officials, it was decided to take a delegation of the western Indians to Washington, so they could be impressed by a view of some of the populous cities in the east. Accordingly, on July 27, Colonel Chouteau was authorized to collect a deputation of Comanche and Kiowa Indians, and accompany them to Washington during the following winter and spring. The Comanche, some time before, said they would go if they were accompanied by a deputation of Osage, with whom they were better acquainted than with any other tribe connected with the United States; and the Osage joined in the request.

It was planned to hold a meeting at Camp Holmes in the autumn where it was hoped there would be a large gathering of the western Indians with whom Chouteau might counsel on the subject of peace. In October, Colonel Chouteau directed his brother Major P. L. Chouteau, to go to Fort Mason [264] and ascertain the points at which the different prairie Indians would be willing to meet Colonel Chouteau, or whether they would prefer to send deputations to meet him at Fort Gibson. The next month Colonel Chouteau was escorted from Fort Gibson by Captain Trenor and a company of dragoons, arriving at Camp Holmes on the twenty-fourth. Two days later Captain Trenor returned to Fort Gibson, leaving with Colonel Chouteau Lieutenant Northrop and twelve men, together with necessary transportation facilities and subsistence to enable Chouteau to carry his operations into effect during the winter and spring.

[264] Colonel Chouteau, who had his trading post at Camp Holmes about five miles northeast of where Purcell, Oklahoma, now is, called the place Fort Mason, for Major Mason who established it. It was commonly known by both names.

Soon after his arrival at Camp Holmes, Colonel Chouteau reported [265] to the Commissioner of Indian Affairs that it was impossible to have a satisfactory interview with the Indians before spring; they were then scattered over a vast extent of country, and almost all of them were at war; "This has in a great measure been caused by the Agents of the Mexican and Texican governments, who, I have every reason to believe, have been for some time among them, making them the most seductive offers if they would take up arms with them in their existing war. They are consequently divided, one part having joined the Mexicans, and the other the Texians; a great many of them are however scattered through the territory of either governments, for predatory purposes alone."

Chouteau reported that the Comanche and associated tribes held thirty or forty white prisoners whom they had captured in Texas and Mexico; that some of them were women of respectable families who were being treated with harshness and cruelty, and he begged for authority to attempt their liberation and relieve them from their wretched condition.

Colonel Chouteau remained at Camp Holmes during the winter, and made two interesting reports in December.[266] They had to do mainly with complaints of Wichita against the Pawnee Mohaw (sic) for attacking them, killing several of the tribe, and stealing all their horses and mules. The Wichita were agriculturalists and tilled the soil with great industry. Shortly after the attack by the "Pawnee Mohaw," they were attacked by the Caddo, and as the Wichita were un-

---

[265] Chouteau to Harris, Commissioner of Indian Affairs, November 25, 1837, Indian Office, *Camp Mason, Western Superintendency,* 1837, C. 510.

[266] A. P. Chouteau to Harris, Dec. 8, and Dec. 16, 1837, *Ibid.* C 511 and C 534.

armed, they were compelled to fly and leave all their property to be destroyed; several were killed and a number of men, women, and children were taken prisoners.

To add to their misery, their village had been devastated by smallpox; they had nearly all been sick during the summer, and many had died; the sickness and mortality were such that in many instances there were not enough well persons to remove the dead from the lodges. "This malady swept through the Missouri Valley in 1837. It first appeared on a steamboat, (the St. Peters,) in the case of a mulatto man, a hand on board, at the Black-Snake Hills, a trading post, 60 miles above Fort Leavenworth, and about 500 miles above St. Louis. It was then supposed to be measles, but, by the time the boat reached the Council Bluffs, it was ascertained to be smallpox, and had of course been communicated to many in whom the disease was still latent. Every precaution appears to have been taken, by sending runners to the Indians, two days ahead of the boat; but in spite of these efforts, the disease spread. It broke out among the Mandans about the 15th of July. This tribe, which consisted of 1600 persons, living in two villages, was reduced to 31 souls." After describing the appalling mortality among many tribes, the writer [267] quotes from an eye witness: "Language, however forcible, can convey but a faint idea of the scene of desolation which the country now presents. In whatever direction you turn, nothing but sad wrecks of mortality meet the eye; lodges standing on every hill, but not a streak of smoke rising from them. Not a sound can be heard to break the awful stillness, save the ominous croak of ravens, and the mournful howl of

[267] Schoolcraft, *op. cit.,* vol. i, 257.

wolves, fattening on the human carcasses that lie
strewed around . . . Many of the handsome
Arickarees, who had recovered, seeing the disfiguration
of their features, committed suicide; some by throwing
themselves from rocks, others by stabbing and shooting.
The prairie has become a grave-yard; its wild flowers
bloom over the sepulchres of Indians. The atmosphere, for miles, is poisoned by the stench of hundreds
of carcasses unburied."

As the Wichita had been consistent friends of the
United States since they had signed the treaty of 1835,
Colonel Chouteau took the liberty of donating to them
a few articles, such as axes, hoes, powder, and lead, to
relieve their most pressing wants and to ameliorate
their shocking condition, for which action he asked the
sanction of the Department. As the Caddo resided
in Texas, Chouteau said he would do nothing toward
intervening in their troubles, but would correspond
with Governor Houston of Texas, and warn him of the
difficulties that would ensue if he did not prevent
further depredations by Indians of his country. He
reported further that as the war parties continued to
move about, it would be impossible to get deputations
together for their visit to Washington until late in the
spring.

In the following June, Colonel Chouteau made
another interesting report from Camp Holmes: [268]
"I was visited on the 27th May by Tabaquena (one of
the principal Chiefs of the Pa-do-kah indians) whom I
had sent immediately after my report to you of the 16th
December last, to visit the Tribes of the Southwest, and
make an arrangement with them to meet me either at

---

[268] Chouteau to Harris, Commissioner of Indian Affairs, June 28, 1838,
Indian Office, *Fort Mason, Western Superintendency* 1838, C 757.

this place or at the Pilot-Mountains about the latter part of March. He brought with him a Deputation from eight of the different tribes – viz, the Ky-oh-wah, Ka-ta-kah, Pa-do-kah, Yam-pa-rhe-kah or Comanche, Sho-sho-nee, Hoish, Co-che-te-kah and Wee-che-tah, among whom were twenty-two of their principal chiefs, and a number of warriors. – There were also present a number of the Osages and Piankashaws. After meeting them in council, and informing them of the wish of the Government to postpone their visit to Washington, they manifested some surprise and regret, and said they had come prepared to make arrangements, to visit their Grand Father the great American Chief. Upon understanding however that the visit was only deferred, they appeared satisfied, and exprefsed a great desire that at some future period I might be permitted to take them." To solace their disappointment, Chouteau gave the chiefs presents as usual. He would have made a treaty with the "Hoish" and other tribes, but a sufficient number of their responsible chiefs were not present, and that matter was deferred to the following October.

Chouteau was informed by the Indians that they were making preparations to go to war against the "Pawnee Mohaw" and "Chians" in consequence of the repeated depredations which both those nations had for a long time committed upon them; and it was expected the Osage would join them, the recent death of their chief Clermont requiring the taking of fresh scalps to facilitate the passage of his spirit to the happy hunting grounds. Colonel Chouteau endeavored to dissuade them from their warlike plans until the Government could intercede with their enemies; his guests agreed only on condition that he would send a message

to their camp north of the fort informing the remainder
of their chiefs and warriors of the arrangement Chouteau had made with them.

Colonel Chouteau was disabled by an injury to his
thigh and could not ride his horse. He accordingly
sent Lieutenant L. B. Northrop and his command, his
nephew E. L. Chouteau, who was also well acquainted
with the western tribes, Tabaquena and the Comanche
chiefs, and eight of their warriors. Chouteau continued: "Messrs. Northrop and Chouteau returned
on the 26th instant, and report that they found the
indians about one hundred and seventy-five miles north
of west of this place, and that they informed them, that
three days before their arrival among them, they were
attacked by a large party of Chians and A-rapeau-ho's,
and that most of the men of the Comanches and their
allies being absent at the time on a Buffalo hunt, the
Enemy entered their towns, which they burnt, by which
means they lost most of their property, and one hundred
of their best horses Killed in the fight. They had also
forty-three men Killed, and many wounded, a number
of women and children were Killed and many taken
prisoners. They told the gentlemen above named, that
had it not been for the ammunition I gave them at this
place, they would have fared much worse than they did,
as without it they would have had only to depend upon
their bows and arrows – The Chians and A-rapeau-ho's
left thirteen slain on the ground and according to report
had many wounded." Colonel Chouteau detailed a
number of other hostilities between the tribes to the
north; the "Pawnee Mohaws" attacked a camp of eight
families of "Pa-do-kah's and stole all their horses consisting of from 140 to 160 head, and not having one
horse left, they were obliged to pack their property on

their backs to the main camp;" an indication of the amazing number of horses the western Indians possessed. "I have information which I believe to be correct, that the Keitsash and Waco indians have been for some time past employed by the Mexican Government to persuade the different wild tribes of this section of the country to join them in their war against Texas, also that the Cherokees who are in Texas, are much in favor of the Mexican cause. I do not however think that any of the tribes have joined them, except the two above named."

Colonel Chouteau concluded his long letter by saying that while awaiting a reply, "I shall return to Gibson, as the indians are now some distance off, and will not be here until October, when I shall again be here to meet them." But Colonel Chouteau never returned to his post in the west. Whether the injury in his leg had anything to do with it, it was not long after this that he was reported sick in Fort Smith, and his recovery thought doubtful, according to Superintendent Armstrong writing October 4. He had recovered sufficiently, however, to go to Fort Gibson, where he died [269] on December 25, 1838. Armstrong wrote on December 31 that Colonel Chouteau had been sick a long time.

Colonel Chouteau was a prominent and useful man in the western country, whose tremendous personal

---

[269] Chouteau's staunch friend Clermont died just a few months before. Governor Stokes wrote (Stokes to Secretary of War, June 5, 1838, Indian Office, Fort Gibson *Western Superintendency* 1838, S 7); "The recent death of their (Osage's) Principal Chief Clermont, will cause their turbulent warriors to go to war before winter with the Pawnees, Kiawas, and other Tribes of the great Prairies, with whom they have been at peace ever since our late Treaties." Clermont had succeeded as chief his father the first Clermont called "The Builder of Towns" who founded Clermont's village and who died in May, 1827.

influence in the winning of the Southwest, overshadowing that of any other individual, should be better known; his outstanding qualities were recognized by his contemporaries, and being a former officer in the army and respected at the post, the officers at Fort Gibson gave him a military funeral with all the pomp the surroundings permitted, and buried him in the cemetery at that post. He was revered by the Indians of many tribes, and their grief is recounted by Gregg, when the latter visited Chouteau's fort the next spring.

Expeditions of Bonneville and Other Early Traders

The Southwest as the theatre of the adventurous trader who braved the dangers and hardships that intervened between him and success, is graphically portrayed by Doctor Josiah Gregg, who left Van Buren the first day of May, 1839, on a trading expedition to Chihuahua by way of Santa Fe, an absorbing account of which is contained in his *Commerce of the Prairies*.[270] The Mexican ports were blockaded by the French and the traders saw an opportunity for handsome profits on goods introduced through the interior. Proceeding from Van Buren they ascended the Arkansas and Canadian rivers to the mouth of the North Fork, which they crossed about a mile above its confluence with the Canadian; passing through the Creek settlement at Eufaula, they proceeded westward past the vicinity of where Holdenville now stands, approaching the Canadian River at Camp Holmes near the site of Purcell, Oklahoma.

The party consisted of thirty-four men, who were expected to qualify as teamsters, hunters, and guards for twenty-five thousand dollars worth of merchandise they were taking to trade to the Mexicans.[271] "We had fourteen road-wagons, half drawn by mules, the others by oxen (eight of each to the team); besides a carriage and a Jersey wagon. Then we had two

---

[270] Thwaites, *op. cit.*, vols. xix, xx.
[271] Thwaites, *op. cit.*, vol. xx, 104.

swivels mounted upon one pair of wheels; but one of them was attached to a movable truckle, so that upon stopping, it could be transferred to the other side of the wagons. One of these was a long brass piece made to order, with a calibre of but an inch and a quarter, yet of sufficient metal to throw a leaden ball to the distance of a mile with suprising accuracy. The other was of iron, and a little larger. Besides these, our party was well supplied with small arms."

Doctor Gregg continued up the north side of Canadian River, keeping on the ridge between that stream and North Fork; June 25, they arrived at Santa Fe, and on the twenty-second of August they set out for Chihuahua. Leaving that city October 31, they returned by way of El Paso to Santa Fe where they arrived December 6. On their return from there to Fort Smith they followed much the same course as their westward route, though they traveled on the south side of Canadian River until they arrived at a point between the ninety-eighth and ninety-ninth meridian, approximately in Blaine County, Oklahoma; there on March 29 they again crossed to the north side and joined the old trail from there to Fort Smith and continued to Van Buren.

The trail followed by Doctor Gregg from Fort Smith to Santa Fe was substantially that of the James and McKnight party in 1823 and became a well known route to Santa Fe; after the discovery of gold in California it was employed by the adventurers to that far country, and for part of the way was the regular mail route to California. On April 4, 1849, Captain R. B. Marcy left Fort Smith over this same route with a body of troops to escort a company of five hundred emigrants who were going to California. Fort Smith was a rendezvous for gold seekers from as far as New York, and for several weeks before the departure of the great caravan, the streets of that village were crowded with California wagons, oxen, and mules. Colonel Bonneville, an ardent adventurer on the prairies, had supposed he would be placed in charge of the great expedition because of his former extensive experience in the west, but greatly to his disappointment Colonel Arbuckle selected Captain Marcy for that adventure.

Benjamin Louis Eulalie de Bonneville was born in France during the Reign of Terror in 1793. His father, publisher of a paper, was a man of classic culture and the intimate friend of General Lafayette. For his indiscretion in denouncing Bonaparte as the Cromwell of France, his paper was suppressed and he and his family were exiled to America. Young Bonneville attended the United States Military Academy at West Point from April 14, 1813, until December 11, 1815, when he was graduated and became a second-lieutenant in the American Army.

After serving in various organizations in the south, he came to Fort Smith in 1822 as first-lieutenant in the Seventh Infantry; and in 1824, upon the abandonment of Fort Smith, accompanied his regiment to Fort Gibson.

The same year, Bonneville secured a leave of absence from his post, and from Fort Gibson went to New York where he became secretary to General Lafayette on his return to Europe on the frigate Brandywine, after his triumphal tour of the United States. On arriving at La Grange, in his native France, Bonneville became the guest of his father's old friend until the following year, when he returned to the United

States and reported to his command at Fort Gibson in November. Here a humdrum, sequestered existence was enlivened by passing traders going or returning by the Arkansas River from the unknown world in the West; stopping at the traders' stores on the Verdigris, or visiting at the post, requiting the hospitality they found there with tales of adventure that fascinated the imaginative French officer; and for neighbors on the Verdigris there were Captain Pryor, with his store of experiences on the epochal adventure with Lewis and Clark to the Pacific Ocean; the capable Chouteau, who could discourse instructively and entertainingly on all subjects relating to the west; Colonel Hugh Glenn, who had followed Chouteau to the glamour of Santa Fe; Pierre Manard, and others whose names have not been preserved for us, but whose tales of daring and of strange scenes long since forgotten, were doubtless detailed to eager ears, stirring in the hearers resolution to see and experience for themselves. It was in this atmosphere that Bonneville spent the next few years without incident or change other than a few months' service at Jefferson Barracks, until he determined to head an expedition to the unexplored West; and in the fall of 1830 he requested an eight months leave of absence beginning the last of the following March, that he might go to New York and visit his parents. After his arrival in the East, he continued to work out his plans and was at last successful in interesting in the enterprise some capitalists of New York, including Alfred Seton, who were willing to advance the large amount of money necessary. And thus equipped, he devoted himself to the details of his expedition, which required extended preparation and time. He next applied to the Secretary of War for

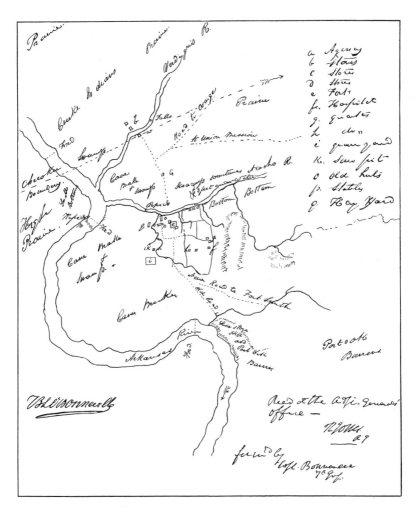

SKETCH MAP OF THREE FORKS AND FORT GIBSON
Made by Captain Bonneville about 1838

At the bottom of the map, Bonneville has noted "At Swallow Rock the river spreads much and is extremely shallow–but there are numerous rapids and one fall located just above the mouth of the Illinois river–impassable except at good stage of water.

"If were decided absolutely necessary to keep a garrison in the neighborhood of the Neosho about the Rapids of the Arkansas is certainly much the best place.–But at Swallow Rock just outside the Arkansas boundary where Fort Coffee stands would probably be most agreeable to the citizens of Arkansas–and as imposing to the Indians–particularly as the Fort I plan is only intended as a depot for stores &c., the army being always in the field or cantoned near the depot "–*B. L. E. Bonneville.*

leave of absence for two years, for the purpose of exploring the country to the Rocky Mountains and beyond, with a view to ascertaining the nature and character of the several tribes of Indians in those regions; the trade possible in those sections; the character of the soil, minerals, climate, geography, topography, geology, and natural history of the regions between the limits of the United States and the Pacific Ocean.[272] Leave was granted him on July 29, 1831, together with certain instructions from the Secretary, requiring him to report, in addition to the matters enumerated, on the number of warriors among the tribes, their disposition toward each other, their method of fighting, and subsisting themselves.

Providing himself with a sextant, telescope, thermometer, microscope, and other instruments to enable him to make the observations desired by the Government, and passports to secure him safe passage through the Indian country, Bonneville left New York by way of Pittsburg, Cincinnati, and Saint Louis, bound for Fort Osage, Missouri, just below the site of Kansas City. Arriving at Saint Louis September 10, he reported to the War Department that he would leave the next day for Liberty, Missouri, near the mouth of Kansas River, but Saint Louis would be his residence during the winter which was to be spent in organizing the expedition.

On May 1, 1832, with one hundred ten men, some of them experienced hunters and trappers, and twenty ox and mule-wagons loaded with provisions, ammunition and trinkets to trade to the Indians, the expedition

[272] The western boundary line of the United States fixed by the treaty with Spain was the one hundredth meridian running through what is now western Kansas.

left Fort Osage for the Rocky Mountains. Immured in the fastnesses of the great West, fascinated by the life he was living, and restricted by tremendous difficulties, he doubtless grew careless of his responsibilities to the Army, and no word was received from him until his return in the fall of 1835. He had sent one letter in June, 1833, which was carried to Washington from Saint Louis by his friend, a Mr. Carre; but, if received, seems not to have been remembered nor to have had the effect of modifying the penalty for overstaying his leave of absence.

At the expiration of Bonneville's two years leave, there was much complaint by the officers at Fort Gibson, where life was monotonous and unhealthy, that an officer could with impunity enjoy the privileges associated with Bonneville's absence in violation of the regulations of the Army. There were reports too that Bonneville had been killed; but it was thought that if the reports of his death were not well founded, as he was engaged in mercantile affairs, and as the officers of his regiment and Colonel Arbuckle in particular were complaining of the number of officers absent, he ought no longer to be continued on the rolls of the Army; accordingly on the recommendation of Major-general Macomb, his name was dropped by the President on May 31, 1834.

On August 22, 1835, Bonneville reached Independence, Missouri, on his return and then learned that his name had been dropped from the army rolls. He went to Washington and on September 26 reported his return to the Secretary of War; he expressed his mortification at learning that he was no longer an officer in the Army and immediately sought to be restored to his rank. He protested that with the instructions of the former Secretary of War, General Eaton, he had devoted himself to securing the information the Government desired, though not attempting to conceal the fact that he was engaged in a trading expedition; he said he had made reports of his progress, but as they were not received at Washington, they had evidently miscarried.

When the report reached Fort Gibson that Bonneville was endeavoring to be reinstated, and with prospects of success, a memorial was prepared and signed by seventeen officers at that post, protesting against his reinstatement. Having been dropped by the highest authority they said, it was a violation of all precedent, justice, and propriety to reinstate him to the prejudice of many still in the regiment. "The inducements to remain in the service are but few; exiled to frontier stations with but a pittance of pay, and with remote prospects of promotion; a violation of the last must necessarily tend to create dissatisfaction by destroying one of the principal rewards held out to us."

His three years of adventure furnished to President Jackson such thrilling and fascinating accounts that with the influence he undoubtedly had in the East, he was enabled to overcome the objections to his reinstatement, and on April 22, 1836, by authority of the President and Senate, an order was issued reinstating Bonneville to his former rank of captain in the Seventh Infantry, to rank as such from October 4, 1825. In the meantime however, while waiting for action by the Senate on his case, Bonneville had returned to the West to close up his affairs, and did not learn of his reinstatement until his return to Fort Leavenworth on August 7, 1836. He immediately started alone on the long ride to Fort Gibson, where he reported early the next month. Naturally, the feeling of the other officers at Fort Gibson was not of the warmest, and Bonneville soon asked to be put in command of a company detached from the regiment, and serving at Fort Coffee.

It appears from the correspondence in the War Department [273] concerning Bonneville's case, that he visited Mr. John Jacob Astor in New York before reporting to Washington on his return. Here he met Washington Irving who wrote the War Department on September 20, saying that Captain Bonneville had just returned from the Rocky Mountains and had "shewed" him his journal; and Irving asked the Secretary if he might have copies of some of the maps of the West that Bonneville had filed with the Department. It was in March, 1836, that Bonneville, still in Washington waiting for decision on his case, wrote the War Department that he was going to leave the next day for New York to see about publishing his journal. "Under the impression that a temporary absence from the metropolis will not prejudice my interests now in the hands of the Senate, I have thought it advisable to publish my journal immediately and with that intention, will proceed to New York tomorrow." He soon departed again for the West.

Irving gives us an interesting picture of Bonneville when he met him at Mr. Astor's home:

"There was something in the whole appearance of the captain that prepossessed me in his favor. He was of the middle size, well made and well set; and a military frock of foreign cut, that had seen service, gave him a look of compactness. His countenance was frank, open, and engaging; well browned by the sun,

---

[273] U.S. War Department. *Case 2742* Appointment, Commission, and Personel, of Adjutant-general's Office 1872.

and had something of a French expression. He had a pleasant black eye, a high forehead, and, while he kept his hat on, the look of a man in the jocund prime of his days; but the moment his head was uncovered, a bald crown gained him credit for a few more years than he was really entitled to.

"Being extremely curious, at the time, about everything connected with the Far West, I addressed numerous questions to him. They drew from him a number of extremely striking details, which were given with mingled modesty and frankness; and in a gentleness of manner, and a soft tone of voice, contrasting singularly with the wild and often startling nature of his themes. It was difficult to conceive of the mild, quiet-looking personage before you, the actual hero of the stirring scenes related." [274]

In the following winter, Irving met Bonneville in Washington, where the latter was whiling away the time he was waiting action by the Senate on his case. There he was rewriting and extending the notes of his travels, and making maps of the regions he had explored. As a result of the interest he felt in the subject, Irving finally bought Bonneville's notes and manuscript for one thousand dollars, and undertook to fit them for publication and bring them before the world.

Irving had become deeply interested in the romance of the West by his visit to Fort Gibson in 1832. Directly after his return from there, he located on the Hudson and while he was working on his *Tour on the Prairies* he was approached by Mr. John Jacob Astor. The latter broached the subject of Mr. Irving's writing a book which would give Mr. Astor and his company their place in the history of the West; and that, as Mr.

---

[274] Irving, Washington. *The Adventures of Captain Bonneville,* 27.

Irving stated it,[275] would secure to him the reputation of having originated the enterprise and founded the colony that were likely to have such important results in the history of commerce and colonization. Astor agreed to place at the disposal of Irving a vast amount of documents, records, and journals, containing the information he hoped Mr. Irving would adapt for his book. Irving was too busy to examine this mass of documents; and in 1833 he wrote to his nephew, Pierre M. Irving, at Jacksonville, Illinois, offering to engage him, with Mr. Astor's consent, to come to the home of Mr. Astor at Hellgate and perform the work of selecting from the manuscripts the material appropriate for the book; his uncle was then to work the material into the book which they named *Astoria*. Pierre accepted the offer, and soon after began his winnowing of dry commercial records from which his uncle, with great literary ability, reproduced scenes and adventures of the Northwest in a book of charm and interest. For this work Mr. Astor gave Pierre three thousand dollars and his uncle gave him one thousand dollars more. It was completed in the early part of 1836 and published in October of that year in London and the United States.

It was with the same deep interest in the romance and adventure of the west, and before *Astoria* was completed, that Irving bought Bonneville's manuscripts and began work on the interesting book that was to be called *The Adventures of Captain Bonneville,* which was published in 1843, and which presents in most attractive manner the remarkable advenures of that soft-spoken officer.

---

[275] Irving, Pierre M. *The Life and Letters of Washington Irving,* vol. iii, 60.

After his return to Fort Gibson, Captain Bonneville spent the next few years there, varied by brief service at Fort Towson and Fort Smith, followed by campaigns in the Florida War and service at posts in the south; as a major he was again stationed at Fort Smith in 1845, and from there went to the War in Mexico, where he was wounded, and was breveted Lieutenant-colonel for gallant and meritorious conduct in the battles of Contreras and Churubusco; he participated in many important engagements in Mexico, and after the war was for some time stationed in the East and remote points in the West.   After his service through the Civil War on the side of the Union, he was on March 13, 1865, made brevet Brigadier-general for long and faithful service in the army.   On June 12, 1878, General Bonneville died at Fort Smith, Arkansas, at the age of eighty-five years, the oldest officer on the retired list of the United States Army.

Governor Stokes's Uncompleted Plans

In March, 1836, Governor Stokes was appointed [276] sub-agent for the Cherokee, Seneca, and Shawnee tribes in place of Captain Vashon who had died the preceding winter. This sub-agency was stationed at Fort Gibson and paid Governor Stokes the munificent salary of seven hundred fifty dollars annually. For an office Governor Stokes had only his bedroom fourteen by sixteen feet; with one letter case, besides his own table and chairs; "the Cherokee papers in one corner of the room; the Seneca papers in another; the Seneca and Shawnee papers in the third corner and the Quapaw in the remaining corner of the room. I am at a place where all the principal Cherokees come to transact their public businefs; and I have not eight feet square vacant in which to do their business."

Governor Stokes complained [277] also to the Secretary of War that his post was an inferior position subject not only to the superintendent but also to the disbursing officer at the post; and that his effort to maintain a commanding influence with the Indians was rendered difficult by the fact that they were daily witnesses of their agent dancing attendance on the second-lieutenant disbursing officer at Fort Gibson who had supervision over his financial transactions with the Indians.

These complaints seem to have borne fruit for in

[276] Herring to Stokes, March 8, 1836, Indian Office, *Letter Book* 18, p. 150.

[277] Stokes to Commissioner of Indian Affairs, August 20, 1836, Indian Office, *Cherokee West* S 39-54.

1837 a law was passed raising the Creek and Cherokee sub-agencies to full agencies and Governor Stokes received a commission [278] dated March 14, 1837, making him Cherokee agent at a salary of fifteen hundred dollars a year. Though ill during the preceding winter, this seventy-seven year old veteran traveled six hundred miles in March and April attending to the payment of the annuities to the Seneca and Shawnee, Quapaw and Osage; and to viewing and appraising the improvements made by the American Board of Commissioners for Foreign Missions at Union and Harmony missions; establishments on the rivers Neosho and Marais de Cygne, consisting of about twenty buildings and improvements which were to be abandoned and removed under the terms of the recent Cherokee treaty.[279] Colonel A. P. Chouteau and Abraham Redfield served with Governor Stokes in making this appraisement, but the extensive report of their work was wholly prepared by Governor Stokes. Four years later, Governor Stokes is found vainly trying to secure his pay for these services for which he and his associates held a formal commission from the Government.

Soon after Governor Stokes was made Cherokee agent he was commanded to remove his agency from Fort Gibson to Bayou Menard, seven or eight miles east of the post. Here he bought from David Biggs a double log house with two rooms twelve by sixteen feet connected by a passage-way; a kitchen fourteen by sixteen and a smokehouse thirteen by sixteen, all boasting shingle roofs and plank floors. In addition, he prepared to erect another building for an office, the total to represent an expense of twenty-two hundred

[278] Herring to Stokes March 14, 1837, *Letter Book* 21, p. 183.
[279] Kappler, *op. cit.*, vol. ii, 326.

dollars, which he was obliged to borrow from a Mr. Harrison, trusting to be reimbursed by a Government that had directed this arrangement without making provision to pay for it. By reason of the new location, Governor Stokes was obliged to spend several hours of each day traveling to and from Fort Gibson to see the young disbursing officer in order that he might perform the services required of him by his Indian charges.

Governor Stokes had not long served as Cherokee agent when there occurred the death of his friend, Colonel A. P. Chouteau. The measure of the loyalty of this good man to Chouteau is found in his efforts to protect the defenseless Osage children of the latter in the meager estate he had tried to secure to them. Chouteau was very much in debt at the time of his death, a judgment for sixty-six thousand dollars having been rendered against him in Saint Louis in July preceding his death; upon execution, less than half that amount was realized, leaving an unsatisfied claim under the judgment of nearly forty thousand dollars.[280]

A letter of Governor Stokes to the Commissioner of Indian Affairs [281] shows how earnestly he tried to protect the objects of the concern of his friend Chouteau:

"You will be good enough to pardon me for addreſsing you on a delicate subject, in which I am called

[280] Letters of administration were issued in Saint Louis to John B. Sarpy, who deputed Captain[later General] Robert E. Lee to act for him in collecting certain of the assets of the estate. About seventy head of mules and a few horses were collected in Indian Territory and sold, and the administrator listed as part of the estate a claim for one-fourth of $73,392.30 against the Government of Mexico for imprisonment, and confiscation of the goods, of Berthold & Chouteau and of Julius DeMun and August P. Chouteau in 1817, a claim that was later adjusted by commissioners by authority of the terms of the treaty with Mexico.

[281] Stokes to Crawford, March 19, 1839, Indian Office, *Osage reserve file* S 1458.

upon to act without authority in consequence of there being no Agent for the Osage Nation of Indians at this time. You will see by the Osage Treaty of 2nd June 1825,[282] Article 5th, that certain reservations of land are made for the benefit of Half-Breeds among which are one to Augustus Clermont [283] 640 acres, valued at $6,000; James, 640 acres valued at $1,000. Paul, 640 acres valued at $1300; Henry, 640 acres valued at $800; Anthony, 640 acres valued at $1,800; Rosalie 640 acres, valued at $1,800; Emilia daughter of Mihanga valued at $1,000; Emilia daughter of Shemianga valued at $1,300. Total $15,000.

"These are Osages, the Indian family of the late A.P. Chouteau. For however it may be considered as a reproach on his character, almost all Traders who continue long in an Indian Country, have Indian wives. – This circumstance does not affect the justice of the claim. – The Osage Nation owned the land, and chose to bestow a part of it in this manner. These reservations are all in country ceded to the Cherokee Nation by the Treaties of 6th May 1828, and Feby 14th, 1833.

"You will see by the 4th Article of the Cherokee Treaty of 29th December 1835, that the United States agree 'to extinguish for the benefit of the Cherokees', the titles to these reservations, which are valued in a Schedule annexed to said last mentioned Treaty, at Fifteen thousand dollars.

"Now Sir, Col. Chouteau, with the best intentions, thought he was doing the best for these reservees by

---

[282] Kappler, *op. cit.,* vol. ii, 154.

[283] Rosalie Chouteau made affidavit, March 17, 1842 [Indian Office, *Osage Reserve File* B. 1463], that she was the widow of A. P. Chouteau and mother of some of his children, and that her sister Masina was the mother of two others, Augustus and Paul. Anthony, who was deceased, was her brother.

stipulating to give them in lieu of the fifteen thousand dollars, about thirty two very valuable negroes, well worth the money. But the title for the greater portion of these negroes was derived from Indians of the Creek Nation, the friends and relations of whom claim the most of them, and it is feared that the reservees will not be able to recover and retain any of them. Since the death of Col. Chouteau, twenty-eight of them have been stolen or enticed away, and most of them are now in the Creek Nation, protected by the Creek Claimants: – Apoth-le-ya-ho-lo a Principal Creek Chief has seven which he claims; and two Half Breed Creeks by the name of Grayson, have most of the remainder. It is ascertained from records, Bonds and authenticated Merchants accounts, that Colo. Chouteau's property both here and in Mifsouri will not pay one fourth his debts: In the meantime a Mr. Bogy the agent of the Administrator at St. Louis, has seized and sold or sent to Saint Louis almost every article of Colo. Chouteau's property to be found in this country, leaving Col. Chouteau's Indian family in this Cherokee Country nearly destitute of the means of subsistence. In this situation of affairs, these helplefs, reservees have applied to me for afsistence and protection: – a request that my limited power affords me but little chance of complying with. In the first place they are Osages, living upon two of their reservations in the Cherokee Country; but they have never been adopted into the Cherokee Nation. My power extends no farther than protecting them in homes, but I can not interfere with their property. I think Sir, that something ought to be done by the Government of the United States to rescue from total lofs, the amount of the value of their reservations; and this the object of my application through you, to the War Department. . . The fifteen thousand dollars ought to be more Equitably divided than is done in the Schedule. The first section amounting to $6000, belongs to Augustus Clermont, the oldest son of Colo. Chouteau, and is rated at more than three times the value of any other: This inequality is owing to the great improvements made by Colo. Chouteau with his own money on that section, which was the residence of the family. One thing more and I will endeavor to close this long letter. It is said that Colo. John Drennan of Van Buren in Arkansas has made a request to the Department to set apart or retain for his use, the value of two of the sections for the payment of a debt due from Colo. Chouteau to him and his partner Colo. David Thompson. This would not be doing justice to the Reservees. The sections are the property of Half-Breed Reservees and they ought to have the value of them. The debt from Colo. Chouteau to Thompson and Drennan originated in this manner. I shall always believe that Colo. Chouteau intended to act honestly and justly by the Half-Breed Reservees, for they were his Indian wife, and most of them his own children: – But being in the pofsefsion of much property, he sold, soon after the Osage Treaty of June 2nd 1825, two of the reservations No. 5 and 8, supposed to have valuable salt springs on them. They were purchased by Gen'. Samuel Houston, then residing in the Cherokee Nation with a Cherokee wife, but not regularly adopted as a Cherokee. Gen'. Houston being unable to carry on salt works, sold the two sections to Thompson and Drennan. Now Gen'. Houston as well as Thompson & Drennan ought to have known, and I expect did know that no white could purchase and hold land in an Indian Country; – I know of no law to authorize such a purchase, but many are the Acts of Congreſs and Treaties expreſsly forbidding such purchases. – The debt from Colo. Chouteau to Thompson & Drennan is therefore a personal debt due from Colo. Chouteau, for which these reservations ought not to be held liable, and I believe Colo. Drennan thinks so too; for since the death of Colo. Chouteau, Colo. Drennan has got six of Chouteau's negroes into his poſseſsion, towards the pay ment of the debt.

"Thompson & Drennan are gentlemen of respectability, and my friends, but I cannot consent that these Half-Breed Reservees shall be wronged without apprising the Department of the nature of the claims upon their property.

"I must again claim your forgiveneſs for calling your attention to this difficult and troublesome affair, which I do at the earnest request of a helpleſs family, suddenly reduced from Independence and Comfort, to great inconvenience if not to absolute want and distreſs. – I enclose a copy of a letter I received a few days ago from Rosalie, the Indian wife of the late Colo. A. P. Chouteau."

Governor Stokes's efforts were unavailing to secure immediate relief for the unfortunate Osage raised in affluence and so suddenly made destitute, but his interest served to assist them until an equally kind hearted successor finally made an adjustment of their difficulties.

During Governor Stokes's four years term as Cherokee agent he witnessed the troubles of the Cherokee Nation, and did much to pacify and conciliate the contending factions. Though he was a very old man and frequently ill, he faithfully looked after his duties as agent.[284]

Lacking an official recording place or repository for such documents, the Cherokee people had placed in his possession their wills, deeds, bills of sale, and guardian's bonds; and he wrote that he was the sole custodian of written evidence of property amounting to over one hundred thousand dollars in value, "belonging to widows and orphans and other legatees; who but for this precaution, might and would have their papers destroyed, and the evidence of ownership left to the uncertain recollection of individuals as formerly. The wealthy Cherokees are too much enlightened to have their property at the hazard of verbal testimony."[285] This evidence of their confidence in their agent, Governor Stokes, must have been gratifying but there was no legal authority for it and therefore no way to compensate him in a pecuniary way for this additional responsibility and labor. At the termination of his office he was most solicitous about the safe-keeping of these papers and he continued on at his post without pay until his successor arrived, so that these documents would be safeguarded.

But at the end of his term the President declined to reappoint him. Richard Adams of Virginia was nominated by the President for the post but the Senate refused to confirm him; thereupon the President nominated Governor Pierce M. Butler [286] of South Carolina,

---

[284] When in 1840, the Secretary of War ordered the Cherokee Nation under the military control of Colonel Arbuckle, Governor Stokes was suspended from office.

[285] Stokes to Commissioner of Indian Affairs, October 26, 1841, Indian Office, *1841 Cherokee File* S. 3036.

[286] Pierce M. Butler, born in Edgefield District, South Carolina, in 1798,

who was confirmed and received his commission on September 20, 1841. And we thus have the spectacle of the Governor of South Carolina coming to Indian Territory to take from the Governor of North Carolina his little office.

Governor Stokes clung to the hope that he might not be forced to give up his post, and as a result the files of the Indian office yield an interesting though pathetic letter written by this veteran to Secretary of War Spencer, telling us something about his life: [287]

"I know that no man ought to addrefs a public functionary on the score of friendship or former acquaintance, and to expect thereby to obtain a favorable consideration of his claims for redrefs of what he may consider as grievances. But I know of no other mode of making my pretensions understood, but by referring to transactions in which I have had a conspicuous share.

"I was in public service, either in the land or Sea service, during the whole of the Revolutionary War,

---

was appointed second-lieutenant in the Fourth Infantry on August 13, 1819, and transferred to the Seventh Infantry on the 13th of the following December and served at Fort Smith and Fort Gibson. He was made first-lieutenant March 1, 1822, and captain in December, 1825. On May 26, 1826, he was married at the home of E. W. duVal of Crawford County, Arkansas, to Miss Miranda Julia duVal, formerly of Washington, D.C. In 1827 he was in charge of the construction of the military road from Fort Gibson to Little Rock. In 1829, while engaged in recruiting work in South Carolina, he was elected cashier of the Branch Bank of South Carolina at Columbia, and October 1, he resigned his commission as captain in the Army.

He served as governor of South Carolina from 1836 to 1838 and on September 17, 1841, was appointed agent to the Cherokee Indians, when he again took up his residence at Fort Gibson. In 1843 and again in 1846 Governor Butler was commissioned to negotiate treaties with the Comanche Indians. He was made colonel of the Palmetto Regiment of South Carolina volunteers on December 22, 1846; he was killed August 20, 1847, at the battle of Churubusco, Mexico.

[287] Stokes to Spencer, Secretary of War, November 20, 1841, Indian Office, *Cherokee File* S 3070.

from 1775 to 1783, and am one among the last of those that remain of that clafs.

"After the close of the War in 1783, I remained in North Carolina, in various public appointments, until December 1816, when I took my seat in the Senate of the United States for seven fefsions, (one Short Sefsion to fill a vacancy and six years under a new Election). . .

"After retiring from Congrefs, I was occasionally in the Legislature of North Carolina, and President of the Board of visitors at West Point, until 1831, when I was Elected Governor of North Carolina and served 1831 and 1832. – I was then appointed at the head of the Commifsion of Indian Affairs West, with Henry L. Ellsworth and John F. Schermerhorn, with considerable power in the regulating of Indian affairs West. . .

"After having trespafsed so long on your patience, I have now only come to the object of this letter. – Some time ago I received a letter from the War Office notifying me that Pierce M. Butler was appointed Cherokee Agent, and directing me to deliver the Cherokee Books, papers and property to him. By the same mail I received a Commission as Register of the Land Office at Fayetteville, Washington County, Arkansas. Now it is not my wish to be in the way of any man; but as Mr. Butler has not yet come, and perhaps may decline the office, I beg leave to submit my humble Claim to the Office of the Agency, with the duties of which I am acquainted, in preference to accepting the office of Register of the Land Office, to the duties of which I am a stranger.

"I am perfectly satisfied that my removal has not been sought by either the Treaty or Ridge party; the old party or first settlers; or the new Emigrants, or Rofs party. — My most influential friends are among them all, and I have seen them all a few weeks ago, as most of them called on me in going or returning from the annual Council in October last. — If it should not be deemed inconsistent with the views and interests of Government to continue an old Revolutionary Veteran in his former office for a short time, I shall be thankful; in as much as my long stay in the Cherokee Nation has caused me businefs which it will take me some time to settle to my satisfaction.

"I now again beg pardon for trespafsing upon your valuable time on matters relating to myself."

Official tyranny followed Governor Stokes to the end of his service. It appears from another letter [288] of his that after the arduous labor of making the treaties of 1835 and 1837, out of an appropriation of ten thousand dollars for expenses, presents, and other demands. there was a balance of $425.15 remaining in the hands of the commissioners, Chouteau, Stokes, and Arbuckle, which amount was by them turned over to Governor Stokes as part compensation for his services. For traveling while sick to Camp Holmes in the summer of 1835 and negotiating the treaty, and negotiating the other treaty at Fort Gibson in 1837, in both of which he not only acted as chairman, but performed all the labor of secretary, he had received no other pay. Nor had he been paid a penny for his services in appraising the improvements at Harmony and Union missions, involving several weeks of labor and hundreds of miles of travel. But on closing up his affairs as Cherokee agent he was forced by the Commissioner of Indian

[288] Stokes to Crawford, November 5, 1841, Indian Office, *Western Superintendency*, S. 3068.

Affairs to pay out of his little salary this amount of money to the Department in favor of a much less meritorious claim of Doctor Richie, who had accompanied Major Chouteau on a western trip.

Governor Stokes either did not accept or did not serve out his term as Register of the Land Office at Fayetteville, and was superseded by another. On the eighth of September, 1842, he was by the President appointed sub-agent for the Seneca, Seneca and Shawnee, and Quapaw at a salary of seven hundred fifty dollars per year.[289] On the fourth day of November, 1842, he died in Fort Gibson at the ripe age of eighty-two.

Governor Stokes's body was interred at Fort Gibson with military honors as was befitting this distinguished public servant and veteran of the Revolutionary War. All the troops of the garrison were turned out and Captain Boone's company of dragoons formed the escort. A large concourse of citizens from the surrounding country attended and immediately after the funeral obsequies, the officers and citizens assembled and adopted fitting testimonials to his memory from which the following is taken: [290]

"The deceased has filled a large space in the history of this country. In his boyhood, he engaged in the struggle for our National Independence, with all the ardor and zeal which characterized his whole career in after life. He was one of the victims of British cruelty on board the Jersey prison ship, and was in confinement on that odious vessel for more than a year. After the war his adventurous spirit led him to differ-

---

[289] Secretary of War to Stokes, September 8, 1842, Indian Office, *Letter Book* 32 p. 443.

[290] Arkansas *Gazette* (Little Rock), December 7, 1842, p. 3, col. 3.

ent quarters of the globe as the captain of a merchant-
man. . . He has filled probably the duties of more
different offices than any man of his day, and in all of
them displayed the highest order of talent. . . He
was, without intermission, a member of the College of
Electors from his state, from the days of Jefferson to
Jackson's last term – the last three elections being president of the College. . .

"From his extensive intercourse with nearly all the
eminent men of the United States of the last century,
his great observation and a most extraordinary memory, he had stored his mind with the prominent facts
in the history of our country, its politics, and great
men, rendering him at all times one of the most agreeable and instructive companions either for the old or
young. . .

"Although far from any kindred, he received during
his last illness all the kind attention that children would
bestow upon a father. His last hours were soothed
by the presence of many of his friends and his exit was
without a struggle."

A man of large experience and extended observation,
Governor Stokes saw many opportunities for improvement and he labored incessantly to help. He wrote
many letters to the Commissioner of Indian Affairs
and the Secretary of War trying, vainly it would seem,
to impress them with some of the information concerning the West which he possessed and of which Washington officials were in appalling ignorance. In some
doubt about how one of his letters would be received
by his superior, the Secretary of War, he said: "You
will pardon me for speaking freely to you upon this
as upon all other subjects. – I am of great age, and it
matters but little to myself or to the Government what

becomes of me, but I will say in respect to my public
employments, that my heart shall never reproach me
so long as I live. I may never [not always] do right,
but I will never wilfully do wrong." To his last days
Governor Stokes wrote a beautiful firm hand that in
no particular revealed his great age.

Warfare on the Texas Border, 1836

It will have been seen how Fort Gibson and the Southwest were gradually being drawn into the struggle between Texas and Mexico. The difficulties of that state with the Mexican government and her aspirations for independence attracted thousands of adventurous and romantic Americans; among them was Sam Houston, who emerged from his self-imposed retirement in Indian Territory, and abandoning his scheme for acquiring riches in that country, decided to take his place again in the affairs and ambitions of his fellow men, and enlisted as champion of Texas against the rule of Mexico.

A government for Texas was proclaimed on November 13, 1835, by a small body of men and Houston was named commander-in-chief of the Texas army. A declaration of independence was published by ninety settlers, all but two of whom were from the United States, and this was followed by a more formal declaration on March 2, 1836. The Mexican government proceeded in its bloody course to put down the insurrection and on March 6, 1836, came the tragedy of the Alamo, which revealed on that Sunday morning the annihilation of the garrison of one hundred eighty Texans at the cost of five hundred twenty-one Mexican lives. And before the end of a month the perfidious Santa Anna had executed three hundred fifty Texan prisoners taken in action while serving under Fannin at Goliad. Santa Anna, little knowing the temper of the men who opposed him, thought he had crushed the revolution and was preparing to relax; but in a few days the redoubtable General Houston with his little army of seven hundred fifty men, faced sixteen hundred Mexicans on the San Jacinto, and, with the Alamo and Goliad to avenge, killed or made prisoners of all of them, including Santa Anna. That day, April 21, 1836, Texas independence was won and Sam Houston hailed as the emancipator.

There were said to be fifty thousand settlers from the United States in Texas and the sympathy of the country was strongly in their favor in their struggle for independence and many sympathizers had gone to Texas solely to fight for her.[291] After the tragedies of the Alamo and Goliad, the wrath of the people of the United States stirred them to action and the desire to help took hold of the country. The Dragoons at Fort Gibson received orders to hold themselves in readiness for an expedition southward. On April 30, 1836, General Arbuckle left Fort Gibson under orders from the War Department to proceed to Fort Jesup on lower Red River and take command of the American forces on the Mexican frontier until relieved by General Gaines who had been ordered there from Florida where he was in command of the troops engaged in the Seminole War.

General Arbuckle with his aide had got only as far as Little Rock when he learned that General Gaines

---

[291] It was just the November preceding that the picturesque Davy Crockett, former member of Congress from Tennessee, at the head of a band of adventurers, arrived at Little Rock on their way to fight for the Texans. The Little Rock Gazette records that "hundreds flocked to see the man who could whip his weight in wild cats." And many remained to hear him abuse Andrew Jackson. Leaving Little Rock well mounted and armed they started for Texas where Davy laid down his life in defense of the Alamo, but not until he had taken a toll of twenty Mexican lives.

had arrived at Fort Jesup and the former immediately retraced his steps to Fort Gibson to put his command in readiness to move at a moment's notice under General Gaines's orders. On May first, during Arbuckle's absence, orders were received at Fort Gibson by express from General Gaines at Natchitoches, by way of forts Towson and Coffee, directing six companies of the Seventh Infantry, together with three companies of dragoons there and the dragoons at Fort Leavenworth, to proceed at once to Fort Towson. The messenger continued to Fort Leavenworth and Lieutenant-colonel Whistler who was in command at Fort Gibson in the absence of General Arbuckle, ordered the troops to make ready for their departure. May 5, six companies of infantry left under Brevet Major Birch and on the eighth the dragoons departed, both detachments proceeding down the north side of Arkansas River and crossing at Fort Coffee, and thence southward to Fort Towson.

General Arbuckle returned to Fort Gibson on the sixth and directed Colonel Whistler to proceed in pursuit of the infantry and relieve Major Birch who was sick. There was a considerable concentration of troops at Fort Towson and, as usual in the summer campaigns, much sickness. By the middle of July the Dragoons, the six companies of the Seventh Infantry from Fort Gibson, and the Third Infantry from Fort Towson were on the march from the latter post to join General Gaines's army at Fort Jesup. A part of the dragoons were engaged at Sulphur Fork, seventy miles below Fort Towson, in preparing rafts for the command to cross the swollen waters of that stream. As time passed the situation seemed to grow more desperate and more threatening, and General Gaines sent orders to Fort Gibson for the few remaining members of the Seventh Infantry at that post to proceed southward at once; officers and troops continued to concentrate at General Gaines's station until late in the fall.

The news from General Gaines's army was war-like and he was assembling all the troops he could to oppose the Mexicans who were reported to have entered Texas twelve thousand strong. A large part of the Mexican force was said to be wild Indians and bandits who were determined to exterminate the Texans. In anticipation of their depredations and outrages, and doubtless hoping for an excuse to cross the line, General Gaines was preparing to join the Texans in resisting them and driving them out. But after the long and fatiguing march from Fort Gibson and extensive efforts made in the concentration and preparation of troops, it was learned that the reports were much exaggerated and the troops that had hoped for the opportunity to punish the Mexicans for their atrocities, were doomed to disappointment; and while the campaign had accomplished little in the way of action, it had demonstrated in a very pronounced manner the friendship of the people of the United States for the Texans.[292]

From Fort Gibson to Natchitoches the troops had marched three hundred seventy miles through excessive heat. Their progress was made the more arduous by the necessity of constructing roads, bridges, causeways, and ferries for the passage of the wagons. On December 26, the dragoons in command of Captain Trenor returned to Fort Towson and departed the next day for Fort Gibson. The infantry passed Fort Towson some weeks later on the return to their station at Fort Gibson

[292] In the fall Major-general Gaines was recalled from personal command on the Mexican frontier, which was entrusted to General Arbuckle.

where they arrived in January after a march of nearly four weeks from Fort Jesup. A detachment of volunteers under Lieutenant Dagley, in charge of a wagon train from Fort Gibson to Fort Jesup carrying clothing for the dragoons and infantry, returned about the same time to Fort Gibson.

There was also a regiment of volunteers recruited in Lawrence and Washington counties, Arkansas, that was retained in camp at Fort Gibson as late as March, 1837, awaiting the arrival of the paymaster. These Arkansas volunteers were encamped about four miles from Fort Gibson within the Cherokee country outside the military reservation.

In October, 1838, a report reached Fort Gibson that another Indian and Mexican attack on the Texans was threatened, and General Arbuckle ordered two dragoon companies from Fort Gibson to proceed at once to Fort Towson, but upon learning that the menace was not so formidable as at first supposed, the order was countermanded.

By Act of Congress July 2, 1836, it was directed that the recommendation of General Macomb for the removal of Fort Gibson be carried into effect.[293] General Macomb suggested Fort Coffee as a location for the garrison, but the Act of Congress did not determine that point, merely directing that all garrisons be placed upon a military road to be constructed through Indian Territory. However, the Secretary of War believed the policy of Congress was wholly wrong, and that the

[293] In December, 1836, Colonel Kearny, Major Smith, and Captain Boone under orders of the War Department were engaged in looking for a site for the Fort Gibson garrison, nearer to Arkansas, but nothing came of it, though they were said to have favored Fort Coffee and Captain Charles Thomas, quartermaster, was ordered to make arrangements for the speedy erection of the new garrison. This was superseded, however, by orders to build a new post near the site of the old Fort Smith.

question of removal should be left to him. In his annual report for 1838 [294] he used language very similar to that contained in the letter of warning written him by Governor Stokes two years before. He said: "So confident am I that the withdrawal of the garrison from Fort Gibson would be the signal of an attack on the part of the Indians,[295] that I have ventured to suspend the execution of that part of the law until an opportunity could be given to Congress to reconsider that order; and would respectfully suggest that the position of the posts, the direction of the lines of communication, and all the details relating to the defenses of the frontiers, should be left to that department of the Government which is responsible for the peace and defence of the country."

After the troops were removed from Fort Smith to Fort Gibson in 1824, the former post was abandoned until 1833, when it was occupied by Company C under Captain Stuart; this company remained there until June 16 of the next year when Stuart evacuated the post and removed his force fourteen miles up Arkansas River to Swallow Rock on the south bank and called the new post Fort Coffee. It was five miles from the Choctaw Agency and was to be the point of debarkation for the Choctaw emigrants coming up Arkansas River by boat. On July 19, 1838, orders [296] were issued directing Captain Bonneville to take his company from Fort Gibson and proceed to Fort Smith there to repair the buildings for receipt of government stores; and ordering Captain Stuart in command of the one com-

---

[294] U.S. House. *Executive Documents,* 25th congress, third session, no. 2, 99, Report of Secretary of War.

[295] But his reference was to the western Indians.

[296] Adjutant-general's Office, Old Records Division, *Fort Gibson Order Book* No. 10, p. 60.

pany at Fort Coffee to abandon that post and remove
all their military, hospital, and other supplies to Fort
Smith and then proceed with his company to Fort
Gibson, the headquarters of the regiment. These
orders were carried into effect in October and Fort
Coffee was evacuated on the nineteenth; but in the
meantime work was begun upon the erection of a new
and permanent fort near the site of the old Fort
Smith.[297] In July, Major Charles Thomas arrived at
the post to superintend the erection of the new garrison.
He came on the steamboat Dayton from Pittsburg and
brought forty laborers and mechanics for the construction of the work. A sawmill formed part of the equipment and the plans contemplated vigorous prosecution
of the work which was not completed, however, for
several years. The fort was to be four hundred fifty
by six hundred feet, with blockhouses at the corners and
the whole was to be of stone and brick and constructed
in the strongest possible manner. While the work on
Fort Smith was under way, Major Thomas and Captain
John Stuart were directed, on October 29, to proceed
to the headwaters of Illinois River, near the Arkansas
line and locate a site for a dragoon garrison.

The unhappy civil disturbances in the Cherokee
Nation were in part responsible for the unusual activity in the construction of these posts on the Arkansas
line; and a wholly unwarranted suspicion of the
intentions of the Indians was responsible for the
extraordinary act of ordering ten thousand troops to
concentrate in the Cherokee Nation. In the summer
of 1838 the Cherokee extended invitations to chiefs
of surrounding tribes to attend a conference for the

---

[297] The new post was erected on a tract of three hundred acres deeded
to the United States by John Rogers on June 17, 1838.

discussion of matters of mutual interest and to renew the ties of friendship between them. At the request of the Cherokee, Governor Stokes wrote the invitations. The council was held in the Cherokee Nation and ten tribes were represented, including the Cherokee, Creek, Seminole, Seneca, Delaware, Shawnee, Quapaw, and Sauk, but the Osage and Kansa were not invited. It was attended by Governor Stokes, General Arbuckle, and Creek Agent James Logan, who reported that the meeting was peaceable and was not in any sense hostile to the United States.

When the invitations had gone out Colonel Mason wrote an alarming letter to General Gaines advising him that the Indians were meeting to plan a concerted attack on the white people, and his letter was given wide circulation in the press. The letter seemed to have produced a panic in General Gaines who ordered out the troops at Jefferson Barracks and Fort Leavenworth toward the meeting place in the Cherokee Nation. He then called on the Governors of Tennessee and Arkansas for volunteers to defend the borders. The Governor of Arkansas immediately issued a proclamation calling for volunteers; but the Governor of Tennessee did not so easily lend himself to the hysterical mood of General Gaines and he received a letter from the War Department advising him that the Government had no authority to call on the Governors of the states for volunteers nor to accept their services and that no occasion existed in any event for the use of troops against the Indians alluded to.

Orders were given for the return to Fort Leavenworth and Jefferson Barracks of the troops that had started to the Cherokee country. Governor Stokes, the Cherokee agent was chagrined and exasperated that the military should have so misjudged the character of his charges and given such unfavorable publicity to them. He, General Arbuckle and Creek Agent Logan joined in a communication to the press [298] vouching for the pacific character of the meeting of the Indians and for the friendship of all of the Indians present except the Sauk of which there was some doubt.

The site selected by Captain Stuart and Major Thomas for a dragoon post was at first called Camp Illinois, but was later named Fort Wayne. In April following, Colonel Mason in command of the dragoons at Fort Gibson, was directed to take post with his four companies at Fort Wayne and build the fort at that place. The excitement attendant on the killing of Ridge and Boudinot [299] caused a considerable concentration of troops at Fort Wayne and Fort Gibson, six companies at Fort Leavenworth being ordered under Colonel Kearny to report to General Arbuckle at Fort Gibson. Fort Wayne contained four companies of Dragoons and one company of the Fourth Infantry, part of whom were engaged in the construction of the barracks and other buildings of the post. The officers who selected the site for Fort Wayne made the same fatal mistake that occurred at Fort Gibson and the post was located in a most unhealtful situation. Soon after the arrival of the troops at that station many of them fell sick and Captain Stuart, himself one of the

---

[298] Batesville *News* (Arkansas), October 18, 1838, p. 2, col. 2.

[299] Elias Boudinot and Major Ridge joined with a small minority of the Cherokee tribe in signing the treaty of 1835 [Kappler, *op. cit.*, vol. ii, 324] agreeing to the removal of the tribe from their ancestral home to the west of the Mississippi. Their action made them so unpopular with the majority of the tribe that on June 22, 1839, while the factions of the tribe were engaged in bitter controversy over the subject of reuniting in Indian Territory, Boudinot was killed at his home at Park Hill and Major Ridge and his son John Ridge were killed near the Arkansas line.

first victims, died December 8, 1838. A number of other deaths followed, including that of Lieutenant James M. Bowman, who died there on July twenty-first. He had just returned from his excursion in the prairies where, at the head of a company of dragoons, he had acted as an escort for the famous expedition to Santa Fe and Chihuahua, headed by Josiah Gregg, whom he left at the limits of the United States.[300]

Fort Wayne was surrounded by a picket fortification and set in the vicinity of a small creek one and one-half miles from Illinois River near the Arkansas line. The quarters occupied by the four dragoon companies stationed there, were placed on a narrow rising ground directly on the bank of this creek. Between the river and the creek was a low canebrake bottom subject to overflow, and after heavy rains the stagnant water in this constantly damp bed of vegetable matter, in the heated season brought about an increase of the prevalent malaria. In the four companies of dragoons and one of infantry stationed there, during the summer of 1839, the sick report ranged from one hundred sixty to one hundred twenty from July to October.

In consequence of the extremely unhealthful situation, further work on the post was ordered stopped in the summer of 1839 and another location was found seventeen miles north, near Spavinaw Creek and across the Arkansas line from the postoffice of Maysville. In the fall the command moved to the new location, a very healthful one, where they were quartered in tents while engaged in the construction of temporary barracks. When completed Fort Wayne consisted of a number of log cabins placed on the lines of a rectangle,

---

[300] Thwaites, *op. cit.,* vol. xx, 127, 128.

defended by three blockhouses. The blockhouse at the southeast corner was located on the bank of the creek forty yards from the fort, and in the upper story was a six-pounder gun mounted on a field carriage. At the northwest corner on the high ground was another blockhouse containing also a six-pounder, both located to command the country around the fort. Much sickness was reported from Fort Wayne caused by numerous whiskey shops a few hundred yards distant across the Arkansas line. A chronicler reported [301] that the inhabitants of Washington County, Arkansas were much opposed to the removal of Fort Wayne, pleading a great fear of exposure to the Cherokee Indians, "when in fact the true cause was, the loss they sustained in losing the good market for the sale of their produce as old Fort Wayne was to them in Washington County and tending to depreciate the value of lands in their vicinity." Government officials held that the posts were established to keep peace among the Indians and to protect the emigrant Indians from the incursions of the indigenous tribes rather than for the protection of the white people who rested in comparative security a long distance from the wild Indians.

In the meantime, a radical change was taking place at Fort Gibson. The Seventh Infantry, General Arbuckle's regiment, that had established the post in 1824, and had been there constantly ever since, was ordered to Florida to engage in the war against the Seminole. The Fourth Infantry, the most of which had been in Florida for three or four years hunting the Seminole Indians, and a part of which had been engaged in driving the Cherokee out of their eastern

[301] *Army and Navy Chronicle,* Vol. xi, p. 249.

homes were ordered to Fort Gibson, where a large detachment arrived on February 6, 1839.[302] The next day the Seventh Infantry in command of Lieutenant-colonel William Whistler, left Fort Gibson in keel boats in which they proceeded down Arkansas River, arriving at Little Rock in about ten days; there they waited for the steamboat Little Rock that towed them down stream enroute to Tampa, Florida. General Arbuckle remained at Fort Gibson in command of the Southwest Division.

The Government employed a body of Creek warriors in the war against the Seminole and in June, 1837, five hundred of them returned to Fort Gibson on the steamboat Black Hawk under Lieutenant Deas. An offer of similar employment was made to Choctaw warriors and by November five hundred of that tribe had rendezvoused at Fort Gibson to enter the service for the Florida War; they had been led to believe they would receive the sum of two hundred seventy-two dollars each for six months service, but after making all preparations they were informed that a mistake had been made by a clerk and that the amount of pay would be seventy-two dollars. Enraged at thus having been misled by the Government, they disbanded, tore off their plumes and war ornaments and washed the war paint from their faces. On the strength of the offer held out to the Indians by the War Department, the traders at Fort Gibson and the Verdigris had sold the warriors twenty thousand dollars worth of goods, intended for their expedition, expecting to be paid on their return from Florida; but to their sorrow they faced a total loss of all the goods furnished the Indians

302 The Fourth Infantry had marched all the way from Tampa, Florida, to Fort Gibson.

and the War Department came in for condemnation from many quarters.

Fort Gibson continued to furnish news for the papers of the country; sickness, death, and desertions required constant replacements and large bodies of recruits coming up Arkansas River to Fort Gibson were so frequent as to become familiar features and to furnish considerable business for the steamboats. It was reported that within a period of three days during their first year at Fort Gibson, all of the field officers of the Fourth Infantry were changed by death and resignations and consequent promotions. Three companies of the Third Infantry had been sent to Fort Gibson and in the spring of 1840 they were ordered to join the garrison at Fort Smith where with the others there they made five companies under command of Brevet Major W. G. Belknap. The whole of the Fourth Regiment remained at Fort Gibson under Colonel Alexander Cummings.

A board of officers composed of General Arbuckle, Colonel Mason, and three others, met in March, 1841 at Fort Gibson to select a more healthful site for a post in that vicinity of strategic value equal to that of the present post. A like investigation was required of them in connection with Fort Wayne. No change of Fort Gibson was effected, though a recommendation was made that the new post be erected just across the Arkansas River at Frozen Rock.

This was about the last service of General Arbuckle at Fort Gibson, for he was ordered to a small garrison at Baton Rouge and General Zachary Taylor succeeded him in command of the troops on the southwest frontier, then called the Second Military Department. The friends of General Arbuckle were aroused by this supposed unjust treatment of the veteran officer and Senator Sevier of Arkansas, on June 3, 1841, offered a resolution asking "the President to inform the Senate why General Matthew Arbuckle has been removed from his command at Fort Gibson West of Arkansas, to Baton Rouge, in Louisiana, where there are no United States Troops."

Senator Sevier charged that Arbuckle was removed to gratify John Ross because he had bitterly opposed Ross in the affairs of the Cherokee Nation. Since the removal of Arbuckle closely followed the visit by Ross and John Howard Payne to Washington and the Congressional investigation of Arbuckle, the charge seems well founded. Sevier declared that Arbuckle was a brave, vigorous veteran officer and that his removal was intended to disgrace him. Upon consideration of the resolution, however, the Senate decided that it could not properly question the motive of the President for the removal of General Arbuckle, and the resolution was tabled.

General Taylor came to Fort Gibson in June, 1841, and relieved General Arbuckle, who had been there most of the time during a period of seventeen years. Immediately after General Taylor's arrival at Fort Gibson,[303] he received a report of a band of lawless Kickapoo, Shawnee, Delaware, Caddo, and Cherokee, and Indians of other tribes from west of the Washita and south of Red River intruding into the country along Blue River belonging to the Chickasaw, where they stole horses and killed stock of those emigrant Indians. Two companies of dragoons and a detachment of the Fourth Infantry were ordered from Fort

---

[303] General Taylor soon removed his headquarters to Fort Smith where he spent the most of his time until the beginning of the Mexican War.

Gibson to the scene of the difficulties to drive out the intruders. In August, a number of armed citizens of Texas crossed Red River and killed two Indians, a man and a woman. Two or three weeks later a company of sixty or eighty armed Texans crossed Red River above the mouth of the Washita and scoured the country between those rivers in quest of roving bands of lawless Indians, and failing to find the objects of their intended chastisement, committed depredations upon a number of Chickasaw Indians.[304]

The Chickasaw Indians for several years had been urging the Government to build a military post in their country as a protection against marauding Indians and white people from Texas, and in September, 1841, General Taylor left Fort Gibson with an escort to select a site for such a post on Washita River. The post subsequently located near the confluence of the Washita and Red rivers near where Colonel Dodge camped in 1834, was named Fort Washita and was under construction during the next year or two. The site was described as commanding and picturesque. The fort was situated in a circular grove crowning the lofty prairie from which there was an uninterrupted view for many miles around the lovely prairie and woodland. "The post, farthest west of any military post in the United States is now occupied by two companies of the Second Regular United States Dragoons, and one company of the Sixth Infantry. The troops are in tents and employed in building the post. Major Fauntleroy, Second Dragoons, is in command."[305]

Emissaries from Mexico and Texas were continually

[304] U.S. Senate. *Executive Documents,* 27th congress, second session, no. 1, 340, Report of Secretary of War.
[305] Arkansas *Gazette* (Little Rock) November 16, 1842, p. 3, col. 4.

circulating among the Indians in the southern part of Indian Territory, seeking to enlist them in their quarrel, and General Taylor and Superintendent Armstrong were alert to keep the Indians from becoming involved. In May, 1842, they were afforded an opportunity to admonish a large number of them on the subject. The Creek Indians called a council to meet near the junction of the Deep Fork and Canadian rivers to discuss in a friendly way matters of mutual interest. There were present participating in the council, delegates from the Creek, Choctaw, Chickasaw, Seminole, Shawnee, Kichai, Wichita, Pawnee, Osage, Caddo, Kickapoo, Quapaw, Delaware, Piankashaw, Tawakoni, and Seneca tribes. General Taylor and Major Armstrong addressed the meeting through interpreters and induced a number of the prairie Indians to go to Fort Gibson to renew their allegiance to the Government. General Taylor had an interview with the Osage, who were then on the way to their summer hunt, and also with the Shawnee, Delaware, Kickapoo, and the wild tribes, upon the subject of American prisoners that might be held by any of them, urging that they be brought in and surrendered. As a result of the efforts of General Taylor, it was reported that much good was expected to follow the conference.

The steadfastness of McIntosh, the Creek chief, was shown the year before when a Mexican general sent him by a Delaware a bundle of documents soliciting the Creeks to join Mexico against Texas and enticing offers were made to him. The chief immediately sent them back to the Mexican with the remark, "it was a bad talk" but kept the offer from becoming known to the members of the tribe.

General Taylor's injunction concerning white prisoners soon bore fruit; on August 23, a party of Kickapoo Indians brought to Fort Gibson a white boy ten or eleven years of age whom they had purchased from the Comanche for four hundred dollars, they said. September twenty-eighth a Delaware Indian brought in a fourteen year old boy named Frederick Parker who also had been purchased from the Comanche. Indians of that tribe had taken both boys in a raid in Texas six or seven years before; and they said the younger boy had a sister older than he, who was still with the Comanche. Neither boy could speak any English but the officers were making some progress in teaching the younger one until the arrival of the second. They found much pleasure in each other's society as both spoke Comanche and it was difficult to induce either to attempt the English language; and it was seriously considered sending one of them to Fort Smith that they might be separated. This was not done however and in September of the following year Fort Gibson was visited by their grandfather Mr. Parker of Texas who had heard of the prisoners and came to claim them. The officers required him to describe the children by their birthmarks and other features and upon finding that the description corresponded with their appearance they were delivered to their grandfather who took them to their home in Texas. [306]

The Comanche Indians had taken many white prisoners in Texas whom they bartered to other tribes to

---

[306] U.S. War Department, Adjutant-general's office, Old Records Division, *Fort Gibson letter book* xvii, pp. 44, 51, 53, 69. General Taylor had ordered the ransom paid; the Act of Congress of March 3, 1843 (5 Statutes 612) included in the Indian Appropriation Bill an item of "$450 paid by order of General Zachary Taylor for two white boys ransomed from the Comanche Indians." A similar provision was made in the Indian Appropriation Bill of June 17, 1844 (5 Statutes 715), "for ransoming a white boy by the name of Frank Lee Witter from the Comanches $200."

be delivered to the whites for ransom. Dr. Dickerson Burt arrived at Fort Gibson on April 13, 1842, and reported [307] that he had just come from the Creek settlement on the Canadian at the mouth of Little River where he had seen a party of Indians from the Wichita village who said that members of the latter tribe had just returned from a plundering expedition in Texas bringing home with them seven or eight white children whose parents they had killed; they brought also a large number of horses they had stolen in Texas. The next year it was reported [308] that George White Hair, an Osage chief had a white girl eight years of age whom he had purchased from the Comanche. She could not speak English and could give no account of herself. White Hair said he bought her because he and his wife had no children, but the Osage agent gave it as his opinion that he had purchased her for the profit he hoped to realize by way of ransom from the white people.

Frequent inquiries came to Fort Gibson from Texas officials concerning these prisoners. On May 2, 1845, General Arbuckle requested Cherokee Agent Butler [309] to secure information concerning two white boys taken prisoners by the Wichita and Comanche early in 1844, their parents having been murdered; and two children of a Mrs. Simpson of Austin, Texas, William, twelve years of age, and Jane, fourteen, taken from their homes the preceding November. It was thought by General Arbuckle that they might be among a number of white

---

[307] Colonel Mason to Adjutant-general Jones, Adjutant-general's Office, Old Records Division, *Fort Gibson letter book* No. 17, p. 31.

[308] Calloway, Osage sub-agent to Captain Armstrong, May 1, 1843, Office Indian Affairs, *1843 Osage File* A 1471.

[309] Adjutant-general's Office, Old Records Division, *Fort Gibson letter book* No. 17, p. 235.

prisoners recently brought to Edwards's trading post near the mouth of Little River, where their captors hoped to realize some money from their sale. Edwards's settlement about five miles south of where is now Holdenville, Oklahoma, became a sort of clearing house for white prisoners captured in Texas, and brought there for barter by their Indian captors who were too wily to approach nearer to Fort Gibson.

Border Warfare and Texas

Governor Butler's commission as Cherokee Agent was dated the seventeenth of September, 1841, and soon afterward he appeared at Fort Gibson to take over the duties of the office on Bayou Menard. In a short time however, he was ordered to remove the agency to Fort Gibson where at first he occupied the former quarters of General Arbuckle, a dilapidated three-room log house, built in 1834, a kitchen, smokehouse, and a double log cabin built for the servants. The officers at the post took exception to the presence of the agency and Butler was requested to remove to the dragoon quarters off the reservation. There he got Captain Nathan Boone to survey a section of land adjoining the reservation on the south, including the dragoon quarters, which was to be kept as an agency reservation. Butler reported that the dragoon barracks were rotten and good for little or nothing – so much so that during the summer Colonel Kearny preferred to occupy tents with his command. Early in the year 1845, Butler removed his agency back to Bayou Menard, which was much more comfortable for himself and family and more convenient to the Indians.

Soon after Governor Butler became Cherokee Agent, he took up the cause of Rosalie Chouteau, the half-breed Osage wife,[310] and others of the family of the late Colonel Chouteau. After Rosalie's relation with Colonel Chouteau began, and especially after their

---

[310] After Colonel Chouteau's death Rosalie was married to a Cherokee.

home was incorporated in the Cherokee Nation in 1825, she and her children became citizens of that tribe and were afterwards recognized as such by the tribe and the Indian agent and superintendent. Governor Butler said he knew Rosalie Chouteau personally;[311] "she has an interesting family now requiring the proper use of their funds to be applied toward their rearing and education." He was finally able to adjust the matter of their claims to their satisfaction and that of some of Colonel Chouteau's creditors. In February 1843, Rosalie came to Fort Gibson and received from Governor Butler the funds due her and the other heirs, of which she paid part to Colonel Chouteau's creditors.

But for the interest of Stokes and Butler in their welfare, the plight of Rosalie Chouteau and Colonel Chouteau's other Indian heirs suddenly bereft of their protector and plunged into penury, would have been desperate indeed. Immediately upon the death of Colonel Chouteau, a number of his slaves were spirited away by the Creeks, and the remainder were seized by his creditors who took also the goods in the trading post on the Verdigris of the value of about six thousand dollars, together with seventy head of mules and horses found at the Saline. Emboldened by the helplessness of the bereft family, the Osage had made a raid and had run off from the establishment at the Saline, four mules, their one fine carriage horse and nine other good horses, a yoke of oxen and eleven other head of cattle, for all of which Rosalie filed a claim with the Government against the Osage. This was disallowed

---

[311] Butler to Crawford, Commissioner of Indian Affairs, March 20, 1842, Indian Office, *Osage Reserve File* B 1463.

by the Indian Office on the ground that she was an Osage. Subsequently Armstrong presented the claim again saying that she had been adopted by the Cherokee tribe and as a member of that tribe she was entitled to be reimbursed for her losses.

In the spring of 1842 another Mexican war scare thrilled Indian Territory; the Secretary of War ordered a rearrangement of the troops in that section, and moved reinforcements toward the Texas border. Eight hundred men were ordered from Jefferson Barracks to Fort Towson and they passed down the Mississippi River in four steamboats and four keel boats. It was estimated that with the troops at Fort Gibson, Fort Towson, Fort Wayne, and other posts, General Taylor would have two thousand at his disposal for service in Texas if needed. Earlier in the year the Texas authorities had complained to Washington that the Osage and other western Indians were having improper relations with Mexico and were carrying off property from citizens of Texas. Colonel James Logan, the Creek agent, was engaged under orders, in delivering to the Creeks three thousand rifles that the Government had taken from them on their removal from the East and had agreed to return on their arrival in the West. But while he was so engaged, reports from Texas were threatening, and acting upon the suggestion of interested parties that these guns might find their way into the hands of wild Indians on the border where they would be used against Texas, he discontinued the delivery of the rifles after having given out three hundred sixty. Logan got himself into difficulty with his superiors for thus acting upon his own judgment, but his action indicated the extreme concern throughout the West for the people of Texas.

In May, 1843, Manuel Flores,[312] an agent of the Mexican Government, accompanied by a Seminole who spoke Spanish, was arrested near Little River while trying to induce the Creek Indians to enter into a treaty with Mexico and take up arms against Texas. He was left in the custody of some of the Creek chiefs who were to bring him in to Fort Gibson and turn him over to the military authorities, but before they were ready to start he made his escape.

The Seminole, hunted out of their homes in the Everglades of Florida by rifle and bloodhounds had been brought west and located near Fort Gibson; the treaty [313] negotiated by Governor Stokes's commission gave them a tract of Creek land extending from the junction of Canadian and North Fork rivers upward to Little River. Some of them removed to that location, but a thousand of them under their leader, Alligator, remained on the bottom lands near the post, unwilling to leave; destitute, they fed themselves by killing the live-stock of the Cherokee, until they became a serious menace to the peace and prosperity of the latter. Governor Butler took vigorous steps to secure their removal from the lands of his charges, with the result that on January 4, 1845, a treaty [314] was entered into between the United States, the Creeks, and Seminole, providing for the location on the Creek lands of the Seminole westward of their former allotment of land, where they were subsisted for six months after their removal.

---

[312] For a number of years Flores had been engaged in negotiating with the Indians in the interest of Mexico. In 1838 he was commissioned by his government to treat with the Cherokee, some of whom had promised to join the Mexicans against Texas.

[313] Kappler, *op. cit.,* vol. ii, 290.

[314] Kappler, *op. cit.,* vol. ii, 407.

Governor Butler reported in February 1845, another alarm of war near Fort Gibson,[315] and it was at first thought the western Indians were about to move against the Creeks who were hunting buffalo on the western prairies. Some time before, a fight had occurred near the Creek settlement at the mouth of Little River between the Creeks and a party of Wichita hunters in which four of the latter were killed. The Creek warriors on the Arkansas and Verdigris under the leadership of Roly McIntosh and Jim Boy went to the aid of their people on the Canadian and general warfare between the tribes was threatened. After the Creek warriors had left, a rumor was circulated along the Verdigris that the Osage were about to embrace that opportunity to make a concerted attack on the undefended homes of the Creeks. Color was lent to the rumor by the visit of a number of Osage men at the home of Ufala Harjo on Arkansas River where they had gone to buy some corn. The Creeks became panic-stricken and women and children came flocking into Fort Gibson. The Creek agent and some of the traders on the Verdigris also rushed to the post for protection. Captain Boone was sent with his company on February 22, to the mouth of Little River and returned a week later; while Captain Cady was sent with two companies of infantry up the Arkansas, but soon returned and reported the Osage scare unfounded.[316]

As the Mexican conflict became more and more imminent, Texas insisted that it was the duty of the United States to restrain Comanche and other southwestern Indians who moved about, some times in

---

[315] Niles Register, vol. lxv, 306.

[316] Adjutant-general's Office, Old Records Division; *Fort Gibson letter book* No. 17, p. 201 ff.

Texas, and at other times north of Red River, and demanded that the northern country endeavor to compel those tribes to enter into treaties of peace with both countries. The Secretary of War promised to send Major Armstrong from Fort Gibson to meet commissioners from Texas at the Waco village on the Brazos River, about the first of March 1843, to treat with the Indians; but later it was decided to assign Governor Pierce M. Butler to that duty. Texas desired the United States to enter into a treaty of alliance with Texas and the Indians, but naturally the Secretary of War declined to so instruct Butler. March 12, 1843, Governor Butler with Captain Blake and an escort of fifteen men from Fort Washita arrived at the Caddo village, and proceeded to the council ground on Tawakoni Creek. There the council was held beginning March 28, in which nine tribes participated. Texas was represented by G. W. Terrell and others; Jim Shaw, Jesse Chisholm, and other famous scouts and interpreters took part. The council lasted three days but accomplished nothing decisive, and another was planned for the early winter; and the last of November, Butler and Colonel Harney started out again in an effort to meet the Comanche and other western tribes. They had an escort of eighty men with two pieces of artillery, and by Thanksgiving 1843, had proceeded as far as Boggy Depot on their way to where they planned to hold the conference on Red River near the mouth of Cache Creek, a short distance above Coffee's Station. Unfortunately this effort was unsuccessful as the former was. The Texas commissioners met some of the smaller tribes at Bird's Fort on the Trinity about twenty miles from Dallas, and were informed that the

Comanche refused to treat at that time and the matter was deferred until the following April.

The next summer the Government made a third attempt and entrusted this enterprise to Captain Nathan Boone, who was stationed at Fort Gibson. The Government was using every effort to assist the Texans to secure peace with the Comanche and other western tribes and remove the menace of the latter while Texas was engaged in her struggle with Mexico. Chiefs of the Comanche, Waco, and Caddo Indians and Texas commissioners met at Tawakoni Creek in Texas and entered into a treaty.

Captain Boone left Fort Gibson on September 25, 1844, with company H of the First Dragoons and his orders required him to be at the rendezvous on the fifteenth of that month. Colonel Mason reported [317] that he could not possibly cover the four hundred miles that intervened before October fifteenth; that the prairies were burning and the horses would suffer for food.

The Indians were restless and would not remain until the arrival of Captain Boone, who after an absence of six weeks returned to Fort Gibson. As if to accentuate the failure, while Boone was gone the Comanche killed a number of white families and Choctaw along Red River, and two companies were compelled to leave Fort Gibson the first of October to drive out the murderers.

Governor Butler persevered, however, and armed with a commission from President Polk, January 1846, saw him and M. G. Lewis in Texas on their way from

[317] Mason to Jones, Sept. 25, 1844, Adjutant-general's Office, Old Records Division; *Fort Gibson letter book* No. 17, p. 158.

Coffee's Station on Red River to Comanche Peak on Brazos River about two hundred miles above. The expedition was a most arduous one, undertaken in a winter of unexampled severity during which the progress of the expedition was much delayed by the rigors of the weather and great distances they were obliged to travel. For some reason General Arbuckle (who again had taken command at Fort Gibson when General Taylor was ordered to the Mexican border) declined to give them a military escort; Governor Butler collected about forty men in civilian life beside two each from the Creek, Cherokee, Chickasaw, and Seminole tribes for the moral effect their presence would have on the wild Indians.

They were obliged to range over a great extent of country in the effort to win the Indians by visiting them at their homes, and these excursions required them to travel with packhorses into well nigh inaccessible places. After a great amount of toil, hardship, and exposure that prostrated Governor Butler with sickness, he was finally successful, and on May 15, 1846, at Council Springs, Texas, negotiated the treaty [318] with the Comanche, Aionai, Anadarko, Caddo, Wichita, Waco, and other western tribes. Texas was not a party to the treaty; by its terms the Indians agreed to deliver up to the United States all white or colored prisoners belonging to Texas or the United States; cease stealing horses and other forms of violence. The United States agreed to establish trading posts among them and furnish blacksmiths to keep their guns and farming utensils in order.

Due to the exceptional range of their efforts, the difficulty of getting the Indians in the proper state of mind

---

[318] Kappler, *op. cit.*, vol. ii, 411.

to treat with them and to get them to forget their griev-
ance against the Texans, and due also to the ill health
of Governor Butler, the commissioners spent more
money than they were expected to, with the result that
they were severely arraigned by the Commissioner of
Indian Affairs, apparently with little consideration for
their having accomplished what the Government upon
three prior efforts had seemed willing to expend a large
sum of money to secure.   Governor Butler was not a
strong man and during the first year of his service at Fort
Gibson as Cherokee Agent, had found it necessary to
secure a leave of absence from his unhealthful surroundings, and went to his home where he was prostrated for some time with what he called bilious fever.
Impelled by his sense of duty to his country, he prepared to enter the war against Mexico and on the
twenty-second of December, 1846, he was made Colonel
of the Palmetto Regiment of South Carolina Volunteers.   With every evidence of deep emotion and
embarrassment, torn between a sense of duty to the
men of his regiment and to the demands of his pride
to have his accounts properly adjusted, Colonel Butler
wrote the Commissioner of Indian Affairs a letter,
promising to go to Washington just as soon as he could
discharge his "present obligation to the country in a
state of war", and assist in adjusting his account.   This
is the last letter from Colonel Butler in the files of the
Indian Office, for he was killed on August 20, 1847, at
Churubusco, Mexico.

To the difficulties of keeping the Indians from becoming embroiled in the conflict between Mexico and
Texas, there were the complications added by the
internal revenue laws of Texas.   That republic enacted
stringent laws on the subject of trade, and imposed

heavy duties on imports, which were sorely felt by the agricultural Indians along Red River, the Choctaw and Chickasaw. While their market south of Red River was taken from them, they were undersold by the Texans without let or hindrance north of that river, the Government of the United States giving them no protection. The Texans were extremely jealous of the proper respect for their laws and bombarded official Washington on account of a number of real or fancied slights.

The Congress of Texas passed an act on December 19, 1836, declaring its boundaries to extend to the source of the Rio Grande, and thereby included within the Republic parts of what are now New Mexico, Colorado, and Kansas. In the summer of 1841 an expedition of several hundred men left Austin, Texas, for Santa Fe. The purpose of the undertaking was partly military and partly commercial. Commissioners had been delegated by Governor Mirabeau B. Lamar to treat with the Mexicans of Santa Fe and surrouding country and invite them to transfer their allegiance from Mexico to Texas; the military force was expected to encourage them to do so, and at the same time enforce Texas's pretentions of sovereignty over that region. A large number of merchants with many wagon-loads of merchandise accompanied the expedition and expected to engage in profitable trade with the Indians and natives of the western country.

The expedition was poorly organized and poorly officered; traveling across a country wholly unknown to them, without competent guides they soon fell into difficulties; they imprudently permitted themselves to be divided and by the time they came near Santa Fe, the treachery of one of their officers made it possible for the Mexicans to make them all prisoners, to the infamous Manuel Armijo, Governor of New Mexico. The same cowardly Armijo who fled from Santa Fe without firing a shot when General Kearny approached on August 18, 1846, permitting this Mexican stronghold defended by seven thousand soldiers to be occupied by less than two thousand Americans. Delivered into the hands of the brutal Salezar these unfortunate Texans were started on their weary march to the city of Mexico. He who reads the account of the sufferings of those men and of the inhuman outrages to which they were subjected, written by one of them, George Wilkins Kendall,[319] cannot wonder that the Texans planned some sort of reprisal.

The government of Texas in 1843 issued to Colonel Jacob Snively a commission [320] to organize an "expedition for the purpose of intercepting and capturing the property of Mexican traders who may pass through the territory of the Republic, to and from Santa Fe." The troops were to mount, equip, and provision themselves at their own expense, and the spoils were to be equally divided between them and the government of Texas. They were directed not to go upon the territory of the United States, as the object of the expedition was that of retaliation against Mexico; the merchandise and all other property of all Mexican citizens was declared to be lawful prize of the captors. It was declared that "goods to an immense amount have been introduced, in violation of our revenue laws, both

---

[319] Kendall, George Wilkins. *Narrative of the Texan Santa Fe Expedition.*

[320] American Historical Association. *Annual Report for 1908* (Washington, 1911), vol. ii, (1) part ii, 217.

by hostile Mexicans, and by citizens of the United States, a state of things which it has become the duty of this government to interrupt and prevent."

An extensive and profitable trade had been carried on between the United States and Santa Fe and the interior of Mexico since 1822. Wagon trains were first employed in 1822 by Captain William Bicknell's party and again in 1824 by a party including Colonel Marmaduke, afterward Governor of Missouri. The Santa Fe Trail was officially located by act of Congress in 1825. However, the depredations of the prairie Indians interposed such hazards in 1828 that the next year the government furnished a military escort for the traders; three companies of infantry and one of riflemen under Major Bennet Riley, accompanied this caravan; Philip St. George Cooke and James F. Izard were lieutenants under Riley. Again in 1834, the Government directed Captain Wharton of the Dragoons, to escort a company of traders to the limits of the United States, a mission in which he was engaged when the remainder of his regiment left Fort Gibson on the memorable expedition to the prairie Indians. After that time the traders had been forced to travel without military escort.

But in 1843 the government of Texas announced its purpose to prevent this trade through what it denominated Texas territory. Application was then made to the War Department of the United States by several American citizens for an escort from Independence, Missouri, to Santa Fe; at the same time, the Mexican Minister made a similar request for the protection of Mexican merchants then in Missouri who desired to transport to Santa Fe a large amount of merchandise they had purchased.

The War Department thereupon gave orders to General Taylor in command of the Second Military Department with headquarters at Fort Smith, and to General Kearny in command of the Third Military Department with headquarters at Fort Leavenworth, to keep the mounted troops in readiness to dash across the prairies as occasion required, or at least yearly, if only to exhibit themselves to the frontier Indians. Under orders of General Taylor to proceed for the protection of the traders going to Santa Fe, on May 14, 1843, Captain Nathan Boone left Fort Gibson with sixty men of companies H and E and the next day all the mounted men of company D followed under the command of Lieutenants Abraham R. Johnston and Richard H. Anderson, and joined Boone three days later seventy-five miles above Fort Gibson.

Boone pursued a route up Arkansas River and the Cimarron. Traveling north from the latter he arrived at the Santa Fe Trail on the north side of the Arkansas where he met a small body of traders; with these he traveled a few days west on the trail and then recrossed to the south side of Arkansas River and on June 13, camped opposite the mouth of Walnut Creek. Here he was joined by Captain Philip St. George Cooke who camped on the north side of the river on Walnut Creek with three companies of dragoons to await the arrival of the trading caravan in his charge. As Captain Cooke thought his force was sufficient to protect the traders, Captain Boone departed in a southerly course and visited the great salt plains. After many exciting buffalo hunts which he described in his journal [321] he reached Canadian River which he descended to Chou-

[321] Pelzer, Louis. *Marches of the Dragoons in the Mississippi Valley,* 183-237.

teau's old trading house near the site of Fort Mason or Camp Holmes; he then proceeded down the Canadian to Edwards's trading house or Old Camp Holmes near the mouth of Little River, and on to Fort Gibson where he arrived on July 31. In August Captain Enoch Steen [322] with a force of dragoons was ordered out from Fort Gibson also for the protection of the Santa Fe traders. [323]

For the convoy of the traders in Missouri who were ready to depart for Santa Fe, Captain Philip St. George Cooke was detailed with one hundred ninety men with instructions to proceed as far as the limits of the United States. These mounted troops with several pieces of artillery rendezvoused at Council Grove on Grand River, June 3, and proceeded on their route with the caravan, joining Captain Boone a few days later. The traders convoyed by Captain Cooke had with them forty-seven covered wagons and three dearborns; the Mexicans were headed by the infamous Armijo, [324] whose capture by the Texans would have given them great joy.

Snively with one hundred eighty men rendezvoused at a place now in the northwest part of Grayson County, Texas; they crossed Red River near Coffee's trading house, and marched northwest to Arkansas River; there they attacked one party of Mexicans of whom they killed eighteen and then at a point [325] where it

---

[322] Born in Kentucky and came to Fort Gibson in 1832 with the Rangers. Distinguished himself in the War with Mexico and died January 22, 1880.

[323] *Army and Navy Chronicle*, vol. ii, p. 303.

[324] According to Captain Boone, Pelzer *op. cit.*, 213, but see Thwaites, *op. cit.*, vol. xx, 233.

[325] Gregg in the *Commerce of the Prairies* [Thwaites, *op. cit.*, vol. xx, 333] locates this occurrence about fifteen miles below the Caches, which is near the intersection of the one hundredth meridian and the Arkansas River, or in the vicinity of where is now Dodge City, Kansas.

was claimed neither party knew whether it was within the limits of the United States, Captain Cooke intercepted Snively's expedition and disarmed them, but permitted them to retain ten guns for their protection. The traders were enabled to proceed in safety and after escorting them to the boundary line, Captain Cooke returned to Missouri, furnishing safe conduct for fifty of Snively's men, the remainder of whom returned to Texas by Fort Washita, except a few who had secreted some of their guns from Captain Cooke, and later clandestinely took out after the caravan. It was reported that Cooke's disarming of Snively's band had made a good impression on the Mexicans in Santa Fe, who showed greater respect for the Americans and treated them with greater hospitality.

A tremendous uproar was raised by the government of Texas for the "enormous outrage" of thus invading Texas territory and arresting her citizens. Van Zandt, the Texas representative at Washington, suggested that the Texan flag ought to be hoisted at some western fort and saluted with a number of guns by way of atonement. The investigation which followed, established that the arrest was well within the limits of the United States and the court of inquiry acquitted Captain Cooke of any misconduct. While demanding some sort of reparation, Van Zandt himself in writing to his government, disclosed his disingenuous attitude: "I have given this subject every attention in my power, and from all that I have been able to discover it is my impression (although as you perceive I maintain the contrary to this Government) that the occurrence took place within the territory of the United States." [326]

[326] American Historical Association. *Annual Report for 1908*, vol. ii, (1) part ii, 254.

That same spring the steamboat Fort Towson was ascending Red River with fifty thousand dollars worth of merchandise, most of it belonging to merchants at Doaksville, Colonel David Fulsom, Joel H. Nail, and Robert M. Jones, all Choctaw citizens. Before reaching their destination they were arrested by lack of water and stored their goods at Bryarly's landing on the Texas bank of the river. There the goods were seized by James Bourland, revenue collector of Texas, who claimed them for the state for the violation of their revenue laws. A few weeks later the commander of the boat with his crew and that of the Hunter, numbering in all thirty men, returned, bound the collector with a rope, took the merchandise and returned it to the boat. After the goods were loaded, Colonel Loomis in command at Fort Towson, was called on to furnish protection against an effort to recover them by the Texan authorities. As part of the merchandise was public property going to the sutlers at forts Towson and Washita, he promptly complied with the request and thereby brought himself and the government within the sweeping condemnation that followed. Upon the investigation that ensued, General Taylor, then stationed at Fort Smith, exonerated Loomis of any misconduct in the matter.[327]

General Zachary Taylor was ordered on April 23, 1844, from Fort Smith to Fort Jesup to assume command of the First Military Department and General Arbuckle was ordered from Fort Gibson to Fort Smith, in command of the Second Military Department. July 7, 1847, the Third Military Department, the head-

[327] By act of Congress of March 3, 1847, thirty thousand dollars was appropriated to settle the claims of the late Republic of Texas for disarming Colonel Snively's command, and for entering the custom-house at Bryarly's landing and taking goods therefrom.

quarters of which was at Fort Leavenworth, was added to General Arbuckle's command, on account of depredations by Comanche, Pawnee, Arapaho, and others on citizens of the frontier and on the Santa Fe and Oregon roads. General Arbuckle was directed to go to Fort Leavenworth and Independence, acquaint himself with conditions and extend his supervision over the route to Oregon; in his absence he left Lieutenant-colonel Loomis in command of the Second Department, with headquarters at Fort Gibson. Arbuckle was directed also, if he could spare them, as quickly as possible to send a company of the First Dragoons to join the army in Mexico under General Taylor.

The Mexican War was now in full tide; it carried the entire Southwest into the flood with an impulse that swept the old boundary away and established a new one. Kearny, Doniphan, Cooke, Fremont, and Carson broke through the barriers at Red River and the Spanish possessions, and they were followed by the frontiersmen who pressed on to the Rio Grande and the Pacific Ocean. The Southwest of the trader, trapper, and explorer gave way to the Southwest of the immigrant, the herdsman, the gold seeker, and agriculturalist. With the birth of a new era was closed the last chapter of an old.

Bibliography

The numerous letters referred to and quoted from in the text constituting part of the files of the Indian Office are included within an arrangement of those files now known as the Retired Classified Files. This arrangement is the result of a recent effort in the Indian Office to change the form of the original filing in which the papers were folded and more or less abstracted and indexed, to a flat filing system by which the former files and definite method of identification were entirely destroyed. After 1834 these old files bore a file number which is preserved in the foot-notes to the text. Because of the destruction of the original method of filing it is possible to refer to the files preceding 1835 only by date and subject as has been done. The letters emanating from the Government are retained in the letter books to which reference has been made.

AMERICAN HISTORICAL ASSOCIATION. Annual report for 1904 (Washington, 1905).

———— Annual report for 1908 (Washington, 1911) Diplomatic correspondence of the republic of Texas, vol. ii (1) part ii.

AMERICAN HISTORICAL REVIEW (Lancaster, Pa.) vol. xxiv, no. 2. Documents, Captain Nathaniel Pryor 253 ff.

AMERICAN STATE PAPERS (Washington, 1834) Foreign relations vol. iv; Indian Affairs vols. i and ii; Claims vol. i; Miscellaneous vols. i and ii; Military Affairs vol. v.

ARKANSAS ADVOCATE (Little Rock), March 31, 1830 - April 20, 1837.

ARKANSAS GAZETTE (Arkansas Post and Little Rock) Nov. 20, 1819 to Dec. 31, 1845.

ARKANSAS HISTORICAL ASSOCIATION. Publications (Conway, Arkansas 1917) vol. iv, Narrative of a Journey in the Prairie by Albert Pike.

ARMY AND NAVY CHRONICLE (Washington, Jan. 3, 1835 - May 21, 1842), vols. 1-12, vol. 13, no. 1-18; merged into the Army and

Navy Chronicle (Washington, Jan. 12, 1843 - June 17, 1844) vols. 1-3.

BANCROFT, HUBERT HOWE. Works vol. xv, History of North Mexican States (San Francisco, 1884).

BATESVILLE NEWS (Arkansas) March 19, 1838 - April 27, 1842.

BRACKETT, ALBERT G. History of the United States Cavalry, from the formation of the Federal Government to June 1, 1863 (New York, 1865).

CATLIN, GEORGE. Letters and notes on the manners, customs, and condition of the North American Indians, written during eight years' travel amongst wildest tribes of indians in North America (Philadelphia, 1857) 2 vols.

CHEROKEE ADVOCATE (Tahlequah, Indian Territory) Sept. 26, 1843 - Sept. 28, 1853.

COOKE, PHILIP ST. GEORGE. Scenes and adventures in army, (Philadelphia, 1859).

COUES, ELLIOTT, editor. Journal of Jacob Fowler, narrating an adventure from Arkansas through the Indian Territory, Oklahoma, Kansas, Colorado, and New Mexico, to the source of Rio Grande del Norte, 1821-1822 (New York, 1898).

COUES, ELLIOTT, editor. Expeditions of Zebulon Montgomery Pike (New York, 1895) 3 vols.

CULLUM, GENERAL GEORGE W. Biographical register of officers and graduates of U.S. Military Academy, 3d edition (Boston, 1891) 4 vols.

DARBY, WILLIAM. Geographical description of state of Louisiana (New York, 1817).

[DAVIS, VARINA JEFFERSON]. Jefferson Davis, memoir by his wife (New York, 1890).

DODGE'S MILITARY ORDER BOOK. An unpublished manuscript document in Colonel Dodge's handwriting, containing his military orders and correspondence from August 1832 to March 1836. The document is in the possession of the Historical Department of Iowa (Des Moines).

DOUGLAS, WALTER B., editor. Three years among Indians and Mexicans, by General Thomas James (St. Louis, Mo. Hist. Soc., 1916).

FLINT, TIMOTHY. History and geography of Mississippi valley (Cincinnati, 1832).

———— Recollections of last ten years in the valley of Mississippi (Boston, 1826).

GUILD, Jo. C. Old times in Tennessee, with historical, personal, and political scraps and sketches (Nashville, 1878).

HALL, JAMES. The West: its commerce and navigation (Cincinnati, 1848).

HEITMAN, FRANCIS B. Historical register and dictionary of United States Army, from its organization September 29, 1789, to March 2, 1903 (Washington, 1903) 2 vols.

HEMSTEAD, FAY. Political history of Arkansas (St. Louis, 1890).

HERMAN, BINGER. The Louisiana purchase (Washington, 1898).

[HILDRETH, J.] Dragoon Campaigns to the Rocky Mountains (New York, 1836).

HOSMER, JAMES K. History of the Lewis and Clark Expedition (Chicago, 1902) 2 vols.

HUGHES, JOHN T. Doniphan's expedition; account of the conquest of New Mexico; General Kearny's overland expedition to California; Doniphan's campaign against the Navajos; his unparalleled march upon Chihuahua and Durango; and the operations of General Price at Santa Fe with a sketch of life of Colonel Doniphan (Cincinnati, 1848).

HUNTER, JOHN D. Memoirs of a captivity among the indians of North America from childhood to the age of nineteen (London, 1823).

INDIAN REMOVAL. Speeches on passage of bill for removal of indians delivered in congress of United States, April and May, 1830 (New York, 1830).

IRVING, JOHN T. Indian sketches taken during an expedition to Pawnee and other tribes of American Indians (London, 1835) 2 vols.

IRVING, PIERRE M. Life and letters of Washington Irving (New York, 1862-1864) vol. iii.

IRVING, WASHINGTON. Adventures of Captain Bonneville U.S.A., in Rocky Mountains and far west, digested from his journal and illustrated from various other sources. Hudson Edition (New York, 1868).

———— Tour on prairies, the Crayon Miscellany (New York, 1868).

JEFFERSON, THOMAS, and Wm. Dunbar. Documents relating to

purchase and exploration of Louisiana (Boston, American Philosophical Society, 1904).

KAPPLER, CHARLES J., compiler and editor. Indian affairs; laws and treaties (United States Senate Documents, 57th congress, first session, no. 452), vol. ii.

KENDALL, GEORGE WILKINS. Narrative of Texan Santa Fe Expedition; description of tour through Texas, and across great southwestern prairies, Comanche and Caygua hunting-grounds, with account of sufferings from want of food, losses from hostile indians, and final capture of Texans and their march as prisoners, to city of Mexico (New York, 1844) 2 vols.

LATROBE, CHARLES JOSEPH. Rambler in North America (New York, 1835), vol. i.

McCALL, MAJOR GENERAL GEORGE A. Letters from frontier written during a period of thirty years' service in Army of United States (Philadelphia, 1868).

McCOY, ISAAC. Annual Register of Indian Affairs within Indian or Western Territory (Shawanoe Baptist Mission Ind. Ter., 1835-1838).

———— History of Baptist Indian Missions; embracing remarks on former and present condition of aboriginal tribes; their settlement within the Indian Territory and their future prospects (Washington, 1840).

McKENNEY, THOMAS L. Memoirs, official and personal with sketches of travels among northern and southern indians; embracing a war excursion, and descriptions of scenes along western borders (New York, 1846) second edition, 2 vols. in one.

MARCY, COLONEL R. B. Thirty Years of army life on border (New York, 1866).

———— The Prairie Traveler, a handbook for overland expeditions, reprint (London, 1863).

MARSHALL, THOMAS MAITLAND, PH.D. History of western boundary of Louisiana purchase, 1819-1841 (Berkeley, 1914).

MILITARY AND NAVAL MAGAZINE OF UNITED STATES (Washington March, 1833 - Feb. 1836) vols. 1-6; merged into Army and Navy Chronicle.

MISSIONARY HERALD (Boston) 1821-1836, vols. 17-32.

MISSOURI GAZETTE AND PUBLIC ADVERTISER (St. Louis Jan. 1, 1819-March 6, 1822).

Morse, Rev. Jedidiah, d.d. Report to Secretary of War of United States on Indian Affairs; a tour performed in summer of 1820, under a commission from President of United States, for purpose of ascertaining for use of Government, actual state of the Indian tribes in our country (Washington, 1822).

Niles Register (Baltimore), vols. 1-12, 13-24 (New series vol. 1-12) 25-36 (3d series vol. 1-12) 37-50 (4th series vol. 1-14).

Pelzer, Louis. Marches of Dragoons in Mississippi valley (Iowa City, Iowa, The State Historical Society of Iowa, 1917).

Powell, Colonel Wm. H. List of officers of Army of United States (New York, 1900).

Presbyterian Board of Publication. Scenes in Indian Country (Philadelphia, 1859).

Robinson, Fayette. Account of organization of Army of United States (Philadelphia, 1848) 2 vols.

Schoolcraft, Henry R., ll.d. Information respecting history, condition, and prospects of Indian tribes of United States (Philadelphia, 1847) vol. iii.

Smithsonian Institution. Annual report of board of regents to July 1885 (Washington, 1886) part v, the George Catlin Indian Gallery.

Stoddard, Major Amos. Sketches, historical, and descriptive of Louisiana (Philadelphia, 1812).

Thwaites, R. G., editor. Original Journals of Lewis and Clark expedition, 1804, 1806 (New York, 1904) 7 vols.

———— Early Western Travels, 1748-1846 (Cleveland, 1904-1908).

Vol. v. Bradbury, John. Travels in Interior of America, including a description of Upper Louisiana, together with States of Ohio, Kentucky, Indiana, and Tennessee, with Illinois, and Western Territories; Dec. 31, 1809 - Jan. 20, 1812, with subsequent data in Appendix; reprint of (second) London edition, 1819.

Vol. xiii. Nuttall, Thomas. Journal of travels into Arkansas Territory, with occasional observations on manners of aborigines; Oct. 2, 1818 - Feb. 18, 1820, reprint of original edition: Philadelphia, 1821.

Vols. xiv, xv, xvi, and xvii. James, Edwin. Account of an expedition from Pittsburgh to Rocky Mountains, performed by order of Hon. J. C. Calhoun, Secretary of War, under command of Maj. S. H. Long, of U.S. Top. Engineers, compiled from notes of Maj. S. H. Long, Mr. T. Say, and other gentlemen of party; March 31, 1819 - Nov. 22, 1820. Text reprinted from the 3 - volume London edition, 1823; preliminary Notice, Long and Swift's calculations of observations, and Say's vocabularies of Indian languages, from the Philadelphia edition of same year.

Vols. xix and xx. Gregg, Josiah. Commerce of Prairies; or, journal of a Santa Fe trader, during eight expeditions across great western prairies, and a residence of nearly nine years in Northern Mexico; 1831-1839; reprint of 2-volume New York edition (second) 1845.

TRENT, WILLIAM P. AND GEORGE S. HELLMAN. Journals of Washington Irving (Boston, The Bibliophile Society, 1919), vol. iii.

U. S. BUREAU OF ETHNOLOGY. Bulletin 30, Handbook of American Indians, fourth impression (1912) 2 vols.

———— Seventeenth annual report, 1895-1896, Calendar History of the Kiowa Indians, by James Mooney (Washington, 1898) part i.

———— Nineteenth annual report, 1897-1898, Myths of Cherokee, by James Mooney (Washington, 1900) part i.

UNITED STATES HOUSE OF REPRESENTATIVES:

Documents, 20th congress, first session, no. 263; letters from Secretary of War transmitting correspondence relative to settlement of Lovely's Purchase in Territory of Arkansas.

Executive Documents, 22d congress, first session, no. 116, president's message upon the subject of the contemplated removal of Indians to west of Mississippi.

Reports, 22d congress, first session, no. 502, report of investigating committee of charges of fraud against Samuel Houston and Secretary of War, in rationing of emigrating Indians together with testimony heard by committee.

Executive Documents, 22d congress, second session, no. 2; president's message transmitting report of Secretary of War of Nov., 1832.

Reports, 23d congress, first session, no. 474; report of the committee on indian affairs submitting a bill to provide for organization of department of indian affairs and a bill to provide for establishment of Western Territory, accompanied by a report of commissioners of indian affairs west, at Fort Gibson.

Executive Documents, 25th congress, second session, no. 3; report of the Secretary of War, with report of office of indian affairs, December 1, 1837.

Documents, 25th congress, second session, no. 311; report of committee on military affairs, submitting a plan for defense of western frontier, furnished by Major-general Gaines, February 28, 1838.

Executive Documents, 25th congress, third session, no. 2; report of Secretary of War.

Documents, 26th congress, first session, no. 129; memorial of delegation of Cherokee Nation, with exhibits.

Executive Documents, 30th congress, first session, no. 41. Notes of a Military Reconnoissance, from Fort Leavenworth, in Missouri, to San Diego, in California, including part of Arkansas, Del Norte, and Gila rivers, by Lieut. Col. W. H. Emory. Made in 1846-47, with advanced guard of Army of West.

UNITED STATES SENATE:

Executive Documents, 23d congress, first session, no. 1; president's message with report of Secretary of War.

Documents, 23d congress, first session, no. 512, v vols., correspondence on the subject of the emigration of Indians between 30th Nov. 1831, and 27th Dec., 1833, furnished in answer to a resolution of Senate, of 27th Dec., 1833.

Executive Documents, 23d congress, second session, no. 1, message of President.

Documents, 24th congress, first session, no. 23; petition of Joseph Bogy praying compensation for spoliations on his property by a numerous party of Choctaw Indians, then at peace with United States, whilst on a trading expedition on Arkansas River, under authority of a license derived from United States.

Documents, 24th congress, second session, no. 47; report of senate committee on indian affairs on petition of George W. Brand with Senate Bill no. 91.

Executive Documents, 27th congress, second session, no. 1; report of Secretary of War.

Executive Documents, 31st congress, first session, no. 64; reports of Secretary of War, with report of Captain R. B. Marcy's route from Fort Smith to Santa Fe.

Executive Documents, 32d congress, second session, no. 54, exploration of Red River of Louisiana, in year 1852, by Captain Randolph B. Marcy, assisted by Captain George B. McClellan.

UNITED STATES STATUTES AT LARGE, vols. ii, iii, iv, and v (Boston, 1846-1850).

UNITED STATES v. TEXAS, United States Supreme Court Reports, vol. clxii, i.

———— no. 4, Original. United States Supreme Court, Printed record, 3 vols.

[WASHINGTON D. C.] Daily National Intelligencer; Jan. 1, 1813 - Dec. 31, 1850.

[WASHINGTON D. C.] United States Telegraph; Feb. 6, 1826 - June 28, 1834.

WYETH, WALTER N. D.D. Isaac McCoy, Early Indian Missions, a Memorial (Philadelphia, 1895).

YOAKUM, H. History of Texas from its first settlement in 1685 to its annexation to United States in 1846 (New York, 1856) 2 vols.

Index